The Power of Ideas

The Power of Ideas

The Heritage Foundation at 25 Years

Lee Edwards

JAMESON BOOKS, INC.
OTTAWA, ILLINOIS

Jameson books are available at special discounts for bulk purchases, for sales promotions, premiums, fund raising or educational use. Special condensed or excerpted paperback editions can also be created to customer specifications.

For information and other requests write:

Jameson Books, Inc.
722 Columbus Street
P.O. Box 738
Ottawa, Illinois 61350

815-434-7905

Printed in the United States of America.

Jameson Books titles are distributed to the book trade by LPC Group, 1436 West Randolph Street, Chicago, IL 60607. To order call 800-243-0138.

Library of Congress Cataloging-in-Publication Data

Edwards, Lee.
    The power of ideas : The Heritage Foundation at 25 years / Lee Edwards.
       p.   cm
    Includes bibliographical references and index.
    ISBN 0-915463-77-6 (alk. paper)
    1. Heritage Foundation (Washington, D.C.)—History.   2. Policy sciences—Research—United States—History.   I. Title.
    H67.W338E38   1997
    320'.06'073—dc21   97-41296
                                                                          CIP

5   4   3   2   1   /   00   99   98   97

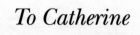
To Catherine

Contents

Acknowledgments

This history is the product of some fourteen months of intense research, interviewing, writing, and rewriting. I conducted over 125 interviews with foundation employees, trustees, supporters, and alumni; with think-tank presidents, journalists, members of Congress, and congressional staffs. I traveled to New York, Connecticut, Florida, California, and Illinois for these interviews and to examine records and correspondence. My one major regret is that I did not have time for more research, but the fast-approaching deadline of Heritage's twenty-fifth anniversary did not allow it.

The Heritage Foundation is a perpetually busy place, but its people—from the president's office to the mailroom—always took time to share their recollections and insights with me. I am particularly grateful to Ed Feulner, Phil Truluck, Dick Allen, John Von Kannon, Hugh Newton, Herb Berkowitz, Richard Odermatt, and William T. Poole for memories of the early days. Heritage alumni who were especially helpful were Paul Weyrich, Chuck Heatherly, Jeff Gayner, Bob Huberty, Willa Johnson, Milt Copulos, and Kate O'Beirne.

Nor could I have told the foundation's history without the cooperation of such analysts as Stuart Butler, Kim Holmes, Robert Rector, Bob Moffit, Pat Fagan, Jim Phillips, and Baker Spring. Former officers—Burt Pines, Bruce Weinrod, and others—were extremely helpful. Adam Meyerson, as always, provided a philosophical perspective.

No one person could have sifted through the several thousand backgrounders, analyses, studies, and books produced by Heritage between 1973 and 1997. I depended heavily on the foundation's annual reports as well as on the summaries prepared by the highly competent professionals in Heritage's public relations office.

The indispensable person in my research was Heritage's librarian John Nixon, the King of Nexis-Lexis, who could always locate an article or a book or a citation, often within a few minutes. I am also indebted to my research assistants, Jason Boffetti, Catherine O'Connor, and Seth Becker. During the writing phase, I was kept on course by the best editor I have ever worked with—Patricia Bozell.

A word here about Heritage's trustees, a remarkable group of truly distinguished Americans: my interviews with Joe Coors, Frank Shakespeare, Midge Decter, Tom Roe, Fritz Rench, Lew Lehrman, and others lightened my labors and made my days.

As a proponent of Truth in Labeling, I want to state that this is an "authorized" history. Selected senior managers of the foundation read the manuscript for content and accuracy, but their revisions were few. No one gave me a list of what or whom to include or exclude. This is a work of which I am enormously proud—as a historian and as a conservative.

—Lee Edwards
Alexandria, Virginia
May 1997

Foreword

An American Institution

by William E. Simon

How much America and the world have changed over the last quarter of a century! In 1973, when The Heritage Foundation was founded, government was seen as the solution to nearly every national problem. Our nation's defenses were inadequate, and our economy was being strangled by anti-growth regulations. How far we have come from those dark days when most policymakers believed that statist ideas would bring peace and prosperity!

At home, we have traded soaring inflation, rising unemployment, and an ever-expanding government for stable prices, millions of new jobs, and the beginning of the end of big government. Abroad, we have gone from Western weakness and uncertainty and an ever-more-aggressive Soviet Union to the collapse of communism and the triumph of democracy and free markets around the world. And how often The Heritage Foundation has been at the center of these extraordinary changes during this dramatic quarter-century!

Heritage's mission, from the beginning, has been to provide timely, credible information for policymakers (especially members of Congress) and the media about the vital issues facing America. No longer would congressmen and their staffs get a useful study *after* debate and a vote. No longer would congressmen and their aides have to plow through a 200- or 300-page tome to learn the pluses and minuses of a bill. No longer would conservative ideas be frozen out of the policy debate. Heritage and its famous "briefcase test" had arrived.

Today, nearly every research organization does it, but Heritage invented the quick, reliable response. A congressman or other public official had to be able to fit a Heritage paper in his briefcase and read it on the go. By so doing, and I know this from personal experience, Heritage reshaped the world of think tanks and Washington policymaking.

And, always, Heritage aggressively marketed its product. It wasn't satisfied with mailing studies to policymakers and the media and hoping they would read them. Heritage perfected a careful strategy of personalized dissemination. It hand-delivered studies to members of Congress and to executive department heads. It telephoned reporters, editors, and columnists. It double-checked to make sure a study had arrived in time and had gone to the right person. As historian James A. Smith concludes in his definitive study of think tanks, "Heritage is the salesman and promoter of ideas par excellence."

Heritage would not have been born without the initial financial backing of a far-sighted businessman from the west—Joseph Coors. And Heritage would not have gone on to prosper if Joe Coors had not been joined by other American leaders like Dick Scaife of Pittsburgh, Ed and Sam Noble and David Brown of Oklahoma, and my colleagues at the John M. Olin Foundation.

It is a sign of Heritage's entrepreneurial spirit that it took the biggest gamble of its young life in 1980 by producing a 1,000-page policy blueprint for a conservative administration—before there was one. I had something to do with that decision, having pointed out at a Heritage trustees meeting that when I and others (like GSA head Jack Eckerd) came to Washington in 1969 to work in the Nixon administration, we spent the first several months learning how things worked in Washington rather than focusing on plans and programs. Why not give the new administration, we asked ourselves, a big head start with a set of policy recommendations for every major department and agency?

While no one could be certain that Ronald Reagan would win, we gambled that he would prevail and would be receptive to what one news agency called "a blueprint for grabbing the government by its frayed New Deal lapels and shaking out 48 years of liberal policies."

Reagan made history with his smashing victory over President Carter. And so too did Heritage with our original *Mandate for Leadership.* At the first meeting of the Reagan cabinet, it was given to every member. President Reagan personally endorsed *Mandate,* and some 60 percent of its recommendations were eventually adopted or implemented by his administration.

Never content and never satisfied, Heritage has continued to transform the nation's policies. Over the last twenty-five years, the foundation has played a key role in almost every major public policy debate in Washington, including the Strategic Defense Initiative (SDI), enterprise zones, health care, Social Security, the flat tax, the North American Free Trade Agreement (NAFTA), welfare reform, telecommunications deregulation, congressional reform, and the culture war. My association with Heritage during the years in which it has fought so many battles in behalf of freedom is a source of great personal pride.

Several of the most influential policy experts in America published their first major study at Heritage, including Charles Murray, author of *Losing Ground;* Marvin Olasky, author of *The Tragedy of American Compassion;* and Dinesh D'Souza, author of *Illiberal Education.* I must also mention the groundbreaking work of Heritage's own scholars, especially Stuart Butler, as well as Kim Holmes and Robert Rector. Time and again, they and their colleagues have made a difference in the direction of our nation's public policy with their shrewd insights and perceptive analyses.

I have always been struck by the fact that Heritage considers itself to be far more than a Washington research organization—it is committed to furthering and strengthening the American conservative movement. The foundation started the Resource Bank to help policy experts from across the country and the world to play a greater role in Washington policymaking. Heritage's *Guide to Public Policy Experts* contains information on more than 2,000 policy specialists and 400 institutions.

The foundation has actively supported the formation of state and regional think tanks from coast to coast. It holds an incredible 700 lectures, debates, conferences, briefings, and other events every year in its Washington headquarters. Today, Heritage is the institutional center of the conservative movement. And, to paraphrase an old Washington saying, what's good for the conservative movement is good for the country!

The Heritage Foundation is driven by the power of ideas. From the beginning, it has invited leading intellectuals to share their thoughts about the direction of the nation and the world. Among those who have been distinguished fellows or lecturers at Heritage are Friedrich A. Hayek, Russell Kirk, Walter Williams, Robert Conquest, Thomas Sowell, Ernest van den Haag, Owen Harries, and William J. Bennett.

Indeed, it is almost impossible to name a prominent conservative who has not visited Heritage—from Ronald Reagan, William F. Buckley Jr., Barry Goldwater, Phyllis Schlafly, Bob Dole, Dan Quayle, Jack Kemp, Jeane Kirkpatrick, and Steve Forbes to Newt Gingrich, Dick Armey, Trent Lott, Jesse Helms, Ralph Reed, and Clarence Thomas. Nor must I neglect to mention the many foreign leaders who have walked through Heritage's doors, like Margaret Thatcher of Great Britain, Poland's Lech Walesa, Prime Minister Lee Kuan Yew of Singapore, freedom fighters Jonas Savimbi and Natan Sharansky, Prime Minister Vaclav Klaus of the Czech Republic, and Israel's Benjamin Netanyahu.

One man has been at the center of The Heritage Foundation for the last twenty years, its president and CEO, Edwin J. Feulner Jr. Ed asked me to join Heritage's board of trustees some twenty years ago, and I have constantly marveled at his ability to handle so many different roles so well—manager, fund-raiser, intellectual, and above all, a perennially optimistic entrepreneur. I know Ed Feulner could be heading up a Fortune 500 company, but he has chosen a different but no less difficult path—to apply the principles of free enterprise, limited government, individual freedom, and traditional values to America's public policies.

Of course, Heritage is not a one-man band. Over 150 people—managers, analysts, fellows, scholars, and professional staffers—work together every day to advance the conservative agenda. More than 200,000 contributors make Heritage the most broadly supported think tank in America. And then there is the board of trustees which has included such distinguished men and women as Shelby Cullom Davis, Clare Boothe Luce, Frank Shakespeare, Jay Van Andel, Midge Decter, Joe Coors, and Richard Scaife. It's been a privilege for me to serve with them for two decades.

The story of The Heritage Foundation—and American politics for the last twenty-five years—is told compellingly in the following pages by author-historian Lee Edwards. He captures brilliantly the remarkable story of a remarkable organization at a remarkable time in our history.

That Heritage remains at the top of its game is evident in its creation and now coauthorship, with the *Wall Street Journal,* of *The Index of Economic Freedom,* which ranks the economies of 150 countries. I have said before that the *Index* will turn out to be the foundation's "most important" publication. It is a seminal work that demonstrates once and for all the indivisibility of political and economic liberty. It proves beyond all doubt that, wherever one looks in the world, where there is freedom, there is also prosperity. In many ways, the *Index* is a capstone to Heritage's work in behalf of freedom here and around the globe.

When it was launched twenty-five years ago, Heritage had one major goal — to create a think tank unlike any the nation's capital had previously known. Ed Feulner and all the other Heritage people have succeeded beyond all expectation. They have made The Heritage Foundation a permanent Washington institution, a uniquely American institution.

Everyone associated with the foundation (and those in public life and the media who have benefited from its work all these years) joins me, I am sure, in wishing Heritage a happy Silver Anniversary and wondering what important new ideas and policies it will produce between now and its Golden Anniversary in 2023!

Introduction

by William F. Buckley Jr.

I n the 1950s young Americans had routine experiences at college, after
college, at work, in the professional schools—business, law, medicine—and on the academic high ground of graduate school. Those who
thought to raise their eyes in search of ideological perspective had reason to wonder whether the infrastructure of marketplace thinking had
quite simply been abandoned by the productive sector of the American
establishment. The only journal of conservative opinion back then was a
tiny but valiant fortnightly published in New York, and an even tinier,
equally bright weekly newsletter/essay in Washington. The entire apparatus of American productivity—the business world—seemed to exist
only as a deposit of yesteryear's detritus, a shapeless hulk which cast darker
shadows with every textbook reference or academic allusion to the mate-
rialist way of life.

Of course there were here and there isolated exceptions, little enclaves
of free-market thought, but theirs was a life in the catacombs. Indeed, it
was the period symbolized by the Ford Foundation, a huge philanthropy
endowed by an heroic American entrepreneur. The foundation went so
far in the direction of trendiness as finally to bring on a disavowal of its
activities by the incumbent CEO. Although by instinct and inclination a
political accommodationist, Henry Ford II had tired of trying to explain
the policies of his family foundation's Fund for the Republic.

The advent of The Heritage Foundation would seem, in the circumstances, almost inevitable. But the inevitable doesn't always happen, viz., see my waistline. The productive community, notoriously indifferent to the laid-back world of thought and discussion, may simply forget that it is necessary to change the oil every three thousand miles. And then too, men of affairs do not everywhere linger over the consequences of intellectual and polemical immobility. I remember experiencing agonies back then, as I saw and heard one after another American businessman try hopelessly to contend against polished representatives of mammoth labor unions, hardwired political enthusiasts for statist activity, and academic establishmentarians whose hoops these and other businessmen jumped through at every trustees' meeting. As often as not the representatives of the marketplace left the stage or studio stripped bare by the prehensile facility of their opponents and exposed by the poverty of their resources and the flabbiness of their resolve.

But the inevitable did happen. An organization materialized that would substantially change the situation. It was one of several attempts, and spirited contemporaneous associations now flourish. But Mr. Lee Edwards has caught here the special magic of a foundation that began as small as the first tinkertoy engine of Henry Ford and grew in twenty-five years—the anniversary celebrated by this book—into a dynamo, the dominant think tank in the country.

The story is told with genuine enthusiasm by a talented and successful journalist and biographer. He recounts the little, almost incidental meetings between Harry and Jim and John and Joe. He reminds us that it was an uppity idea, to look the political scene in the face and make available to critically situated Americans—most specifically, legislators and chief executives—pertinent material, a familiarity with which could guide them to right reason. And he describes how the labors of The Heritage Foundation continue: the heavy task of maintaining a data base, and the delicate task of a tenderly swing of the compass. The objective? The reanimation and survival of the great productive enterprise that, though beset by taxation and manhandled by regulation, still manages to maintain a standard of living for the quarter-billion people here who are the envy of the world.

Lee Edwards tells the story from its earliest moment, generating dramatic tension in a half-dozen mini-episodes. The reader gasps with relief when he turns the page to find that, after all, Ed Feulner turned that other invitation down, electing to stick with Heritage. We wonder, Is it possible to find six Americans who would stake $250,000 each to come up with suitable quarters for Heritage? Yes, it proved possible. There are too many heroes in this book for the author to risk singling out one or two, and Edwards leaves the reader with a felt sense of gratitude to all those American men and women who saw an opportunity, recognized the scope of what needed to be done, and financed an enterprise that took wings.

Lee Edwards has given us a book comprehensive in scope and laced with nice detail. I learned in it the heart-warming fact that in its short history The Heritage Foundation's staff and invited friends heard sixty (60!) lectures by Russell Kirk. The datum is testimony to Mr. Feulner's loyalty to a neglected prince of conservative thought, as also to Feulner's ongoing concern that the mission of Heritage be continually examined at the profoundest level. Although his ways are entirely unassuming, one pauses, reading this book, to wonder how Ed Feulner can manage as he does. It helps that he disposes of the requisite biological and temperamental attributes—the capacity to go many hours without sleep, to travel endlessly attending to caseloads of work, to endure a day of meetings that begin at breakfast and end after midnight. Moreover, he exercises managerial responsibility so deftly and unpretentiously as to leave apparently unaffected the operation of his huge enterprise even when he is half a world away.

The idea of Heritage is to heighten economic and political literacy among those men and women whose decisions affect the course of the republic. In this endeavor the foundation had a great hour when Ronald Reagan was elected president and found waiting for him three volumes of material designed to help him chart the nation's course in the right direction. Sixty percent of the suggestions enjoined on the new president were acted upon (which is why Mr. Reagan's tenure was 60 percent successful).

Nor is the broader community of journalists, opinion makers, and academics ignored. The material generated by Heritage research and analysis flows out into the major arteries of American thought. We breathe more securely in the knowledge that high ideals, and right reason, are maintaining their eternal equilibrium in the awful tumult of an age that struggles so very hard to suppress American idealism. The power of ideas, indeed.

The Power of Ideas

1

A Modest Beginning

The early 1970s were the worst of times, and the best of times in which to launch a conservative think tank in Washington, D.C. Conservative leaders and conservative ideas were out of public favor. Vice President Spiro T. Agnew, the hero of many on the Right, resigned in disgrace in September 1973. Congressman Gerald Ford of Michigan, Agnew's successor, was the choice of the Republican establishment, not a conservative like Governor Ronald Reagan or Senator Barry M. Goldwater. The preceding year, Congressman John Ashbrook of Ohio, who had helped start the Draft Goldwater movement a decade earlier, had been trounced by President Nixon in the New Hampshire Republican presidential primary.

In foreign parts, détente was riding high in the saddle. The president traveled to Communist China to kowtow to Mao Zedong; an old ally and friend, the Republic of China, was kicked out of the United Nations. The United States withdrew from Vietnam despite conservative warnings about falling dominos in Southeast Asia, and Nixon signed SALT I, giving the Soviet Union nuclear parity with America. On the domestic front, the president instituted wage and price controls and tried to implement such welfarist proposals as the Family Assistance Plan. Nixon proudly proclaimed, "I am now a Keynesian in economics."[1]

As for think tanks, the American Enterprise Institute and the Center for Strategic and International Studies at Georgetown University were

1

providing most of the analysis for Washington conservatives, with AEI focusing on domestic policy and CSIS on foreign and national security affairs. A confidential memorandum for the February 1974 dinner celebrating William J. Baroody Sr.'s twentieth year with AEI listed a staff of fifty, twenty-four adjunct scholars, a "Talent Bank" of six thousand scholars and experts, the publication of sixty-four books and studies in 1973, the production of twelve one-hour television programs the previous year, and an annual budget of $3 million.[2]

And yet, given liberalism's dominance, there was a real need for an aggressively conservative think tank in one place—on Capitol Hill. Liberals had been kings of Congress for more years than anyone could count, and conservatives seemed unable to make more than a sporadic difference in the people's branch of government.

Envious conservatives watched the powerful liberal coalition of academics, think tank analysts, members of Congress, White House aides, interest group officials, and journalists run much of the business of the nation's capital and wondered: "Why can't *we* put together an operation like that?" And wondered some more. Yet the answer was clear: there was no conservative alternative to the Brookings Institution, the catalyst for many of the legislative successes of the liberals during the 1960s and early 1970s.

Time and again, a liberal professor would write an article suggesting the creation of a new federal program. The article would be quoted approvingly in the pages of the *New York Times* or the *Washington Post*. Studies of the suggested program would be underwritten by the Ford or Rockefeller Foundation. Scholars at Brookings would meet with members of Congress and their staffs to discuss how the program might be legislatively framed. Special interest groups would endorse the proposed legislation and contact their congressmen and senators. And, finally, a broad-based coalition would emerge—seemingly out of nowhere—backing the bill. The rest would roll smoothly into place: The liberal idea would become law, a new government agency would be created, a new social experiment would begin, and taxes would be raised.

A key moment in this alchemy occurred when Brookings' experts transmuted the academic's theoretical suggestion into a legislative proposal.

Such legislative legerdemain was old hat to Brookings, which had been an advocate for expanding the federal government since 1921. That year,

Brookings' predecessor, the Institute for Government Research (IGR), engineered passage of the Budget and Accounting Act, creating the Bureau of the Budget. According to Brookings historian James Allen Smith, the IGR drafted House and Senate versions of the budget reform bill, organized congressional testimony, and arranged publicity to generate public support. The institute was so committed to the idea of an executive-controlled budget process at the federal level that it even housed the new bureau and provided staff "until it could secure its own offices and personnel."[3]

Brookings performed the same service for the Kennedy transition team four decades later, supplying offices, a library, and meeting rooms at the institution's headquarters on Massachusetts Avenue, a block from Dupont Circle. According to Smith, the Kennedy transition task forces "relied heavily" on nearly one hundred scholars who were working on policy issues for Brookings.[4]

The liberal think tank's direct influence continued into the Carter years. A Brookings study in 1976, for example, recommended that the B-1 bomber be dropped from the Pentagon's arsenal. Six months after taking office, President Carter announced his decision to scrap plans for producing and deploying the B-1. Another 1976 Brookings report urged that the United States withdraw its ground troops from South Korea. One year later, in the face of strong military objections, Carter released plans for just such a withdrawal, although he later changed his mind.[5]

As the future head of The Heritage Foundation described the state of legislative affairs in the early 1970s, "The Left had a finely tuned policy-making machine, and the Right had nothing to match it."[6]

Timing Is Everything

The congressional debate over the supersonic transport (SST) in the spring of 1971 was the catalyst for the founding of a conservative public policy organization that could get the right information to members of Congress and to their staffs *on time*.

Prior to votes in the House and Senate in March, supporters and opponents of the SST lobbied Congress furiously. Backers argued that continuing development of the giant high-speed airliner (federally funded since 1962) was necessary to maintain American superiority in aerospace technology and marketing, and to avoid unemployment in the aerospace industry. The opposition charged that a fleet of SSTs would contaminate the atmosphere and could even "trigger a cancer-producing fallout." It also asserted that no broad-based market existed for the aircraft which, they said, would cater only to wealthy travelers.[7]

Most conservatives felt that funds for the supersonic transport should come from the private rather than the public sector, although some favored continuing the program at taxpayer expense to maintain U.S. technological superiority over the Soviets (who began SST test flights that year). But where was the authoritative analysis that could be used in a floor debate?

Shortly after the Senate voted—by only 51–46—to halt government support of a supersonic transport plane, two young conservative staffers met for one of their frequent breakfasts in the basement cafeteria of the U.S. Capitol. Twenty-eight-year-old Paul M. Weyrich was press secretary to Senator Gordon Allott (R-Colo.). Edwin J. Feulner Jr., just thirty, was administrative assistant to Congressman Philip Crane, an outspoken conservative Republican from Illinois. Both young men had been inspired by Barry Goldwater's principled run for the presidency in 1964 and called themselves movement conservatives.

Weyrich was visibly upset. He held aloft a monograph by the American Enterprise Institute that presented the pros and cons of the SST issue, fairly and concisely. It was just what busy Hill staffers needed to prepare their members for debate. But the study had arrived in Senator Allott's offices and been placed on Weyrich's desk a couple of days *after* the Senate vote. Informed by fellow conservative Morton Blackwell, then on the senior staff of AEI, that the institute's tardiness was deliberate, a curious Weyrich called William J. Baroody Sr., AEI's president.

"Great study," said Weyrich. "Why didn't we get it sooner?"

Baroody's response was to the point, "We didn't want to try to affect the outcome of the vote."[8]

Baroody's caution was understandable. As early as 1950, AEI (then called the American Enterprise Association) had been criticized by a congressional committee for presenting "only the viewpoint of big business" in its materials.[9] In 1964, Bill Baroody was deeply involved in Barry Goldwater's presidential campaign, coordinating the writing of the candidate's speeches and position papers and consulting on an almost daily basis with Goldwater. Although Baroody had taken full official leave from AEI, his political role had been noted by President Lyndon Johnson. In 1965, according to Charles Lichenstein, a long-time Baroody associate, there was a "quite thorough IRS investigation" of AEI. That same year, AEI's board of trustees seriously debated whether it should replace Baroody as the organization's president. Baroody survived, but he never forgot that think tanks and politics can be a dangerous mixture.

Among the changes Baroody instituted over the next several years were a withdrawal from current issues (e.g., the legislative analysis division was eliminated) and an emphasis on a longer-range agenda.[10] For young true believers like Weyrich and Feulner, AEI's deliberate noninvolvement in a timely policy debate was inexplicable.

"It was at that moment," recalls Feulner, "that Paul and I decided that conservatives needed an independent research institute designed to influence the policy debate as it was occurring in Congress—*before* decisions were made."[11] They envisioned an activist think tank but separate from Congress and not officially connected to any political party.

Although Weyrich and Feulner never talked with him about it, Patrick J. Buchanan, then working for Nixon aide H. R. Haldeman, had developed a plan similar to the Weyrich-Feulner analysis. Buchanan had made himself the White House expert on "how the liberal beast operated" in Washington, and within days of Nixon's reelection in November 1972, he presented the president with a lengthy memorandum on how "to make permanent the New Majority."[12]

An enduring Republican majority, Buchanan wrote, required the building of an institute that would serve as "the repository of its political beliefs." Such an institute would have three roles: a "talent bank" for Republicans in office, a "tax-exempt refuge" for them when out of office, and a "communications center" for Republican thinkers across the nation. "AEI is not the answer," Buchanan said flatly. The tough young conservative wanted an institution with imaginative leadership that would provide "a realistic and principled alternative" to programs and policies emanating from "an essentially liberal-left bureaucracy" and its allies like the Brookings Institution.[13]

The foundation for such an institute was, in fact, being laid.

Founding the Foundation

The idea of a conservative research organization surfaced in 1968 when James Lucier, an assistant to Senator Strom Thurmond (R-S.C.), introduced Paul Weyrich to Victor Fediay, an analyst at the Library of Congress. Fediay kept talking about the need for some kind of "outside" organization that would provide studies about current issues for senators. The three conservatives agreed that conservative senators were often unable to get a grip on key issues for want of information, while liberal senators could always depend on the Brookings Institution. But, Fediay argued, what was needed was not a conservative think tank but a research firm that would provide conservatively oriented materials gratis to members of Congress and would charge corporations a fee for the same materials. Throughout that year, Lucier, Weyrich, and Fediay expounded their idea to corporate representatives whenever they could but were unable to spark any serious interest.

Frustrated by the lack of response to their plan and the continued ineffectiveness of conservatives in Washington, Weyrich in early 1969 telephoned a longtime friend and mentor, J. Frederic (Fritz) Rench, in Racine, Wisconsin, and asked for his help. Rench, a successful businessman and Republican activist, drafted a prospectus, and that spring, Weyrich, Lucier, Fediay, and Dr. William Roberts, a professor of law at the Catholic University of America, flew to Wisconsin to confer with him.

Rench listened to the four men complain loudly about the shortsightedness of the business community and then asked quietly, "Where is your business plan?"

Weyrich and the others admitted they didn't have one.

"What is your budget?"

They hadn't prepared one.

"How can you expect businessmen," Rench asked, "to support something that doesn't have a business plan or a budget?"

There was no answer until Weyrich, rarely at a loss for words, said, "Will you write one for us?"

Rench agreed and found himself, in the summer of 1969, ensconced in Senator Strom Thurmond's hideaway office in the bowels of the U.S. Capitol, writing and rewriting a business plan (including salaries, rent, telephone, printing, and office equipment) for a new venture called

Analysis and Research Association, Inc. (ARA). Its annual budget was a modest $80,000.[14]

The four would-be entrepreneurs thanked Rench warmly for his labors and began showing their new business plan to prospective corporate clients, but were still unable to find any takers. The future of ARA (and The Heritage Foundation) now turned on the high temperature of Barbara Hughes, an assistant to Senator Allott. One morning in the summer of 1970, Hughes called in sick.

That day a letter addressed to Allott arrived in the office. Ordinarily, it would have been directed by Hughes to the senator or his administrative assistant. Instead, it was given by an intern to press secretary Weyrich. The letter was from Jack Wilson, who had just become the assistant for political affairs to Joseph Coors, the president of the largest brewery west of the Mississippi and an outspoken conservative.

Determined to have his company more involved in the political process, Coors told Jack Wilson to conduct a nationwide search for the right "investment" in the conservative movement. Wilson sent letters to a long list of prominent political figures, including Colorado's senior U.S. senator, Gordon Allott, asking for suggestions.

Weyrich recalls that his hands "began to tremble" as he read the letter. He immediately called Wilson and said, "We need to talk—I have an opportunity in mind for Mr. Coors."[15]

Wilson traveled to Washington where Weyrich, Lucier, and the others explained the urgent need on Capitol Hill for an independent research operation. "We razzle-dazzled him" so well, remembers Weyrich, that Joseph Coors himself came to Washington for an in-depth briefing. Weyrich laid on an impressive program for the Colorado businessman, featuring Senator Cliff Hansen (R-Wyo.), Senator Strom Thurmond, Congressman Henry C. Schadeberg (R-Wis.), Congressman Ed Foreman (R-N.Mex.), and Walter Mote, an aide to Vice President Agnew. Hansen described how "the other side" controlled the information flow in Washington and asserted that Weyrich and his associates were "the guys" who could counter the liberals.[16]

Weyrich was excited about how well the presentation had gone until he learned that Coors was also considering "investing" in the American Enterprise Institute. His high hopes collapsed. How could an unknown, untested research firm compete with a respected think tank that had been operating for nearly thirty years? Casting about for help, Weyrich arranged for Coors and Wilson to talk with fellow conservative Lyn Nofziger, a deputy assistant to President Nixon for congressional relations. Along with Ed Feulner, they met in Nofziger's large pastel-blue office in the Old Executive Office Building next to the White House.

So, what about AEI? Coors asked Nofziger.

"AEI?" repeated the White House aide. And, according to Weyrich, he strolled over to a bookshelf and blew some dust off an AEI study. "That's what they're good for—collecting dust. They do great work but they're not timely. What we need are studies for Congress while legislation is being considered."[17]

Coors later told Weyrich that two things made him decide to go with Analysis and Research Association, despite the obvious youth of its principals: Lyn Nofziger's dismissal of AEI as too academic and ARA's "tremendous business plan."[18]

And that was the beginning. If there had been no ARA, and no Robert M. Schuchman Memorial Foundation (ARA's successor), there would, in all likelihood, have been no Heritage Foundation.

The Coors Connection

ARA started as a joint venture with the Adolph Coors Company, with Coors investing some $250,000 for 1971–1972. Jim Lucier served as ARA's president, and Jack Wilson as its treasurer. Its first offices were in a basement apartment behind the Supreme Court. ARA became immediately involved in researching and analyzing a number of key issues on Capitol Hill, including the Family Assistance Plan. It contracted with Roger Freeman at the Hoover Institution to write an anti-FAP report. And it was Freeman who, despite the objections of other Reagan aides, persuaded Reagan, then governor of California, to testify against FAP before the Senate Finance Committee in February 1972. Weyrich recalls that Senator Russell Long (D-La.) told Senator Carl T. Curtis (R-Neb.) that if Reagan came out publicly against the Family Assistance Plan, "we can kill it." At the conclusion of Reagan's statement, Senator Long praised it as "truly magnificent" and the "most eloquent" of any testimony before the committee.[19]

Joe Coors' decision to commit his company to a prominent role in public affairs was reinforced when he read a confidential 5,000-word memorandum by Lewis F. Powell, a prominent Democratic attorney in Richmond, Virginia (later named to the Supreme Court by President Nixon). At the invitation of the U.S. Chamber of Commerce, Powell detailed what he called the "broad attack" on the free enterprise system, criticized the general "apathy and default" of American business, and urged business executives to take "effective action" against the threat. After making a number of recommendations (such as naming an executive vice president to coordinate corporate action), Powell ended his memorandum bluntly: "Business and the enterprise system are in deep trouble, and the hour is late."[20]

Coors recalls that the Powell memorandum "stirred" him up and convinced him that American business was "ignoring" a crisis.[21] He wondered why business leaders and organizations weren't speaking out more forcefully against President Nixon's "new economic policy" which included a ninety-day freeze on all wages and prices and a Cost of Living Council that would work with labor and business to achieve continued wage and price "stability."[22] The Colorado conservative was also impressed by a speech given by former Treasury Secretary Henry Fowler, who exhorted him and other business leaders to become more politically involved.

But the political vehicle that Coors chose had organizational problems from the start. Lucier was at heart an academician; Weyrich was a political activist; Fediay would take off on unexplained trips to Europe; and Roberts was knowledgeable but unpredictable. Coors did not want to remain the sole sponsor, but ARA was unable to attract other major backers. "They were dedicated," recalls Joseph Coors, "but not unified." In the fall of 1972, Wilson told Weyrich to find another vehicle—ARA wasn't working.[23]

A concerned Weyrich mentioned his predicament to fellow conservative Dan Joy, who mentioned a dormant tax-exempt organization that could be easily taken over—the Robert M. Schuchman Memorial Foundation, named after the first president of Young Americans for Freedom who had died at twenty-seven of a brain embolism. Shortly after the Weyrich-Joy conversation, a reconstituted, Coors-funded Schuchman Foundation opened offices in a small office building at Second Street and Massachusetts Avenue, N.E., half a block from the present Heritage headquarters.

The new president was Paul Weyrich, and Weyrich, Joseph Coors, Jack Wilson, and Ed Feulner were elected to the board of directors. Richard M. Scaife, a generous backer of many conservative and anticommunist causes, soon joined Coors as a financial supporter of the Schuchman Foundation. A few other conservative businessmen, like industrialist William Brady of Milwaukee, also contributed to the new research organization. It seemed that Schuchman might find a niche in the Washington community.

But the board of directors became increasingly divided over the organization's direction. Members of the old board preferred a more traditional approach to public policy, relying on conferences and the publication of papers. The new members, led by Weyrich and Feulner, wanted to affect the legislative process promptly and directly. Before long, recalls Joy, "divorce became inevitable."[24]

But first it was decided that Schuchman would be converted into a public-interest law center (with Ed Feulner as president), while a new and separate public-policy foundation with its own 501(c)(3) status would be created. The lawyers, led by Edward McCabe, who had worked in the 1964 Goldwater presidential campaign, prepared the necessary papers for the IRS. But they needed a name for the new entity.

Weyrich studied a list of possibilities. The James Madison Foundation? One already existed. The Commonwealth Foundation? Too vague. He considered using the name of a Wisconsin congressman whom he had long admired, but the family objected. Finally, one evening an impatient Joseph Coors telephoned Weyrich and told him, "You *will* have a name by tomorrow morning." The next morning, still uninspired, Weyrich and his wife Joyce went for their usual walk near their home in Annandale, Virginia. As they strolled along, Weyrich noted a new sign on a vacant lot: "Coming Soon: Heritage Town Houses." He turned to his wife and said triumphantly, "That's it!" Lawyers confirmed there was no Heritage Foundation on the books; Weyrich informed Coors, who enthusiastically endorsed the name.[25]

The Heritage Foundation was formally incorporated in the District of Columbia on February 16, 1973. The three original trustees were Marvin H. (Mickey) Edwards, later a Republican member of Congress from Oklahoma; businessman John Perrino of Rhode Island; and Fritz Rench. On March 23, the board of trustees was increased to six with the addition of Ed Feulner, Jack Wilson, and Forrest Rettgers, who would become executive vice president of the National Association of Manufacturers. On that same date, Rettgers was elected chairman of the board and Weyrich president of Heritage.[26]

On Their Own

The long-developing divorce between Schuchman and Heritage became final following a heated board meeting at Thanksgiving time 1973. After being told repeatedly what he could and could not do with the money he had contributed to the foundation, Coors, usually the most even-tempered of men, stood up suddenly, remarked that this was not the way the real world operated, and announced that he, Weyrich, Wilson, and Feulner were resigning from the Schuchman board. Back in the foundation offices behind the gas station, the four conservatives looked questioningly at each other.

"What are we going to do now?" someone asked.[27]

Unsure how to answer the question, Weyrich began sorting through the mail on his desk. Abruptly, he stopped. He could not believe his eyes: There was a letter from the IRS. Eagerly, he opened it and learned that, effective November 27, 1973, tax-deductible status had been granted to The Heritage Foundation.

"Gentlemen," said Weyrich, "I have the answer." Waving the IRS letter, he said, "Tomorrow, we begin operating as The Heritage Foundation."[28]

They stayed up much of the night, separating files, papers, and financial accounts, leaving Schuchman a reasonable bank balance. The next morning, Weyrich told the staff of ten that they were now working for The Heritage Foundation. Heritage stayed in the Wheat Growers Building, while Schuchman moved its public-interest law activities (without Feulner, who returned to Capitol Hill as administrative assistant to Congressman Crane) to offices near the Supreme Court. Jeffrey B. Gayner, who would work for Heritage in a variety of top research positions for nearly twenty years, recalls a "seamless change" from Schuchman to Heritage.[29]

In late January, the Schuchman Foundation sponsored a highly successful one-day program on "the energy crisis," featuring a luncheon "dialogue" between Senator James L. Buckley (R-N.Y.) and Senator William

Proxmire (D-Wis.) that drew several hundred people. During an after-noon panel, Milton Friedman argued that the market, not the govern-ment, should determine oil prices. "What we need," Friedman said, "is *not* a specific, detailed [government] blueprint for the future but an adapt-able adjustment machine"—i.e., the "price system."[30] Plans for another conference, with Friedman again a featured speaker, were drawn up, but funds ran short. Within eighteen months, the Robert M. Schuchman Memorial Foundation quietly faded from view.

For its part, The Heritage Foundation would undergo several more changes over the next three years before finally finding the right combi-nation of leadership and issues that would make it during the Reagan years "a major player in national policy."[31]

The Watergate Factor

Like every other institution in the nation's capital, Heritage was affected by the Watergate scandal. Even before President Nixon resigned in August 1974 rather than face certain impeachment, Weyrich had concluded that the fall elections could well be a disaster for the Republican Party. Guided as usual by his activist impulses, Weyrich resigned as president of Heritage in March and started the Committee for the Survival of a Free Congress. Jerry P. James, a legislative veteran of many Hill battles, was picked to suc-ceed Weyrich. Lawrence D. Pratt became treasurer, and Mrs. Charles E. Thomann, secretary. Jeff Gayner, who was pursuing a doctoral program at the University of North Carolina at Chapel Hill, became foreign pol-icy studies director.

But over the ensuing months it became clear that James, an excellent speechwriter and legislative analyst, was not suited for the position of chief executive of a Washington public-policy organization. Besides, James wanted to return to his native Oklahoma. Before he left, however, he and others at the foundation produced a prospectus that offers revealing insights into the early Heritage. Pointing to the "disproportionate influ-ence" of the Ford Foundation and "the Brookings Institute" [sic] on pub-lic policy, the foundation promised to provide in-depth research based on "traditional American economic and social values" and the Constitu-tion. Its audience would be "the public at large" and members of Congress "who struggle to cope with the initiatives of the liberal-socialist 'think tanks.'"

The prospectus mentioned several areas that would receive "particular [research] emphasis" in 1974, including international trade, energy, federal spending, public campaign financing, tax reform, environmental issues, legal services, public education, and Social Security—an ambitious list considering that Heritage had only a handful of analysts. The foundation also committed to a "Washington Semester Plan program" that would educate "mature college level students" about the "practical, inside operation of Congress" and interest them "in legislative government as a career." Finally, it planned to sponsor lectures and debates, particularly at colleges and universities, and to disseminate information about its activities to the "press and news media." The "annual projected budget" was to be $525,000.[32]

Heritage has come a long way since this first, amateurish prospectus. Today, the foundation is careful to get the names of its competitors and colleagues right (e.g., the Brookings *Institution*). It does not indulge in rhetorical overkill by describing liberal think tanks as "socialist." And it does not bite off more than it can chew. Even the present Heritage, with a professional staff of some seventy analysts and fellows, is hard pressed to deal adequately with every major issue before Congress. It was clearly an impossible task in 1974 for a brand new think tank with only three or four professionals.

The Reagan Connection

A search committee for a new Heritage Foundation president was formed, and Frank J. Walton, former secretary of business and transportation for Governor Reagan in California, was hired. He took up his duties as president on June 9, 1975.

In his late fifties, Walton had been a successful California businessman before joining the Reagan administration in Sacramento. He was tall, charming, and almost as good a storyteller as Reagan. And there was no question about his conservative credentials: his California license plate had read: "CUT TAXES." Reagan was by now indubitably the future of the Republican Party, and to have someone from his gubernatorial cabinet as head of Heritage gave the new foundation instant credibility. Walton, moreover, delighted in calling on U.S. senators and congressmen and telling them about Heritage. He once remarked to Russell Long, chairman of the Senate Finance Committee, "Think of us as an extension of your committee staff." Long, who commanded a staff twice the size of Heritage, must have been amused. But Walton could get in to see Long when a Weyrich or Feulner could not—at least not yet.[33]

And Walton was not shy about asking foundations and corporate executives for money. During his tenure as president (Walton informed the board that he would stay for two years and no longer), Heritage's income more than doubled, from $413,497 at the end of 1974 to just over $1 million in 1976. Also, in one of the most important decisions in the foundation's history, Walton introduced direct-mail fund-raising to Heritage. Written by Mary Elizabeth Lewis of Steve Winchell & Associates, the first mailing focused on the unionization of the military and featured a photo of a very small Heritage Foundation and a very large Brookings Institution—David vs. Goliath. The mailing was succeessful, producing several thousand donors, the first in an ever-increasing flow of individual supporters that would yield over 200,000 donors some twenty-five years later.[34] Winchell & Associates has remained the foundation's direct mail fundraising agency, a relationship that probably belongs in the *Guiness World Book of Records*.

An Historic Challenge

Meanwhile, Walton's former boss announced in November 1975 that, although a Republican already sat in the White House, he would be a candidate for his party's 1976 presidential nomination. Ronald Reagan declared that "the American dream" had been mislaid and promised to reduce "the power centralized in Washington."[35] A Gallup Poll subsequently showed that Reagan had surged ahead of President Ford among Republicans and independents. In an NBC survey, the former California governor led Democrat Hubert Humphrey by 48–44 percent while Ford trailed, 44–46 percent.

The New Hampshire primary was, as usual, the first in the nation and accordingly a key contest although only twenty delegates were at stake. A heavily favored Reagan received 49.4 percent of the popular vote and lost New Hampshire by a razor-thin margin of 1,587 votes. Ford won succeeding primaries in Florida, Illinois (Reagan's birthplace), and Wisconsin, thus establishing himself as the clear front-runner.

But suddenly an aroused Reagan began hitting the president hard on the Panama Canal treaties, détente, and deficit spending. With the guidance of Senator Jesse Helms and his campaign aide Tom Ellis, Reagan gave a brilliant TV performance on the eve of the March North Carolina primary. He defeated Ford in the Tarheel State and began a comeback that almost made political history.

But Republicans are loyalist to a fault. They knew and liked Jerry Ford, they were comfortable with him, and they felt Ford had earned the nomination through his years of service to the party. Thus, despite Reagan wins in delegate-rich Texas and California, the advantage began shifting inexorably to President Ford. At the national convention in Kansas City, Reagan lost the nomination to Ford by a mere 1,187 to 1,070 delegates. He would have been the first candidate in ninety-two years to take the nomination from an incumbent president seeking reelection.

After his nomination, a magnanimous Ford asked Reagan to say a few words. His remarks were the rhetorical highlight of the 1976 convention and a foretaste of 1980 and beyond. Without notes or TelePrompTer, Reagan spoke of the problems confronting the nation—"the erosion of freedom," "the invasion of private rights," "the controls and restrictions" on the economy. And he described the "missiles of destruction" that the great powers had "aimed at each other."

What will Americans of the Tricentennial, Reagan wondered, say about the Americans of the Bicentennial? "Will they look back with appreciation and say, 'Thank God for those people in 1976 who headed off that loss of freedom; who kept us now a hundred years later free; who kept our world from nuclear destruction'?... This is our challenge."[36]

Four years later, Ronald Reagan used these same themes—an unfettered economy, individual freedom, and peace through strength—to win the Republican nomination and the presidency, and to launch what came to be called the Reagan Revolution.

Moving Up

While Reagan was trying to move into 1600 Pennsylvania Avenue, The Heritage Foundation—thanks to a $300,000 gift from Joseph Coors—was moving to 513 C Street, N.E., a renovated movie theater facing Stanton Park, six blocks from the Capitol. But things were still cramped: Milton R. Copulos recalls that one analyst worked out of a one-time broom closet.[37]

There was much to analyze. According to an OMB study cited by Heritage, the total cost of federal regulations to the American economy in 1976 was as much as $130 billion. The Kremlin, warned foreign affairs analyst Miles M. Costick, viewed U.S.-Soviet trade not merely as a commercial transaction, but also as a political act. George Washington University professor Charles Moser pointed out that the federal budget had grown so large that the percentage of national income taken by all levels of government had reached an alarming 40 percent. And then there was the American health system.

That same year, Heritage published a sixty-two-page monograph entitled, *The British National Health Service in Theory and Practice: A Critical Analysis of Socialized Medicine*. The coauthors, who taught at St. Andrew's University in Scotland, were Eamonn F. Butler and Stuart M. Butler. The latter would become vice president of domestic and economic policy studies at The Heritage Foundation. The Butlers found "startling parallels" between British socialized medicine, which had produced "unsatisfied demands and shortages" in every health sector in Britain at an ever-increasing cost, and America's Medicare and Medicaid programs. They stated that "virtually all [cost] restraint has been stripped away" from the U.S. programs since Congress elected to reimburse users of the system on the basis of "reasonable cost."

The inevitable result, the Butlers said, was "inflationary cost increases, declining efficiency of medical services in terms of their costs, and over-equipping of many hospitals."[38] The only workable solution was "a system of private medical insurance" with tax concessions for those who could provide for themselves and "direct assistance to those who cannot."[39] Led by Stuart Butler, Heritage would make much the same arguments twenty years later during the fierce public debate over the Clinton health care plan.

Along with a steady stream of monographs, Heritage also emphasized its "quick response capability." Elected representatives, Walton asserted in an early foundation newsletter, are "quickly and accurately informed on any topic of national consequence."[40] The means most frequently used by Heritage were the *Backgrounder* and the *Issue Bulletin*. The first *Backgrounders* usually ran four pages, and were printed on beige paper. The very earliest ones did not carry the disclaimer that is now as much a part of Heritage literature as its Liberty Bell symbol: "Nothing written here is to be construed as an attempt to aid or hinder the passage of any bill before Congress." The research was dependable, the language adequate. But the studies fell far short of the fact-filled, fast-moving style that came to characterize Heritage's publications in the 1980s.

Conscious of its responsibility to further the conservative movement, Heritage published a monthly newsletter with items about organizations ranging from the Pacific Legal Foundation to the American Legislative Exchange Council, the Intercollegiate Studies Institute, the National Federation of Independent Business, Young America's Foundation, and the Hoover Institution at Stanford University.

Another Heritage project, the Communications Network, helped place speakers like Congressman Phil Crane, Senator Jake Garn of Utah, Dr. Phil Gramm (then a professor at Texas A&M University), Congressman Jack Kemp of New York, and Dr. Henry Manne (director of the University of Miami Law & Economics Center), who supported "the free enterprise system." Once a sponsoring group had requested a speaker, the foundation arranged all the details, including transportation and media coverage free of charge. In April 1977 alone, Heritage booked thirty "free enterprise" speeches to counteract the liberal themes of the Carter years.

That same year, the foundation published the transcript of a debate held at St. Olaf College in Minnesota between syndicated columnist and author Jeffrey St. John and Jeremy Rifkin, a veteran radical and head of the People's Bicentennial Commission. Rifkin called for a second American revolution against "Big Business," which, he said, was running and ruining the country. St. John responded that the People's Bicentennial Commission wanted not a second American revolution, but a replay of the blood-stained French Revolution of 1789, which "centralized power in the hands of an elite few who claimed to be acting in the name of the people."[41] An introduction explained that Heritage was pledged "to the preservation and furthering of traditional American values" and hoped that publication of the debate would contribute "to that goal."[42]

However, the phrase "traditional American values" was not formally added to Heritage's mission statement until 1993. As a matter of policy, the foundation decided in the late 1970s to concentrate on economic and foreign policy/national security questions, leaving social issues like abortion, gay rights, and prayer in the schools in the main to other public-policy organizations. But by the early 1990s, the decline of American culture had become so pronounced that Heritage felt compelled to start a cultural policy studies program. William J. Bennett, former secretary of education and chairman of the National Endowment for the Humanities, served as its major spokesman.

At the Crossroads

As the fireworks of America's bicentennial year faded, citizens speculated about their new Democratic president, looking for clues in the 1976 Democratic platform, which, according to the *New York Times,* "was fashioned in the image of Jimmy Carter."[43] For conservatives, the platform made ominous reading. It said, for example, that the United States "must set annual targets for employment, production and price stability"—a clear endorsement of national economic planning. The platform also endorsed national health insurance, a guaranteed annual income, "mandatory" school busing, gun control, repeal of Section 14(b) of the Taft-Hartley Law (allowing state right-to-work laws), a reduction of defense spending, and a new Panama Canal treaty. The estimated cost of the Carter platform was $750 billion—suggesting why workers from the 1972 McGovern campaign labored so hard for Carter's victory in November 1976.[44]

The trustees and staff of The Heritage Foundation, meanwhile, completed a third year with mixed feelings about their performance and their future. The foundation was producing some solid work and was being quoted, at least in the conservative media. But Heritage was seen by most of the Washington establishment as part of the emerging New Right and was relegated to the fringe of politics and policy. The *Washington Post,* for example, described Heritage as "controlled" by Joseph Coors, who, according to the *Post,* believed that the United States had to be rescued from liberalism lest it become "another version of godless communism."[45]

The media again stressed the Heritage-New Right connection when the foundation's legal counsel, James McKenna, paid frequent visits to Kanawha County, West Virginia, to help parents who objected to the liberal textbooks chosen for their schools. The struggle of the Kanawha County parents against West Virginia's educational establishment (and the National Education Association) was prominently featured in *Conservative Digest* and other New Right publications.[46] Further evidence of Heritage's tilt to the New Right was provided by its publication, in late 1976, of a *Critical Issues* study entitled "Secular Humanism and the Schools: The Issue Whose Time Has Come," by Dr. Onalee McGraw. The thirty-page pamphlet was described as "a case study of the growth of humanistic teaching in the public schools and the efforts of local parent groups to stymie the humanistic trend."[47] It quickly went into a second printing and became one of Heritage's most popular early studies.

But some trustees wondered whether this was the right direction for the foundation. Wasn't Heritage's primary target the Congress? If so, then policy analyst Milt Copulos's testimony before the Environmental Protection Agency about the potential serious burdens to small and medium-sized businesses of the Toxic Substances Control Act was more important than the McGraw pamphlet about secular humanism—an issue over which Congress had little effective control.

At this critical moment in Heritage's history, Frank Walton announced at a trustees' meeting in February 1977 that his two years as president would soon be up, and he wanted to go home to California as quickly as possible. Suddenly, trustees were forced to ask themselves: Who should succeed Walton? Indeed, there was even some question as to who would *want* to succeed him.

In those early days, Heritage did not resemble the flagship of a mighty conservative fleet. It was only a small, overcrowded oil tanker. The foundation's staff of twenty-five worked cheek by jowl out of a small two-story building. They had only one Xerox machine, several electric typewriters, and no computers, but they did have a compulsory prayer meeting every Monday morning. Distribution of Heritage publications was unorganized. Richard Odermatt, longtime director of research production, recalls that once or twice a week he would make a circuit of perhaps twenty or thirty congressional offices, dropping off copies of the latest Heritage study, fresh from the foundation's copying machine.[48]

What was needed was someone who would take command of Heritage and enable the foundation to realize its promise and fulfill the intentions of its founders.

2

A New President

In March 1977, President Jimmy Carter proposed four radical changes in American election laws that would materially affect the emerging conservative presence in Congress: federal financing of all congressional elections, "instant" voter registration, active participation in politics by federal employees, and the direct election of the president—i.e., the elimination of the electoral college.

Republican senators met and gloomily decided that nothing could be done to stop the changes which would seriously damage the party. However, a group of youthful conservative activists outside Congress stepped in with a strategy to block Carter's pseudo-populist plan. Led by Paul Weyrich and direct-mail expert Richard A. Viguerie, they sent special mailings to major Republican donors, asking them to call their senators. They wrote op-ed articles for leading newspapers in key states and held frequent briefings for the news media to explain—on one occasion by using a Heritage study—why they opposed the changes. And they mailed "millions of letters," urging people to contact their congressmen by telephone, postcard, and letter.[1]

Unlike the wooden, often pompous Old Right, these new conservatives were particularly adroit at public relations. At a July news conference, for example, Congressmen Steve Symms of Idaho and Robert Dornan of California displayed poster-size voter ID cards to demonstrate the possibilities for fraud inherent in the instant registration proposal. The cards featured photos of Symms and Dornan but carried the names of liberal Democrats on the House Administration Committee who favored the Carter registration plan. The influential (now defunct) *Washington Star* responded to the GOP satire by featuring the phony IDs on page one. The Democratic chairman of the House Administration Committee kept the story going by losing his temper and publicly railing at the Republicans.

Another proof of the New Right's political sophistication was its willingness to join forces with the liberal National Committee for an Effective Congress and with Common Cause. NCEC opposed parts of the campaign finance bill while Common Cause objected to Carter's amendments to the Hatch Act. Inside the Senate, Senator Paul Laxalt of Nevada organized and led a successful filibuster that blocked the combined efforts of the president, Senate Majority Leader Robert Byrd of West Virginia, liberal icon Edward M. Kennedy of Massachusetts, and other liberal Democrats to pass taxpayer financing of congressional elections.

On August 2, 1977, the liberals gave up, and the election law "reforms" designed to put conservatives out of business were laid to rest. The *New York Times* remarked that "the New Right ... is more tightly organized, better financed, more sophisticated and more pragmatic than their predecessors." Lyn Nofziger, the once and future presidential aide, commented that "the Old Right were talkers and pamphleteers. They would just as soon go down in flames as win. But the New Right has moved toward a more pragmatic goal of accomplishing things."[2]

Although not an official organ of the New Right, The Heritage Foundation nevertheless benefited from its energetic efforts in Washington and across the country. For example, a more conscious conservative force in Congress, one that required policy research and analysis, was forged. And the conservative grassroots was made more receptive to fund-raising appeals from a right-minded think tank in Washington.

Less than four years after it had been launched against enormous odds, The Heritage Foundation seemed poised to make a real difference. But first it had to find a new leader.

The Obvious Choice

"Ed Feulner was our choice from the beginning," remembers Fritz Rench, a member of the search committee for a new Heritage president. Joseph Coors concurs, remarking, "Ed was the right person for the job."[3] To begin with, Feulner knew the foundation, having been a founding member of the board of trustees since March 1973 and the corporate secretary since 1975. And he knew Capitol Hill with his decade of experience as an aide to Congressman Melvin R. Laird, then chairman of the House Republican Conference; as administrative assistant to Congressman Phil Crane; and as the executive director of the Republican Study Committee for the preceding three years.

Feulner had immersed himself in the conservative movement as an undergraduate at Regis College in Denver where he first read *The Conservative Mind* by Russell Kirk, *God and Man at Yale* by William F. Buckley Jr., and *The Conscience of a Conservative* by Barry Goldwater.[4] Since then, he had been a Weaver Fellow of the Intercollegiate Studies Institute; had helped found the Philadelphia Society with Bill Buckley, Milton Friedman, and Donald Lipsett; had been elected to the prestigious Mont Pelerin Society at age thirty-two; and had become a member of the core group of young conservatives that guided much of the movement's activities in Washington. And he knew how to get things done, as the increasing impact of the Republican Study Committee on House legislation demonstrated.

Feulner was interested in the Heritage presidency, but he had a problem: he was on the verge of becoming the head of another think tank. Antony Fisher, founder of the London-based Institute for Economic Affairs (IEA), had known Feulner since his graduate days at the London School of Economics and had approached him about starting an American IEA either in New York City or Washington, D.C. Like its British counterpart, the new organization would be a scholarly free-market think tank that produced mostly books and monographs intended to influence the academic world and the media.

Feulner agreed to help Fisher, and the two men met with a third conservative, New York lawyer William Casey. (Casey would later serve President Reagan as his extremely effective but often controversial CIA director.) Fisher, Casey, and Feulner were the original incorporators of the International Center for Economic Policy Studies (ICEPS), which became the influential Manhattan Institute for Policy Research. Feulner was on the verge of accepting Fisher's invitation to be ICEPS founding president when he was offered the leadership of Heritage.

But Feulner had real doubts about Heritage. As he later recalled, "Heritage was still in its embryonic stages and was almost as iffy a proposition as Fisher's think tank. I did not know whether Heritage would even be around in two years."[5] But, on the other hand, Heritage was in place and had a defined mission. Either way, Feulner was ready to leave Capitol Hill (the frustrations generated by a 270–150 Democratic majority in the House were many and mounting), and in the end he decided to go with the more established Heritage rather than a brand new public-policy organization.

He also knew from direct personal experience that conservatives on the Hill were "in desperate need" of the kind of free-market, anticommunist research Heritage was producing. "I thought," he said, "that Heritage, if properly managed with clarity of purpose, could develop into something really big."[6]

It took the Heritage board of trustees little time to agree that Ed Feulner was the right man. Walton announced his intention to retire as president on February 9; at a special meeting on February 25, the board elected Edwin J. Feulner Jr. executive vice president, effective April 1, with the stipulation that he succeed Walton as president on June 1, 1977. Feulner spent the intervening two months closely observing the foundation's operations and taking extensive notes; he was determined to make a fast start.

Upon taking office, the new CEO immediately added several key members to the Heritage team. Phillip N. Truluck, a longtime associate at the Republican Study Committee, was named director of research. Truluck's assignment: to build a new kind of research department that did not then exist in Washington. It would take complicated public-policy questions and translate them into concise, credible research papers that could be quickly read by policymakers in Congress and the executive branch. While almost all think tanks now use such a format for policy analysis, Heritage, under Truluck's guidance, was the first to do so.

But Truluck was much more than the foundation's research director; he soon became Heritage's chief operating officer—its COO. Truluck and Feulner learned to share the responsibility of managing the foundation so well that when the president was away, Heritage continued to run smoothly under the executive vice president's steady hand. Even when Ed Feulner took a three-month leave of absence in the fall of 1996 to work for Republican vice presidential nominee Jack Kemp, the foundation, under Acting President Phil Truluck, did not miss a beat. It produced, for example, the 568-page *Issues '96* for congressional candidates and almost all of *Mandate for Leadership IV: Turning Ideas into Action*. The unique Feulner-Truluck partnership is a major reason for the enduring success of The Heritage Foundation.

The other significant people whom Feulner brought on board when he assumed the presidency were:

- Hugh C. Newton, the seasoned professional public relations director for the National Right to Work Committee, was named public relations counsel. Newton's task: To get Heritage's product into the hands and minds of opinion makers in Washington and across the country and to build a success-oriented public relations program. Within a week of Newton's arrival, syndicated columnist Andrew Tully (not a conservative) quoted a Heritage study that roundly criticized the Carter administration's "Universal Voter Registration" bill.[7] Newton recommended the hiring of Herb B. Berkowitz, another Right to Work Committee publicist, as the foundation's public relations director. The third member of the public relations "department" was Newton's and Berkowitz's omnicompetent assistant, Shelia Myles. All three are still with Heritage twenty years later. Berkowitz was promoted in 1983 to vice president for public relations and became a member of senior management, a rare honor among Washington think tanks.
- Willa Johnson, former legislative assistant to Congressman Phil Crane and Senator George Murphy, was chosen as director of the Resource Bank. Johnson's responsibility: to create a national network of conservative groups and individuals. "I wanted Heritage to become a clearing house," Feulner later explained, "not only *for* conservative information but also *of* conservative people; we wanted Heritage to identify conservative policy experts on university campuses and connect them to the Washington policy community."[8]

In its first year under Johnson, the Resource Bank arranged for several conservative experts—like Ernest van den Haag of Fordham, Thomas Sowell of UCLA, and Charles Hobbs, an architect of Ronald Reagan's welfare program in California—to testify before congressional committees. "Policymakers," Johnson points out, "were being exposed to views they had never heard before." Under Johnson and her successors Robert Huberty and Thomas C. Atwood, the Resource Bank helped make Heritage "a hub for the conservative movement."[9]

- Robert L. Schuettinger, an American-born, Oxford-educated intellectual who had worked under Feulner at the Republican Study Committee, was hired as editor of the foundation's new quarterly journal, *Policy Review.* Then as now, Feulner considered *Policy Review* Heritage's intellectual agora—a place where academics and politicians of differing conservative viewpoints could debate ideas and policies. The journal's very first issue made a strong impression, offering probing articles by historian Robert Conquest, economists Peter Bauer and Kenneth W. Clarkson, and journalist Robert Moss. In the second issue, black economist Walter E. Williams argued that the minimum wage had not only failed to help minorities—it had hurt them. C. Sumner (Chuck) Stone, a nationally respected black columnist for the *Philadelphia Daily News,* referred to Williams' "persuasive data" and argued that the Temple University professor offered remedies that "ought to be considered seriously.... Imagine," concluded Stone, "a black man sounding like Barry Goldwater. Is nothing sacred?"[10] Despite its pedantic title, "Government Sanctioned Restraints That Reduce Economic Opportunities for Minorities," Williams' analysis is one of the most cited articles in *Policy Review*'s history.

Christopher DeMuth, then director of the John F. Kennedy School of Government's Regulatory Reform Project and now president of Heritage's friendly rival, the American Enterprise Institute, wrote to Schuettinger: "If you can sustain the high quality of the articles in the first two issues you should move very quickly into the top rank of policy journals."[11]

Seeking to strengthen the organization's overall performance and morale, Feulner discharged several employees, had personal conferences with those whom he asked to stay, and quietly dropped the compulsory weekly prayer meeting. The enhanced reputation of the foundation was confirmed when Freedoms Foundation at Valley Forge presented its top 1977 award in the "Americana" category to Heritage. The same award was given in 1976 to the internationally praised "Tall Ships" program commemorating the U.S. bicentennial. In accepting the award, Heritage Chairman Ben Blackburn, a former Republican congressman from Georgia, remarked that the foundation's goal was to convince policymakers and the public that conservative ideas "are better. And just as important, why we think they will work."[12] Further to the left on the political spectrum, Senator Daniel P. Moynihan (D-N.Y.) described Heritage's *Backgrounders* as "accurate, thorough and balanced presentations of facts surrounding the issues."[13]

Heritage also met a critical market test: it increased its base of grassroots financial supporters to some 120,000 and its annual budget to $2.8 million by the end of Feulner's first eighteen months in office. It could also point to a growing number of corporate supporters including Amway, Chase Manhattan, Dow Chemical, General Motors, Loctite, Milliken, Mobil, Pfizer, Sears Roebuck, and SmithKline. The new president upgraded the board of trustees, adding William E. Simon, former secretary of the treasury; J. Robert Fluor, president of the Fluor Corporation; and Joseph Coors, president of the Adolph Coors Company. In keeping with the foundation's entrepreneurial spirit, the new trustees were all creative, self-made leaders, not play-it-safe corporate managers.

Sometimes consciously, sometimes unconsciously, Heritage was creating a new kind of public-policy institute—what *Time* magazine would later call an "advocacy tank."[14]

The Idea Brokers

As James Smith sets forth in his definitive study of think tanks, *The Idea Brokers,* the first generation of policy research institutions emerged about 1910 as an outgrowth of Progressivism and the "scientific management" movement. They operated in an era when the federal government had limited intellectual resources of its own and welcomed outside knowledge and counsel. Brookings, founded in 1916, is the foremost example of this first generation of think tanks which was sustained by private philanthropy.

The second generation—the first to carry the label "think tank"—was created in the years following World War II when the government openly sought "sophisticated technical expertise" for the Cold War and the War on Poverty. Their services were primarily underwritten by federal funds. The RAND Corporation is the prototype of this post-World War II generation of research institutes.

The third generation of think tanks was founded in the 1970s, and was an outgrowth of the ideological battle between conservatives and liberals that has characterized American politics for the past several decades. The Heritage Foundation is the exemplar of this newest generation which spurns government money and is deliberately more political than previous research organizations.[15]

The think tank is a uniquely American institution which seeks to link knowledge and power and to turn ideas into public policy. Conservative historian George H. Nash suggests that the think tank has become an increasingly influential institution because of "the continuing growth of government and the deepening politicization of our society."[16] The inevitable result was an explosion of public-policy organizations. By the mid-1990s, over one thousand private, not-for-profit think tanks were operating in the United States, one hundred of them in the greater Washington area.[17]

What Is Conservatism?

Among all these think tanks, The Heritage Foundation is unique because from its beginning it has explicitly described itself as "conservative." And what, one may reasonably ask, does that mean? What is conservatism? It is not an easy question. Some of the most knowledgeable conservatives in America have declined to answer it.

In his 1970 survey of conservative thought in the twentieth century, William F. Buckley Jr. defended his determination not to give a brief definition of conservatism by saying, "I could not give you a definition of Christianity in one sentence, but that does not mean that Christianity is undefinable." In his seminal work on the conservative movement, historian George Nash explained that he offered "no compact definition" of conservatism because conservatives themselves have "no such agreed-upon definition." He went on to describe the three kinds of conservatives who had emerged in the post-World War II period—"classical liberals" or libertarians, traditionalists, and militant anticommunists.[18]

In his introduction to a 1990 anthology of modern American conservative thought, academician Charles R. Kesler argued that American conservatism is divided into three parts, each with its own interpretation of the moral and intellectual crisis confronting America but all agreeing that its root cause was communism. Traditionalists see communism as "only the latest and most radical form of the deracination of man in the modern world." Libertarians concur as to the inherent evil of communism but offer "the morality of free choice" and the marketplace as antidotes to tyrannical government, left or right.[19]

The neoconservatives (famously described by Irving Kristol as liberals who have been "mugged by reality") are latecomers to American conservatism. They were driven out of the Democratic Party by the New Left during and after George McGovern's 1972 presidential campaign. On foreign policy, the neoconservatives found themselves at "the cutting edge of conservatism's resistance" to the Soviet Union's military and diplomatic offensives of the 1970s and 1980s.[20] Their *realpolitik* produced a strong distrust of collectivist ideology that linked them with traditionalists, but the latter's enthusiasm for Christianity and agrarianism separated them from the mostly Jewish urban neoconservatives.

The general editors of the 1970 Buckley anthology provided a crisp description of what they called "Mr. Buckley's conservatism," which is as good an answer to the question "What is conservatism?" as we are likely to get:

> [It] is vigorously individualistic, in favor of ordered liberty, hostile to promiscuous equalitarianism, and pronouncedly tolerant. While theistic in character, it welcomes non-believers. Though tradition-oriented and partial to continuity rather than experiment, it has a deep streak of romantic utopianism.[21]

The Carter Opportunity

The Carter years from 1977 to 1980 were mostly a time of economic misery for the American people and of communist gains around the world.

But they were golden days for conservatives. The president and his Georgia "mafia" offered almost daily targets for analysis and commentary. In 1974, following Nixon's ignominious departure from office, Republicans had been told that their party was finished. Some conservatives advocated the formation of a third party led by Ronald Reagan and/or George Wallace. But in the 1978 off-year elections, after two years of Jimmy Carter, Republicans gained three seats in the Senate and thirteen seats in the House of Representatives. It seemed that America was not ready to abandon its traditional two-party system.

By the end of 1979, the inflation rate stood at 13.3 percent—the highest since the Korean War and nearly double the 7.2 percent rate Carter had inherited from Ford. Confronted by mounting economic woes, Carter did not blame his administration's maladroit decisions. Instead, he faulted the American people who, he said, were deep in the throes of a spiritual "crisis of confidence."[22] While the president was lecturing Americans and demanding that they "snap out of it," they were being slowly strangled by "stagflation"—double-digit inflation coupled with zero economic growth.

Problems proliferated—the energy crisis, the plummeting dollar, soaring interest rates, the uncertain future of the Panama Canal, the fall of the shah of Iran, the usurpation of power by the Sandinistas in Nicaragua, the unbalanced SALT II treaty, the brutal Soviet invasion of Afghanistan. Casting about for an explanation of this communist aggression, Andrew Young, Carter's ambassador to the United Nations, went Orwellian, asserting that the thirty thousand Cuban troops in Angola brought "a certain stability and order" to the country.[23]

Meeting the Energy Crisis

Heritage set out to offer practical solutions, starting with an issue that affected everyone—energy policy. The foundation adamantly opposed Carter's proposal to create a Department of Energy, arguing, in a series of papers and monographs by Milt Copulos, that the way out of the energy crisis was through deregulation and an "energy mix" of oil, gas, hydroelectric, coal, and nuclear power. To dramatize the broad support for its prescriptions, Heritage presented a three-day "National Conference on Energy Advocacy" in February 1979.

Among the major speakers at the conference, cosponsored by fifty national organizations, were Senator James A. McClure (R-Idaho), Congressman Mike McCormack (D-Wash.), and Margaret Bush Wilson, the chairwoman of the NAACP (National Association for the Advancement of Colored People). The meeting produced a 414-page source book, *Energy Perspectives: An Advocate's Guide,* edited by the hard-working Copulos, which called on the Carter administration to decontrol domestic oil prices and relax various EPA restrictions, thereby allowing more domestic oil exploration. As a result of Heritage's and other groups' efforts, the government began to lift controls on oil prices and reduce EPA regulations on oil exploration in the United States. When President Reagan swept away many more regulations in 1981, prices fell sharply. In very short order, as Heritage had predicted, the United States "had a glut of oil."[24]

Heritage's reputation in the energy field was strengthened by a prescient study, "The Iranian Oil Crisis," by Middle East expert James Phillips, published in February 1979, before deregulation. Phillips predicted there would soon be worldwide oil shortages and long gas lines in America. One month later, the CIA publicly came to essentially the same conclusion. Soon Phillips, who had come to Heritage from the Fletcher School of Law and Diplomacy at Tufts University, was briefing Washington's intelligence community on the politics of the region.[25]

As a result of Carter's neo-Keynesian policies and the continuing economic ripples from Nixon's centrist impulses, inflation in America hit double digits. There was increasing talk in Washington of retrying the oft-failed tactic of wage and price controls. *Policy Review* editor Schuettinger decided to drive a stake into the heart of that idea. In *Forty Centuries of Wage and Price Controls: How Not to Fight Inflation,* coauthored by British political scientist Eamonn Butler, Schuettinger declared that four thousand years of human history showed that government controls did only one thing well—produce inflation.[26] The book, published in February 1979, was an expanded version of an article Schuettinger had written in the summer 1978 issue of *Policy Review.*

Heritage quickly went to work. A four-part serialization of the book was mailed to major daily newspapers; an op-ed article of 750 words was sent to several hundred editorial page editors; copies of the book with a covering news release went out to editors, business writers, columnists, and book reviewers. Many newspapers used the work to explain their opposition to economic controls. Several more—including the *Detroit News,* then the largest afternoon daily in the country—published the serialization. Lindley H. Clark Jr., writing in the *Wall Street Journal,* called the book "an admirable survey of controls' sorry history."[27]

When President Carter announced his anti-inflation program in October 1978, he called for "voluntary" wage and price guidelines and was careful to say that he opposed mandatory controls and did not intend to ask Congress for the authority to impose them.[28] Indeed, despite the predictions of many, Carter never requested wage and price controls—testimony to his good sense and the climate of public opinion created, in part, by Heritage.

A New Conservative Coalition

Under Ed Feulner, an increasingly confident Heritage Foundation set an ambitious goal: to establish itself as a significant force in the policymaking process and to help build a new conservative coalition that would replace the New Deal coalition which had dominated American politics and policy for half a century. In the field of domestic policy, the foundation focused on (1) choice in education, (2) urban enterprise zones, (3) supply-side economics, (4) deregulation of the economy, and (5) significant reduction in the size of government.

Education and jobs were key components of the conservative strategy to truly reduce poverty. Giving poor families a tuition voucher would allow inner-city parents the option of removing their children from substandard and often dangerous public schools and placing them in better, safer schools. Vouchers, tuition tax credits, magnet schools, and other mechanisms to inject market competition into education would break the iron hold of the teachers unions on public schools. Heritage published a widely read monograph, *Family Choice in Education: The New Imperative* by policy analyst Onalee McGraw, in early 1978. The seeds planted by Heritage took time to mature, but by the mid-1990s, educational choice had become an accepted alternative in many school districts across the nation.

An Enterprising Idea

In 1979, economist Stuart Butler introduced a new concept to Washington with his paper "Enterprise Zones: A Unique Solution to Urban Decay." Butler urged the elimination of taxes and regulations on businesses operating in depressed inner-city areas, thus spurring commercial activity and creating the jobs people needed to pull themselves out of poverty. The following year Butler published a longer version of the same paper under the title "Enterprise Zones: Pioneering in the Inner City." the *New York Times* acknowledged the cogency of his idea by publishing an op-ed article by Butler; that article led to a book contract.

Butler pointed out that three years earlier, President Carter had stood amidst the rubble and burned-out tenements of the South Bronx and promised federal aid to rebuild the area "brick by brick and block by block." The pledge, Butler said, was symptomatic of the "grandiose" government projects that were introduced with great fanfare but invariably produced disappointing results. In the words of one disillusioned senator, "all we have been doing is bulldozing great holes in our cities and throwing billions of federal dollars down them."[29]

In the fall of 1980, Butler led a day-long editorial seminar at Heritage. He explained his proposal to thirty influential journalists and to leaders of the NAACP, the Booker T. Washington Foundation, and the National League of Cities. Sensitive to the needs of the less advantaged, conservative Republican Congressmen Jack Kemp from upstate New York and liberal Democrat Robert Garcia from New York City introduced legislation to establish enterprise zones in selected inner cities. The idea was adopted as a plank in the 1980 Republican platform and was formally implemented during the Reagan administration in the 1982 Enterprise Zone Tax Act. Connecticut became the first state that same year to create an enterprise zone. Butler pointed out, however, that the act emphasized tax credits rather than investor incentives and tended "to help those who are already on the ladder." He also criticized the measure for requiring twenty-eight single-spaced pages of official explanation. "The Administration's long-delayed plan," in Butler's judgment, "clearly has some serious flaws, but they are correctable."[30]

Stuart Butler's paper on enterprise zones was only the first in the series of groundbreaking domestic studies for The Heritage Foundation that made him, by the mid-1980s, one of the most influential policy analysts in Washington, D.C. Phil Truluck, who hired Butler, says, "Many people can analyze issues. Only a very few can predict what the major issues are going to be and stay out front on them."[31]

The Real Enemy

The need to reduce taxes to spur the economy and promote greater prosperity has been a core Heritage theme from the beginning. In 1978, legislative analyst Donald J. Senese authored a monograph entitled *Indexing the Inflationary Impact of Taxes: The Necessary Economic Reform,* based on an idea long advocated by Nobel economist Milton Friedman. As Senese pointed out:

> Government officials, politicians, and special-interest groups who advocate larger and larger programs are not enthusiastic about indexation since it would take the "profit" out of inflation for the government and provide a reduction of government revenues and, thus, less government funds to cover their particular programs.[32]

Liberals used tax bracket creep to increase federal spending from $97.72 billion in 1961 (John Kennedy's first year) to $210.17 billion in 1971 (Nixon's third year) and then to $579.6 billion in 1980 (Carter's fourth year). Inflation was pushing citizens automatically into ever higher tax brackets, so indexing tax rates became a central pillar of the Reagan economic recovery program in 1981.

One early study in particular, Ed Feulner recalls, helped establish The Heritage Foundation as a credible source of information on domestic policy. In August 1977, President Carter introduced a much-ballyhooed "welfare reform" plan. After careful study, Heritage policy analyst Samuel T. Francis concluded that instead of increasing the cost of welfare by $2.8 billion, as the administration estimated, the Carter welfare reforms would cost taxpayers "at least" $17.8 billion more per year than the existing program. Francis asserted that the administration erred at both ends, overstating present welfare costs by some $8.8 billion and underestimating the cost of the reforms by at least $9 billion.[33]

The administration and its congressional supporters quickly challenged the findings of the Heritage document and insisted that the Congressional Budget Office (CBO) resolve the dispute over the true cost of the welfare reform program. After studying the relevant figures, CBO analysts reported that the Carter proposal would increase by almost twenty-two million the number of Americans who received some form of welfare, and they estimated the additional annual cost at about $20 billion—$2 billion *over* the Heritage estimate. The president and his allies were devastated. Furthermore, the CBO added, the reforms would have a minimal effect on people in poverty. Of the twenty-two million new people on welfare, 74 percent would come from families with incomes of over $10,000 a year (in 1977 figures). As Martin Anderson wrote in *Policy Review,* the thrust of Carter's plan was not to reform welfare but "to further the idea of a guaranteed annual income."[34]

In June 1978, congressional leaders told President Carter that his proposed welfare reform plan was dead for that session of Congress. There was not even enough support in the House to approve a compromise bill that halved the price tag of the original Carter bill. In the course of the welfare reform debate, The Heritage Foundation established itself as a think tank to be listened to.

Rolling Back Communism

Meanwhile, Heritage strove to develop a more effective American foreign policy and national security strategy, not simply to contain communism but to roll it back. There were four components to the Heritage plan:

1. Find ways to increase the cost to the Soviet Union of maintaining its empire.
2. Build up both our defenses and the NATO's resolve to deter a Soviet attack on Western Europe.
3. Protect ourselves from the single greatest threat to the United States—Soviet long-range nuclear missiles (ICBMs).
4. Seize every opportunity to contrast the prosperity produced by the free-market system with communism's inability to provide more than subsistence living to anyone except its elite.

The foundation's studies on foreign policy and national security issues during the Carter years included analyses of the flaws of the SALT II treaty; basing options for the MX missile; the importance of the neutron bomb to America's defense arsenal; and Senate abrogation of the defense treaty between the United States and the Republic of China on Taiwan.

Reflecting the views of most conservatives, Heritage subjected SALT II to frequent, skeptical examination. In April 1978, for example, it suggested that the United States revise its negotiating strategy to include the controversial Soviet "Backfire" bomber in any new U.S.-Soviet strategic arms agreement. More than a year later, in August 1979, the foundation warned that SALT II could prevent the United States from taking steps to meet the "growing Soviet strategic threat" predicted for the early 1980s. In November 1979, Heritage analyst Jeffrey G. Barlow stated that ambiguities in the language of SALT II left two important Soviet weapons systems—the SS-20 and the Backfire bomber—"unconstrained by the new treaty."[35]

Following the Soviet invasion of Afghanistan in December 1979, the Carter administration "delayed" Senate consideration of SALT II. Washington observers agreed that Heritage and other public-policy institutes had raised so many serious questions about the proposed treaty that approval by two thirds of the Senate was no longer obtainable—if it had ever been.

The Soviet Union's "Vietnam"

The study that established Heritage as a major player in the foreign policy debate was James Phillips' insightful *Backgrounder,* "Afghanistan: The Soviet Quagmire," distributed on October 25, 1979, thirty-two days *before* the Soviet invasion of Afghanistan.

Phillips pointed out that Afghanistan had been "convulsed" for over a year by a "brutal" civil war that showed no signs of abating. He described the broad spectrum of opposition to the Hafizollah Amin regime, the pervasive "xenophobia" of Afghans, and their strong resentment of the influence of "omnipresent Soviet advisers." The Heritage analyst outlined the Soviet Union's options, ranging from military escalation to political compromise. He argued that Afghanistan was important to Moscow for regional as well as global political and strategic reasons. If the Soviets permitted Kabul to fall into the hands of religious/nationalist forces, Phillips wrote, "they would be setting a dangerous precedent for Warsaw" and other Eastern European satellites.[36]

With remarkable foresight, he concluded his single-spaced, eighteen-page analysis with these words:

> The chronic turbulence in the Afghan political scene makes it more than likely that Amin will be (according to an old Afghan folk-expression) *Barre Duroz Shah*—"King for two days." If and when Amin falls prey to the same fate that befell his predecessors, it can be expected that Moscow will have other candidates for power waiting in the wings.[37]

On a bleak December 27, 1979, a Soviet airborne brigade overthrew the regime of President Hafizollah Amin, executed Amin for "crimes against the people," and installed the puppet Karmal regime. Within days, Soviet armored columns were fanning out across Afghanistan to occupy major population centers and begin waging a "full-fledged counterinsurgency campaign" against rebellious Moslem tribesmen.[38]

Phillips could barely handle the flood of requests for media interviews; he was besieged by telephone calls from government officials wanting briefings. Speculation was widespread that Phillips must have gotten classified information from the Central Intelligence Agency, even that he might be a CIA employee. The truth was that Phillips, like all good analysts, had used his knowledge of the region, his understanding of geopolitics, and a careful reading of the public record to conclude that the Soviets would have to take decisive action to preserve their interests in Afghanistan.

Becoming a Major Player

By early 1980, Heritage had taken several significant steps toward becoming an influential Washington think tank. Phil Truluck had put together a young, talented research team made up mostly of men and women in their thirties working toward Ph.D.s. They prided themselves on being able to turn out a good paper in a matter of days and sometimes even hours. In 1979, the foundation produced 100 studies and books which were praised by Democrats as well as Republicans. Congressman Thomas A. Daschle of South Dakota (now Senate Democratic leader) remarked that Heritage's "SALT Handbook [was] superbly written and a great deal of help to my staff and me."[39]

Heritage marketed its product aggressively and shrewdly to the policy-making community and the news media. Columnist Patrick J. Buchanan, discussing the new self-confidence of American conservatives, quoted United Auto Workers president Douglas Fraser as saying, "[Conservatives] are out-lobbying, out-working, outspending and outhustling us and, unfortunately, at times they are out-thinking us." Buchanan marveled at the way the new conservative think tanks had pushed their way into the public-policy mainstream, and he credited Heritage with "turning out, weekly, the timeliest, best-researched position papers floating around the Capitol."[40] Not satisfied to be just a Washington think tank, no matter how influential, Heritage was reaching some 1,400 daily and weekly newspapers with its syndicated column, "The Heritage News Forum," by-lined by Ed Feulner.

The foundation continued to broaden its financial base. Feulner reported that in 1979 Heritage received money from eighty-seven corporations. Its budget for the year topped $4 million for the first time, a 40 percent increase over the previous year. The board of trustees was expanded with the addition of such heavyweights as Shelby Cullom Davis, investment banker and former U.S. ambassador to Switzerland; Frank Shakespeare, president of RKO General and former director of the U.S. Information Agency; Dr. Robert H. Krieble, board chairman of Loctite Corporation; and Dr. David R. Brown, a distinguished Oklahoma orthopedic surgeon and member of the board of the Noble Foundation, one of Heritage's earliest and most generous supporters.

But Heritage trustees were always more than financial donors. They were men and women of deep experience and proven ideas who were expected to share both with the foundation's management. What Washington needed most, Ambassador Davis said, were "architects and engineers." F. A. Hayek, Russell Kirk, and Milton Friedman had convincingly explained "why totalitarianism is wrong and why freedom is right. But this doesn't tell us how to create policies and laws based on conservative principles. That's where Heritage comes in." Dr. Brown took a long view of what needed to be done, saying that "the huge growth of government over the last several decades is impossible to roll back quickly." He believed that conservatives should concentrate on economic and foreign policy issues and leave controversial moral questions to the "individual conscience."

Frank Shakespeare was convinced that, through the force of their ideas, conservatives had "set the parameters" of the public-policy debate. But he also knew that their ideas, however popular, would not automatically produce victories at the polls.[41]

In 1979, John O'Sullivan, former assistant editor of the London *Daily Telegraph* (and later successor to William F. Buckley Jr. as editor of *National Review*, the conservative movement's most influential journal), replaced Robert Schuettinger as editor of *Policy Review*. O'Sullivan maintained *Policy Review*'s reputation for lively, controversial discourse. Among the journal's highlights that year were a debate between Senators Barry Goldwater of Arizona and Edward Kennedy of Massachusetts over President Carter's abrogation of the Mutual Defense Treaty with the Republic of China, and an article by business leaders Jay Van Andel and Richard DeVos detailing how government regulation harmed the consumer and stifled business competition.

As always, Heritage sought to strengthen and enlarge the conservative movement through the Resource Bank and other networking tactics. It began hosting a monthly luncheon of conservative public-interest law groups. It sponsored an annual Resource Bank meeting outside Washington; the 1979 meeting, smoothly coordinated by Willa Johnson, was attended by forty groups from across the country. Through its employment service, the Talent Bank, Heritage placed twenty conservatives in jobs on Capitol Hill that year. Its Academic Bank, a national roster of conservative intellectuals, linked more than a thousand scholars across the country. In all these efforts, Heritage functioned as the honest broker among the principal strains of American conservatism—the traditional right, the economic libertarians, the anticommunist/pro-defense right, the New Right, and the neoconservatives.

As part of its campaign to foster a conservative intellectual renaissance in America, Heritage named Sovietologist Robert Conquest, historian Russell Kirk, Professor Pedro Schwartz of Spain, and Professor Patrick

O'Brien of Australia as Distinguished Scholars in 1979. The foundation also arranged for younger American scholars—e.g., Thomas Sowell of UCLA and Walter Williams of Temple University (both Heritage adjunct scholars)—to brief members of Congress and key aides on such issues as the Davis-Bacon Act, which calls for the payment of "prevailing" wages to workers on federal and federally assisted projects.

In the spring of 1980, Heritage dedicated its expanded headquarters on C Street facing Stanton Park—two buildings obtained through a gift from Mr. and Mrs. Joseph Coors and a $500,000 contribution from the Samuel Roberts Noble Foundation. A $270,000 donation by Jack Eckerd, founder of the drug store chain, subsequently enabled the foundation to purchase a third building at 509 C St., N.E. To complete the expansion, a fourth row house was leased by the foundation. At a celebratory dinner, featured speaker William F. Buckley Jr. remarked that "it seems incredible that we ever managed to do without the Heritage Foundation." Every American, he said, "live[s] off the fruits of its research which ... fortifies the resolve to be free."[42]

Still, Heritage could not yet seriously challenge Brookings or AEI. But Ed Feulner and the rest of his colleagues were always on the lookout for the right opportunity to elevate Heritage to its rightful place in the front rank of Washington public-policy organizations. That opportunity presented itself when a former Hollywood actor and two-time governor of our most populous state announced his candidacy for the 1980 Republican presidential nomination.

3

The Big Gamble

There are only ten weeks between a presidential election and a presidential inauguration, and yet, in that brief period, a president-elect must pick his cabinet and his chief advisers, including his national security adviser and his chief budget officer; write his inaugural address setting the tone for his administration; and decide which of his campaign pledges he is going to implement in his first hundred days. He must shift, literally overnight, from a politicking to a governing mode and become the president, not just of the political coalition that elected him, but of all the people. So complex a task is made even more difficult when the incoming president is of a different political party and governing philosophy from that of the outgoing chief executive.

Several trustees of The Heritage Foundation had been involved in this very experience in 1968. It was Jack Eckerd, head of the General Services Administration under President Nixon, who first suggested, at a trustees' meeting in October 1979, that the foundation should help the process by drawing up a plan of action for a possible conservative administration in January 1981. While no one could say with certainty who the Republican nominee would be, he was bound to be to the right of President Carter, and stood an excellent chance of being elected.

41

Heritage should take on this enormous task because, it was argued, the new administration, preoccupied with electoral politics, would have given little thought to governing. William E. Simon, another Heritage trustee and secretary of the treasury under Presidents Nixon and Ford, strongly endorsed Eckerd's suggestion. The two men recalled that when they came to Washington, they spent so much time learning who was who that months went by before they took a serious look at policy and programs. Robert Krieble proposed that the foundation produce a manual that would help policymakers "cut the size of government and manage it more effectively."[1]

"Our strong feeling," explained Ed Feulner, "was that the people of the new and hopefully conservative administration should have some source of information and guidance other than what you get from the incumbents whom you replace." In the Nixon transition, he pointed out, "Republicans were briefed by Democrats, the very people whose jobs were at stake and who had a vested interest in maintaining the status quo."[2]

The status quo was the *last* thing The Heritage Foundation wanted to preserve. Here, Heritage was not "conservative" at all but "radical," eager to return to the limited government roots of the republic.

Feulner, Phil Truluck, Willa Johnson, and others went to work. Knowing they needed a top-flight editorial director for the "manual," Feulner telephoned Charles Heatherly, a former field director of the Intercollegiate Studies Institute now working for the National Federation of Independent Business in California. Heatherly recalls that Feulner talked about the need for "our own agenda—a detailed blueprint" for an incoming conservative administration. Heatherly had already decided to leave NFIB after six years and move to Washington. He agreed to undertake the overall direction of the Heritage study, beginning November 15, 1979.[3]

Heatherly, Feulner, Truluck, and Johnson began by drawing up a list of key conservatives to talk to, starting with Paul Weyrich and experienced Senate staffer Margo Carlisle, who joined Heritage in the late 1980s as vice president and director of government relations. They also began listing people in the Nixon administration, like William Simon and Caspar Weinberger, from whom they could draw lessons. "Willa was my partner and my mentor," says Heatherly of Johnson, who became a senior vice president of Heritage. While Heatherly concentrated on the policy blueprint, Johnson was tasked with "organizing a Talent Bank for the new administration."[4] All agreed from the beginning that policy and personnel had to fit together.

At the trustees meeting in December 1979, Feulner submitted a general plan based on the notion that conservatives had to be prepared to answer the question, "What is the conservative agenda, particularly for the First Hundred Days?" As Feulner later explained in the foreword to *Mandate for Leadership,* the recommendations were not offered as "cure-alls" for the nation's problems nor as a catalogue of every concept in the "conservative storehouse of ideas." They were, rather, concrete proposals which if implemented would help "revitalize our economy, strengthen our national security and halt the centralization of power in the federal government."[5]

But in the final days of 1979, Heatherly and his colleagues were still trying to figure out how to do something that had never been done before. Then in late January 1980, Heatherly wrote a five-page outline titled *Mandate for Leadership.* He proposed a team approach that would "scope out" every key department and agency of the government. Each team would have a chairman and a co-chairman, and would include academics, conservatives who had been Nixon and Ford appointees, and congressional staff. He set a deadline of June 1 for the first-draft manuscript of each team. "I insisted," Heatherly remembers, "that every draft had to have continuity and conformity."[6]

The choice of some team chairs was obvious (Treasury and Defense), while some didn't work out, or made false starts. For some agencies, there just weren't many knowledgeable or experienced conservatives. "Commerce was a nightmare for us," recalls Heatherly, and "transportation was difficult." For several months, there were "endless, endless meetings of teams, inside and outside Heritage."[7]

Nevertheless, Heritage always seemed to know where to find the right analyst for the right department or agency. For example, there was unanimous agreement that the best man to head the team on regulatory agencies was James E. Hinish Jr. Not one American in a hundred thousand had heard of Hinish, but Heritage knew that he was counsel for the Senate Republican Policy Committee and one of the chief architects of the National Republican Convention's regulatory proposals. According to

Heatherly, Hinish "recruited an outstanding team and did yeoman's work in coordinating the regulatory reform study."[8]

Ultimately, more than 250 experts served on twenty teams, while dozens more contributed ideas and information. To maintain the foundation's nonpartisan status, Heatherly wrote to both the Reagan-Bush and Carter-Mondale campaigns, offering to meet with them on the Heritage project. No one from Carter-Mondale headquarters ever called back, but Reagan-Bush quickly responded.[9]

Not one of the *Mandate* team members received a penny for his participation in the months of research and writing that produced twenty volumes totaling over 3,000 manuscript pages. But the cost of the luncheons and late night snacks was considerable—sometimes reaching $6,000 in a single month.[10] The final cost of producing *Mandate for Leadership: Policy Management in a Conservative Administration* was approximately $250,000, a major sum for any think tank. The typesetting and printing costs of the book version, in those days before personal computers and desk-top publishing, came close to $100,000. Along with the hundreds of hours expended and the inevitable diversion of staff and other resources, *Mandate* represented an enormous gamble for the seven-year-old public-policy institute.

Waiting for Reagan

But the trustees gave their full backing, convinced that President Carter was in serious trouble and a conservative Republican had an excellent chance of winning the presidency. They hoped that the GOP's presidential nominee would be Ronald Reagan, who, when he announced his candidacy in November 1979, pledged an income tax cut along the lines of the Kemp-Roth bill; an orderly transfer of federal programs—and the funds to pay for them—to state and local governments; a revitalized energy program based on increased production of oil, natural gas, and coal; and the development of a long-range strategy to meet the challenge of the Soviet Union.[11] The Heritage Foundation had made the very same recommendations in studies it had published.

But to get the nomination, Reagan first had to overcome six experienced opponents—former Senator Howard Baker of Tennessee, former Governor John Connally of Texas, Senator Robert J. Dole of Kansas,

Congressman Phil Crane, Congressman John Anderson of Illinois, and former Ambassador George Bush. Rarely has a national political party offered so impressive a field of candidates for the nation's highest office.

By June, having won twenty-nine of thirty-three primaries and received 60 percent of the popular vote, Reagan had far more than the 998 delegates he needed for the nomination. He spent the six weeks before the GOP convention overseeing the writing of the party platform and mulling over his vice presidential choice. He turned over the major responsibility for what he should do if elected to his longtime aide Edwin Meese III, who was also serving as deputy campaign director under William Casey.

Meese visited Heritage in the early spring and was briefed on *Mandate*. On another occasion, campaign manager William Casey dropped by. In July, Heritage decided to hold a dinner for the team chairmen and co-chairmen at the University Club in Washington. Ed Meese was a surprise guest and gave *Mandate* "his blessing," removing any doubt as to how the study would be received by the Reagan administration.[12]

By now, everyone realized he was working on an unprecedented document, unprecedented for Washington and for Heritage. Ed Feulner became so concerned about its size that he once asked Heatherly, "Can you cut it in half?"

"Sure," responded the editor of *Mandate*, "if you can postpone Election Day. We don't have time for the additional editing."[13]

The final product looked at thirteen cabinet-level departments, most of the regulatory agencies, the Office of Management and Budget, the Environmental Protection Agency, the Senior Executive Service, and key smaller agencies like the National Endowments for the Arts and Humanities, ACTION, and other "poverty" agencies. But in keeping with the focus on management and administration, the report did not take a stand on such social issues as abortion, busing, and public school prayer.

Of all the Washington think tanks, only Heritage could have produced a volume the size of Tolstoy's *War and Peace* so quickly and inexpensively. Indeed, only Heritage, the master of quick response, would have attempted to research and write a government-wide study in less than a year. Only a *conservative* organization like Heritage could have asked several hundred *conservatives* to donate their time and expertise to writing a programmatic blueprint for a *conservative* administration. Only Heritage, moreover, could have put together so large a team of political and academic experts—a classic application of the inside-outside principle—committed to conservative goals.

Indeed, never before had such a critical mass of conservatives come together to debate and determine their positions on such a wide range of subjects. The process gave the Reagan administration and the conservative movement itself a running start in going to bat for the initiatives. Many potential objections by conservatives were anticipated and answered in *Mandate's* recommendations.

And only Heritage believed that "major, fundamental changes in the size, scope, and direction of the federal government are possible" and was prepared to show, specifically, how the changes could be effected.[14]

A Time of Opportunity

The historical importance of *Mandate* was underscored by conservative philosopher Russell Kirk in a lecture he delivered at Heritage that summer. Kirk called the present time "an hour of conservative opportunity." Thirty years ago, he noted, there were no organizations like The Heritage Foundation, and its increasingly influential journal, *Policy Review.* Thirty years earlier, he said, it would have been inconceivable that "two economists believing in a free economy [i.e., F. A. Hayek and Milton Friedman] would be awarded Nobel Prizes." Thirty years ago, he continued, it would have been most improbable for both national political parties to nominate those candidates "who seemed the more conservative of the lot." Kirk predicted that America was "entering upon a period of conservative policies" and, more important, that "the conservative political imagination will set to work to allay our present discontents and to renew our order."[15] The central purpose of *Mandate for Leadership* was to take full advantage of the conservative opportunity offered by a conservative president.

On Thursday evening, November 6, 1980, just two days after Reagan was elected the fortieth president of the United States, Ed Feulner, Phil Truluck, and Chuck Heatherly personally delivered manuscript copies (each numbering twenty volumes and weighing thirty pounds) of *Mandate for Leadership* to Ed Meese; Martin Anderson, the president-elect's top domestic policy adviser; and Richard Allen, Reagan's national security adviser. The six men met in a private dining room in the basement of the Hay-Adams Hotel, opposite the White House. Meese had a good idea of what was coming, but none of the Reagan aides was prepared for the magnitude of *Mandate.*

Even Meese did not expect to receive more than 2,000 specific recommendations to move the federal government in a conservative direction, including boosting the defense budget by $20 billion in fiscal year 1981 and increasing it by an average of $35 billion over the next five years; establishing urban "enterprise zones" to breathe life into the nation's cities; reducing personal income tax rates by 10 percent across the board; calling for line item veto power by the president and developing a new strategic bomber by using B-1 and advanced bomber technology.[16]

Shaking Up Washington

Mandate hit Washington like a hurricane. Meese publicly expressed his gratitude to Heritage and promised that the Reagan administration would "rely heavily" on the study. E. Pendleton James, personnel chief of the transition group, called the report "valuable because it is all concrete recommendations rather than generalities ... we can get our teeth into it." And President Reagan himself passed out copies of *Mandate* in book form at the very first meeting of his cabinet. "Leaders in both the new administration and the Congress," said new OMB director David Stockman, "will find in this work all of the tools they need to `hit the ground running.'" "This will be the first time a president has ever been this well prepared to take over," added Robert Terrell, a House Interior Committee staff member who chaired the Heritage team assigned to the Interior Department. Congressman Trent Lott of Mississippi, then House Minority Whip, described *Mandate* as "unparalleled in scope" and "a useful guide, not only for the Administration but also for many of us on Capitol Hill."[17]

The news media were also impressed—some despite themselves. The *New York Times* dubbed the mammoth report "a guideline [for] the Reagan team." The *Washington Post* called it "an action plan for turning the government toward the right as fast as possible." And United Press International described it as "a blueprint for grabbing the government by its frayed New Deal lapels and shaking out 48 years of liberal policies."[18]

Mandate's extraordinary impact was heightened by shrewd marketing. Prior to its formal release at a packed news conference, portions of the study were leaked to targeted journalists. Thus, the chapter on national defense was given to reporters who covered the Pentagon, and the chapter on environmental regulations was hand-delivered to journalists who wrote about the EPA. Dozens of stories about *Mandate* recommendations appeared in most of the leading media.[19]

Unlike many conservative documents of the past, *Mandate* was not a work of political rhetoric but a policy document. It was specific and realistic. For example, several administrations had called for acceleration of offshore oil leasing programs. What made The Heritage Foundation's analysis unique was that it specified particular lease parcels—Nos. 53 and 68 in California and No. 68 in the Gulf of Mexico—that should be moved up in the schedule. Inevitably, some *Mandate* positions reflected divisions within the Right. The Interior report called for a return of control over most mining, reclamation, and water rights to the states, but did not specifically recommend legal action to transfer land to the states—a goal of the "Sagebrush Revolution" that Reagan had supported.[20]

One of the report's more prescient passages dealt with the real possibility that PATCO, the air traffic controllers' union, would order an illegal strike shutting down the U.S. air transport system. "Barring a major air disaster," said the study, "a controllers' strike will far overshadow all other short-term problems of a new administration." *Mandate* warned that the administration could not afford to take "a weak and wishy-washy stance."[21] When the controllers did go out on strike in the spring of 1981, President Reagan followed the strategy outlined by Heritage: he quickly replaced the striking controllers and kept the nation's planes flying, thereby serving notice that he would be a firm and decisive chief executive.

A Washington Bestseller

Heritage rushed into print a 1,093-page edition of *Mandate for Leadership*, which quickly won a place on the *Washington Post*'s paperback bestseller list as Washington's power brokers consulted it for clues to the new administration's direction. Heatherly says that the foundation could have sold advance copies to desperate lobbyists for $1,000 or more.[22] Heritage officials were surprised by *Mandate*'s bestselling status (some 15,000 copies were sold in 1981—remarkable for a book only a policy wonk could love). The authors never expected even the most dedicated policymaker to read the book from cover to cover. They had in mind a very select audience: those who would be appointed to run the various departments and agencies. In consequence, they did not give the original work in its entirety to most Reagan appointees. They divided *Mandate* into volumes, each dealing with a particular area of government, and hand-delivered that volume to the appropriate official.

For Ed Feulner, the direction and the final destination of the new administration depended in large part on the mindset of those in charge. "In the past," he said, "so many of our activities have been *against* things. Now how do you start thinking more positively in terms of conservative initiatives?"[23] Feulner told one reporter that he hoped the Reagan administration would get off to a fast start, making as many dramatic changes as possible to show the country "that this is a new day." Otherwise, he warned, "the honeymoon is so short. After you've been here more than sixty or ninety days, people start looking on you as part of the problem rather than part of the solution."[24]

Reagan must have been listening. At his first news conference in late January, the president denounced the Soviet leadership as still dedicated to "world revolution and a one-world Socialist-Communist state," removed price controls on oil and gasoline, and repeated his intention to abolish the Departments of Energy and Education. The *New York Times* did not care for his anticommunist rhetoric but said he was "right" to end oil controls "eight months ahead of schedule."[25]

A week later, Reagan delivered his first televised "fireside chat," explaining that Americans must accept cuts in nearly every government program if the nation were to avoid an "economic calamity." He also pledged a 30 percent income tax cut over the next three years—the Kemp-Roth proposal—but promised to retain a "social safety net" for the truly needy. *Newsweek* called Reagan's plan to cut spending *and* income taxes a "second New Deal potentially as profound in its impact as the first was a half century ago."[26]

At the same time, the president increased the 1981 and 1982 defense budgets by $32.6 billion. (The 1982 hike amounted to a 15 percent increase over Carter's Pentagon budget.) The *New York Times* termed Reagan's military budget "a reversal of national priorities as basic and significant as the Great Society programs of President Johnson in the mid-1960s." President Reagan was determined that after a decade of decline, the United States would again achieve military superiority over the Soviet Union.[27]

In late March, in an address to the 1981 Conservative Political Action Conference in Washington, President Reagan sounded a familiar theme:

> Fellow citizens, fellow conservatives—our time is now, our moment has arrived .... Because ours is a consistent philosophy of government, we can be very clear: we do not have a separate social agenda, a separate economic agenda, and a separate foreign agenda. We have one agenda. Just as surely as we seek to put our financial house in order and rebuild our nation's defenses, so too we seek to protect the unborn, to end the manipulation of school children by utopian planners, and permit the acknowledgment of a supreme being in our classrooms.
>
> If we carry the day and turn the tide we can hope that as long as men speak of freedom and those who have protected it they will remember us and they will say, "Here were the brave and here their place of honor."[28]

As it went about the business of staffing, the White House turned to many of the authors of *Mandate for Leadership*. Reagan aides decided that anyone expert enough to write a chapter on how to run a government department would also be qualified to run that department. In fact, one of the main objectives of the Heritage study had been to spotlight the many conservatives in Washington who could head federal agencies or departments. There was no need to rely on political retreads from the Nixon and Ford administrations who did not understand—or were not interested in carrying out—the Reagan Revolution.

The Reagan administration thus offered high-level executive branch positions to several dozen *Mandate* authors. Norman Ture, the primary author of the chapter on the Treasury Department, was named treasury undersecretary for tax and economic affairs—a new position suggested by Heritage. Economist Manuel Johnson also joined Treasury and was later appointed vice chairman of the board of governors of the Federal Reserve.

Heritage vice president and Resource Bank director Willa Johnson served for six months as deputy director of the White House Personnel Office under Pendleton James. Her job was to fill defense and foreign policy posts with qualified conservatives. Charles Heatherly became special assistant to the secretary of education, and budget analyst Eugene J. McAllister worked under OMB director David Stockman. During the Reagan era, The Heritage Foundation placed more than two hundred conservatives a year in government jobs, implementing one of Feulner's favorite maxims, "People are policy."[29]

Other *Mandate* contributors joining the administration at the policy-making level included:

- James C. Miller, III, chairman of the Federal Trade Commission and later director of the Office of Management and Budget (OMB). Since Miller is a Senior AEI Fellow, the institute asserts an equally valid claim to him (see below)
- Interior Secretary James Watt
- William J. Bennett, chairman of the National Endowment for the Humanities and later secretary of education
- Paul Craig Roberts, assistant treasury secretary for economic policy
- John A. Svahn, commissioner, Social Security Administration
- Robert Hunter, member, National Labor Relations Board
- James Hackett, associate director, International Communications Agency
- Tidal McCoy, assistant secretary of the Air Force
- Richard T. Kennedy, undersecretary of state
- Michael Horowitz, OMB special counsel
- Danny Boggs, White House senior policy adviser for natural resources, later named a federal judge
- Stephen Entin, deputy assistant secretary of the treasury for economic policy
- Lloyd Aubrey, special assistant to the Secretary of Labor
- William Gribbin, deputy assistant to the president for legislative affairs
- Donald Senese, assistant secretary of agriculture

- James L. Malone, head of the U.S. delegation to the Law of the Sea Conference in Geneva and New York

Of course, Heritage was not the only conservative think tank supplying the administration with top appointees. The American Enterprise Institute sent twenty-seven of its senior people to work for Reagan, including United Nations Ambassador Jeane J. Kirkpatrick, James C. Miller III, economist Robert Helms (Health and Human Services), Larry Korb (Department of Defense), Anne Brunsdale (International Trade Commission), and David Gergen (the White House).

The Center for Strategic and International Studies at Georgetown University provided a base for Secretary of State Alexander Haig. Chester Crocker, who would devise the Reagan administration's "constructive engagement" policy toward South Africa, was one prominent CSIS alumnus.

Keeping an Eye on Congress

Even with Reagan in the White House, Heritage did not ignore Congress, its first and still major market for its policy products. After all, Republicans were in control of the Senate for the first time in nearly thirty years, and there were thirty-three new and mostly conservative House members. In December 1980, Heritage held its largest-ever training seminar for congressional staff, drawing an audience of over two hundred.

In the meantime, liberals, trying to sort out the reasons for Reagan's victory and the ascendency of conservative ideas, pointed to the role of think tanks. Writing in the *New Republic,* Morton Kondracke suggested that "the liberal movement in America needs its own counterpart to the conservative Heritage Foundation—a fast-moving, well-financed, highly visible research and propaganda organization capable of analyzing issues from a liberal perspective and getting its product quickly into the hands of members of Congress and the press."[30]

Kondracke erred in calling Heritage's product "propaganda"—indeed, he contradicted himself in the same article by referring to the foundation's "dependable research." But most of his article was on the mark, particularly his description of Heritage's twenty-five analysts and research assistants: all under the age of forty, recent or soon-to-be Ph.D.s, earning between $15,000 and $25,000 a year, "who look forward to advancing to Congressional staff jobs rather than walnut-lined slots in the upper bureaucracy."[31] In fact, their motivation was to advance the conservative cause as much as their own careers.

For conservatives, who had been lonely voices in the wilderness for decades, Reagan's victory and the ascendency of conservative ideas produced rare feelings of euphoria. Nobel Laureate Milton Friedman said, "Today our side—the side of truth, the side of freedom, the side of individual rights—has a strength and appeal which years ago one could hardly have imagined." Heritage, for one, was determined to take advantage of what the *Washington Post* called a political "tidal wave" to move the public-policy agenda decisively to the right.[32]

Cutting Taxes

One of the most important achievements of the Reagan presidency was the passage of the Economic Recovery Plan of 1981, in which Heritage played an important role. The act would put $749 billion—more money than the federal government spent in all of 1982—back in the hands of individual taxpayers and businesses over the next five years. In approving Reagan's tax-cut bill, Congress "veered sharply away" from the tax policies that had guided liberal Congresses since the New Deal.[33]

Heritage expected the Republican Senate to pass the measure easily, but the Democratic House, under the astute leadership of Speaker Thomas P. (Tip) O'Neill and Ways and Means Chairman Dan Rostenkowski, was a far less receptive chamber. In a Machiavellian move, House liberals crafted an alternative to the Reagan proposal, giving two thirds of the tax cuts to Americans earning $20,000 to $50,000 a year, and pitting the middle class against the wealthy. O'Neill and Rostenkowski hoped that their tax-cut package would prevent any defection by conservative southern Democrats—the so-called Boll Weevils—who appeared ready to support the Reagan plan.

Responding to the liberal initiative, Heritage published "An Analysis of the Reagan Tax Cuts and the Democratic Alternative" by analyst Thomas

M. Humbert. The seventeen-page study conceded that the Democratic bill had some good provisions, but argued that the Reagan proposal was more satisfactory to supply-siders for three principal reasons:

1. The Reagan tax cut was bigger, 25 percent as compared with the Democrats' 15 percent.
2. The Reagan cuts would be enacted over three years, the Democratic plan over two years.
3. The Reagan proposal cut marginal tax rates across the board while the Democratic alternative aimed about two thirds of its cuts at low- and middle-income taxpayers.

The Democrats' proposed tax bill, suggested Humbert, could be compared to "a Christmas tree decorated with an assortment of ornaments and lights, each placed to attract the support of some special interest." In contrast, the Reagan tax cut set aside the old liberal practice of trying to redistribute income and relied on the allocation of resources through the free market and individual initiative. "The underlying assumption" of the Reagan approach, said Humbert, is that when individuals are left to pursue their self-interest "unhindered by government," they will generate "enormous productive activity" to the benefit of the entire nation.[34]

Humbert's paper was distributed to all members of Congress and their staff aides dealing with economic issues, to reporters covering the story in Washington, and to editorial page editors across the country. It was quoted in and served as the basis for dozens of speeches by members of Congress as well as newspaper editorials backing the Reagan bill. Congressman Kent Hance of Texas, a leader of southern conservative Democrats in the House, acknowledged that Heritage research is "one of the most valuable tools that Congress can use."[35] The tax-bill analysis established Humbert as an expert on taxes, eventually earning him a position with Jack Kemp as one of his senior economic advisers.

Reagan's tax-cut triumph was assured on July 29 when the Democratic-controlled House bowed to a "tidal wave of public pressure" generated by the president's TV appeal for support and adopted his package in place of the Rostenkowski version. Forty-eight Democrats defected to Reagan as the Democrat-controlled House voted 238–195 to adopt the bill sponsored by Republican Barber Conable and Democrat Kent Hance.

Conservatives carried the day, calling for a "new economic beginning" and an end to the "worn-out" policies of the past.[36]

Trimming the Fat

Determined to help sustain the new beginning, Heritage published, only two months after *Mandate,* a 378-page companion volume, *Agenda for Progress: Examining Federal Spending.* Written by a twenty-member panel of university scholars and economists, and edited by Eugene McAllister (the foundation's Walker Fellow in Economics), the study named dozens of programs that could be eliminated or curtailed for savings of $58.6 billion in 1982 alone. At the heart of the critique was a philosophical realignment of nearly all federal spending programs, giving private-sector institutions and individuals a larger role in implementing public policy. The Reagan administration again expressed its public gratitude, with OMB Director David Stockman commenting, "The ideas that we received from The Heritage Foundation were used, were implemented, and have now become the law of the land." Summing up Heritage's contribution, Stockman asserted: "What has become known as the 'Reagan Revolution' in federal tax and spending policy would have literally been impossible without the invaluable ... work done by The Heritage Foundation."[37]

Always mindful of national defense, Heritage released a major study, *Reforming the Military,* edited by Jeffrey G. Barlow, which outlined how military planners could greatly increase the effectiveness of defense spending. A five-member panel of defense analysts and military scholars recommended sweeping changes in manpower and procurement policies as well as shifts in combat strategy. The main criterion in making military decisions, said the experts, should be that of "combat effectiveness—improving our ability to defeat the enemy rather than economic efficiency." Surprising some observers, the study argued that "dollars alone" would not bridge the chasm between American and Soviet military capabilities: the Maginot Line would not have been "any more useful" to France in World War II had it cost less to build. What was needed, argued Edward Luttwak, Senior Fellow at Georgetown University's Center for Strategic and International Studies, was a comprehensive, coordinated strategy, "not bureaucratically-preferred procedures."[38]

Reacting to a sharply increased demand for its product, Heritage doubled the press run for a typical background paper from 3,700 to 7,500 copies, but still kept them timely. A few days before Jamaica's new prime minister, Edward Seaga, visited the United States, the foundation issued a report on the island's economy. Twenty-four hours after Secretary of State Alexander Haig declared that combating terrorism would be one of his top priorities, Heritage published *The Soviet Strategy of Terror* by Samuel T. Francis, revealing Moscow as one of the world's major sponsors of terrorism. And in the middle of congressional debate on whether to maintain the U.S. grain embargo against the Soviet Union (initiated by Carter in response to the Soviet invasion of Afghanistan), Heritage released a study urging that the embargo be strengthened.

A New Vice President

In September 1981, the Heritage Foundation made a longlasting personnel decision when it hired a brilliant, often volcanic, magazine editor and author, Burton Yale Pines, to be its vice president of research. Pines came to the foundation from *Time* magazine where, during a fifteen-year career, he served in its Bonn, Vienna, Chicago, and Saigon bureaus. In the 1960s, he was *Time*'s youngest foreign correspondent. Pines also had solid academic credentials, having completed his course work for a Ph.D. in modern European history at the University of Wisconsin. He spent two years, 1980–1981, at the American Enterprise Institute (at the recommendation of neoconservative Irving Kristol) writing *Back to Basics*, an examination of what he called "traditionalist America." Pines traveled throughout America for nearly a year where he discovered a strong yearning for a return to old-fashioned traditional values and conservative ideas.[39] His office at AEI was next to Jeane Kirkpatrick's (she was not yet at the United Nations), whose foreign policy stance reinforced his own hard-line attitude about the Cold War.

One evening, Pines dined with Herb Berkowitz, who was highly impressed by his intellectual and ideological views, and his journalistic talents. Pines strongly implied that he wanted to stay in Washington, so Berkowitz suggested to his Heritage colleagues that they bring the ex-*Time* editor on board as head of research. Pines had an enormous impact during his ten years at the foundation.[40]

First, he multiplied Heritage's research output from about one paper every week or so in 1980 to 250 papers a year by the mid-1980s. And he did so without a commensurate increase in staff. Pines wanted the foundation to look at *all* aspects of public policy so that when any topic came up at the White House, someone would remark, "Let's see what Heritage has to say." Within three years, Heritage was no longer "the feisty new kid on the conservative block," as Reagan described the foundation in 1981, but "the basic intellectual resource for the administration."[41]

Heritage now had three specific targets: (1) Reaganauts inside the White House and other executive agencies who were constantly battling pragmatists and moderates over the direction of the administration; (2) Reaganauts in Congress, especially in the House of Representatives, who wanted to make deep (not superficial) cuts in government; (3) the news media, which, according to Pines, "are not lost to us. They are lemmings who follow the pack. You can change their minds, but slowly." Pines saw Heritage's role as providing ammunition for those who "wanted to change history, and we did it!"[42]

Second, Pines insisted that every Heritage study read quickly and be factually sound. The first two or three paragraphs had to present the author's main findings or arguments and the last paragraphs had to repeat them. He was fond of quoting *Time* founder Henry R. Luce that "the less you write, the more they remember." The writer's challenge, Pines emphasized, was to keep the reader reading. He edited every single Heritage paper (totaling about 2.5 million words a year) and often sent a paper back for a second or third rewrite. Pines is proud that he "trained a generation of conservatives to write better and understand better what conservatism is."[43]

Third, he launched several new publications, including the two-page *Executive Memo,* which enabled the foundation to comment on an issue within hours. In early 1984, for example, the communist Sandinista government of Nicaragua filed a suit in the World Court seeking to stop the United States from funding the anticommunist resistance movement, the Contras. When the White House chose to ignore the World Court's demand that the United States appear before the tribunal to defend itself, liberals jumped on the Reagan administration, accusing it of ignoring the rule of international law. Drawing on his foreign policy experience, Pines quickly wrote a memo personally defending the White House decision as legally and politically justified.

Pines pointed out that the Soviet Union and its satellites had never accepted the World Court's jurisdiction. It would be "foolish," he added, for the United States to engage in a legal dispute with "a regime that routinely disregards international law and norms, violates its citizens' human rights, suppresses dissent, imposes censorship, and refuses to hold free elections."[44] Conservative members of Congress cited the Heritage memo, Pines was invited to appear on a number of network television programs, and public opinion shifted in favor of the White House. A potential embarrassment for the Reagan administration was turned into a setback for the Sandinista regime.

Fourth, Pines greatly expanded the lecture series from about one formal address a month to over one hundred talks, panels, and other events a year. At the suggestion of William F. Buckley Jr., he hired Ben Hart, a former editor of the combative *Dartmouth Review*, as director of lectures and seminars. Pines told Hart that he didn't care about the size of the audience—"all those who turned up at Heritage" were participants in the Reagan Revolution. If a speaker said something significant, Heritage would reprint the remarks in its print shop, quickly and cheaply.[45]

Remembering Vietnam

Pines also played an important supportive role in one of the most emotional issues of the early 1980s—the Vietnam War Memorial, located on Washington's Mall within view of the Lincoln Memorial. When a blue-ribbon panel selected the black wall design of Maya Ying Lin, a Yale undergraduate, many veterans were quick to protest, calling it a "black gash of shame and sorrow" and "the black trench." Contributors had expected that the design would honor the living (some 2.7 million men and women served in Vietnam) as well as the dead.

Heritage policy analyst Milt Copulos, a combat veteran who served two consecutive tours of duty in Vietnam, worked with Pines, Senator John Warner (R-Va.), an original sponsor of the memorial, and Interior Secretary James Watt to resolve an impasse. It was agreed that there would be three additions to the original design: a flag, a statue of a serviceman near the wall, and additional wording for the inscription. The changes reassured Vietnam veterans that future generations would understand that "the soldier who fought in Vietnam did so honorably and for an honorable purpose."[46]

Safety Nets and Charles Murray

One of those who remember Burt Pines well and are grateful for his encouragement is social scientist Charles A. Murray, author of the seminal work about the American welfare system, *Losing Ground*. In the fall of 1981, Murray decided to leave his job as chief scientist for the American Institutes for Research in Washington, D.C., and try to make a living as an independent researcher and writer. He wrote to several think tanks in town inquiring about possible adjunct fellowships. The only response came from Burt Pines, who invited Murray to drop by for a chat.

At the time, liberals were charging that Reagan's budget cuts would "shred" the safety net that protected millions of needy Americans. Murray declared that criticism of Reagan was "silly." Trained as a journalist to follow the money trail, Pines wanted to know what had happened to the billions of dollars spent fighting the War on Poverty. He suggested that Murray write a monograph on whether Lyndon B. Johnson's welfare programs had been a success or a failure. He offered a fee of $2,500 which was "fine" with Murray.[47] The result was a 1982 study that made history: *Safety Nets and the Truly Needy: Rethinking the Social Welfare System*.

Digging deep into the Library of Congress and other repositories, Murray showed that the percentage of Americans in poverty had been dropping since World War II, but slowed in the late 1960s and then stopped in the mid-1970s—just as government spending on poverty programs rose sharply. In the central argument of his study, Murray declared that welfare programs, which were supposed to lift people out of poverty, did just the opposite. They undermined the work ethic and created a culture of dependency. By making poverty more bearable, they created a permanent dependent underclass. Even worse, the combination of public assistance and free time had contributed to the breakdown of the family and the community, especially in the inner cities. As Murray summed up, "the poor are living in worse conditions now than they were twenty years ago.

The social ills that a progressive social welfare policy proposed to eradicate have accelerated under its aegis."[48]

Murray proposed four reforms of social welfare policy in America: (1) assistance should be provided only for those unable to work; (2) holding a full-time job is preferable to "any combination of work and welfare"; (3) a stigma should be attached to anyone who is able-bodied and on welfare; and (4) rewards for those who "achieve" should be greater than rewards for those who do not.

While conceding that the reforms would be fiercely resisted by "an entrenched social service bureaucracy," Murray argued that they were required if the objective was to construct a true safety net that would raise "the poor to independence."[49]

Irving Kristol was so taken with Murray's thesis, which appeared as an op-ed article in the *Wall Street Journal,* that he asked Murray to write the lead article for the fall 1982 issue of the *Public Interest.* That article, "Two Wars Against Poverty: Economic Growth and the Great Society," led William Hammett of the Manhattan Institute to offer Murray a position which enabled him to write *Losing Ground,* one of the most influential public-policy books of the last twenty years.

Restructuring the Management

Pines's appointment as vice president of research was part of a new management structure which Ed Feulner and Phil Truluck designed in the spring of 1981. In addition to his duties as director of research, Truluck had been overseeing the activities of the entire foundation when Feulner was out of town, so that about forty people reported directly to him. But the research and running the foundation were too much for any one person to handle—even the quietly efficient, never complaining South Carolinian. Truluck became executive vice president and chief operating officer with direct responsibility for daily operations.

"Suddenly," explained Truluck, "we were playing on a public-policy stage whose audience had doubled to include not only the United States Congress but a philosophically receptive new administration." Heritage's COO feels strongly that the action was a milestone of the foundation: "We created a management structure that is still in place."[50] In effect, Phil

Truluck became Mr. Inside (the coordinator/implementer) and Ed Feulner Mr. Outside (the visionary/salesman) of the Heritage Foundation—although when he was in the building, Feulner remained a hands-on president. It is a sign of Feulner's personal security and his strength as a chief executive that he welcomes in the number two position a strong and independent thinker like Truluck.

Around the same time, John Von Kannon, former publisher of the *American Spectator,* was named treasurer and took over the financial affairs of the foundation, including fund-raising and liaison with the corporate sector. Von Kannon is widely acknowledged to be one of the most effective fund-raisers in America. Richard Larry, who directs the Sarah Scaife Foundation, calls him "the premier development guy today."[51] A central reason is that Von Kannon believes deeply in the product he is selling—Heritage and conservatism. "Money does not lead the mission," Von Kannon says, "the mission comes first." He recalls that one year Heritage lost $200,000 when five steel companies and a prominent textile manufacturer stopped giving because of the foundation's free trade stance. One steel executive became so angry when Heritage would not compromise its position that he tore up a check for $10,000 in front of Feulner, who later remarked to his colleagues, "We're not for sale."[52]

Confident that the foundation would run smoothly under Truluck, Von Kannon, and the rest of the new senior management, Feulner increased his time outside Washington (1) talking to present and potential donors about Heritage; (2) strengthening conservatism at home and abroad through groups like the Philadelphia Society, the Intercollegiate Studies Institute, and the Mont Pelerin Society; and (3) making useful governmental and nongovernmental overseas contacts for Heritage and the conservative movement. With Reagan in the White House and Feulner on the road, Heritage's income soared 34 percent in one year, from $5.3 million in 1980 to almost $7.1 million in 1981, while its staff increased to eighty-seven full-time employees.

A significant change also occurred in the leadership of the Heritage board of trustees when Frank Shakespeare succeeded Ben B. Blackburn as chairman and Ambassador Shelby Cullom Davis became vice chairman. Shakespeare, president of the RKO General Corporation, brought more than thirty years of broadcast communications and political experience to the board. President Reagan would later appoint Shakespeare U.S. ambassador to the sensitive post of the Vatican and then to Portugal. Davis had combined a highly successful business career in New York with diplomacy, having served as U.S. ambassador to Switzerland. Davis succeeded Shakespeare as board chairman when the broadcasting executive went to Rome. Under their decade of combined leadership, Heritage experienced what a senior foundation official calls the "glory days."[53]

On the Go

Ed Feulner has loved to travel since his student days in London. Longtime friend Richard V. Allen says, "Ed never met an airplane ticket he didn't like."[54] Feulner's appointment-packed visits to Europe and Asia in the 1980s paid high dividends in prestige and support for Heritage. In 1981, the foundation, in cooperation with the Hanns Seidel Stiftung (the foundation of Bavaria's leading political party), hosted the visit of several dozen members of the West German Bundestag, who met with their American counterparts on Capitol Hill as well as State Department and other officials.

Heritage also sponsored a Washington dinner for Jonas Savimbi, head of UNITA, Angola's anticommunist nationalist movement, and urged the administration, in the October issue of *National Security Record,* the foundation's monthly publication devoted to big picture security issues, to funnel arms and supplies to Savimbi. Savimbi met all the criteria: he was friendly to the West, antagonistic toward communism, a leader of the largest tribal group in the country, and one of the most popular figures in Angola. It was widely speculated that he would win a free election if the Angolan Marxists ever dared to hold one. Before long, Savimbi began receiving assistance from the United States under the Reagan Doctrine. The Angolan leader once told Heritage policy analyst Michael Johns that Heritage's support was "critical" to his survival. Johns, who traveled extensively throughout Africa and was the foundation's leading expert on the Third World, says flatly that "UNITA and Savimbi would have been destroyed without Heritage."[55]

In 1982, Heritage established the Asian Studies Center, chaired by Richard V. Allen, former national security adviser to President Reagan, a

Heritage Distinguished Fellow, and a longtime colleague of Ed Feulner. Allen and Feulner assured Heritage trustees that the center would be funded through its own endowment. The two men were as good as their word, raising more than $13 million over the next decade and a half, almost all of it from South Korean, Taiwanese, and other Asian foundations and corporations. Much of the center's attention focused on the lessons to be learned from the "economic miracles" of Korea, Hong Kong, Singapore, and Taiwan. Over the years, center analysts frequently discussed the People's Republic of China, usually taking a hard line on its brutal violations of human rights, but gradually adopting a softer line toward the question of U.S.-PRC trade. Allen insists that the "real conservative position" on MFN (Most Favored Nation) status for China "is renewal—to help our friends there." He includes Taiwan and Hong Kong among those who benefit from MFN. "I prefer a weak and fractured China," says Allen, "but MFN is not the vehicle to do that."[56]

Heading for the High Frontier

Of Heritage's many projects in a crowded 1982, none was more important to America's national defense and the course of the Cold War than its sponsorship of a new space strategy called "High Frontier." At a packed March 3 news conference, Ed Feulner and Lt. Gen. Daniel O. Graham, former director of the Pentagon's Defense Intelligence Agency, outlined the results of a months-long, $50,000 study that urged the Reagan administration and the Congress to adopt an all-out effort to develop both military and peaceful uses of space. The study's most dramatic recommendation was the development of a multi-satellite global ballistic missile defense system capable of knocking out enemy nuclear missiles aimed at the United States.

High Frontier, explained General Graham, constituted a change of U.S. strategy "from the bankrupt and basically immoral precepts of Mutual Assured Destruction (MAD) to a stable and morally defensible strategy of Assured Survival." He asserted that a layered strategic defense, including a "spaceborne capability to intercept" Soviet missiles midcourse, could be accomplished in a remarkably short time if there was "a national commitment to do so."[57]

Graham had been a military adviser to Ronald Reagan during the 1980 presidential campaign and the leader of a group that advocated "a fundamental change in U.S. grand strategy by making a technological end-run around the Soviets." However, once in office, the Reagan administration became involved in plugging up the "yawning" gaps between American and Soviet military capabilities. While not denying that weapons like the MX missile and the B-1 bomber were needed, Ed Feulner said at the February 1982 Heritage news conference that the High Frontier strategy would enable the administration and the nation to make greater use of "the industrialized and peaceful applications of space as well as the tapping of its military potential."[58]

The Heritage study found a receptive audience in the Oval Office. President Reagan had favored an alternative to MAD since at least July 1979 when he toured the headquarters of the North American Aerospace Defense Command (NORAD) in Colorado. As Reagan biographer Lou Cannon tells the story, Reagan asked Air Force General James Hill what could be done if the Soviets fired a missile at an American city. Nothing, Hill replied. NORAD would track the incoming missile and then give city officials ten to fifteen minutes warning before it hit. "That's all we can do," said Hill. "We can't stop it." According to Reagan aide Martin Anderson, the soon-to-be presidential candidate couldn't believe that the United States had no defense against Soviet missiles. "We have spent all that money and have all that equipment, and there is nothing we can do to prevent a nuclear missile from hitting us," he later remarked.[59] Reagan kept pushing for a better way, which turned out to be the Strategic Defense Initiative (SDI), about which the normally modest Reagan says flatly, "SDI was my idea."[60]

Although in charge of domestic policy in the Reagan White House, Anderson in 1981 formed a small informal group (including the president's science adviser, George Keyworth) to discuss strategic missile defense. In September and again in October, the group met with Edward Teller, the father of the H-Bomb, and military experts Karl Bendetsen and Daniel Graham. What Anderson called a "critical turning point for SDI" came in January 1982 when the group—almost all of whom were involved in the soon-to-be-released High Frontier report—met with the president.[61] Also in attendance at the January meeting were Jaquelin Hume and Joseph Coors, both members of Reagan's "kitchen cabinet." Anderson recalled that although the president did not commit himself, he asked questions about the feasibility and cost of missile defense. "It was clear from his demeanor that he was convinced it could be done." Coors later told Feulner that Reagan's eyes lit up during the presentation.[62]

There were many more meetings inside and outside the White House, including a visit by Keyworth to The Heritage Foundation. Keyworth's support of SDI was critical. By his own admission, the science adviser had been skeptical about strategic defense since his days at Los Alamos in the late 1960s. But he was brought around by long conversations with his mentor Edward Teller, his own reading and research, and interactions with advocates like Graham and others at Heritage.[63] There was also strong, often violent opposition within the administration. Secretary of State George Shultz once called Keyworth "a lunatic" in front of the president for his advocacy of SDI, arguing that it would "destroy" NATO. But Reagan did not budge from his commitment to the concept of strategic defense, causing an admiring Keyworth to remark that the president "has this marvelous ability to work the whole while everybody else is working the parts."[64]

Finally, on March 23, 1983, President Reagan, in a nationally televised address, announced that development and deployment of a comprehensive antiballistic missile system would be his top defense priority—his "ultimate goal." "I call upon the scientific community in our country," he said, "those who gave us nuclear weapons, to turn their great talents now to the cause of mankind and world peace, to give us the means of rendering these nuclear weapons impotent and obsolete." He called the system the Strategic Defense Initiative (SDI), but it was ridiculed as "Star Wars" by its detractors.[65] But more than any other strategic action he took, Reagan's unflinching commitment to SDI convinced the Kremlin it could not win the arms race and led Gorbachev and his communist colleagues into suing for peace and ending the Cold War. As Alexander Solzhenitsyn later put it, Gorbachev "had no choice but to disarm."[66]

Master Fusionist

Seemingly never too busy, Feulner found time to earn a Ph.D. in political science from the University of Edinburgh (writing his dissertation about the Republican Study Committee between 5:30 and 7:30 every morning for three years), serve as chairman of the U.S. Advisory Commission on Public Diplomacy, and preside for one year over the Institute for Research on the Economics of Taxation (IRET). He was an active participant in every organization. As Kathy Rowan, his executive assistant for more than twenty years, says, "When Ed joins something, he really joins."[67]

Feulner kept faith with Heritage's mission to represent all major strains of conservatism by inviting Midge Decter, author, social critic, and leading neoconservative, to join the board of trustees in the spring of 1981. It was a calculated and even courageous act. At the time, traditional conservatives and neoconservatives were still getting used to each other— some paleoconservatives have never made the adjustment. Decter recalls a meeting in New York City where for the first time she met Paul Weyrich and Phyllis Schlafly, the head of the anti-Equal Rights Amendment effort. To the surprise of many, she and Schlafly "got along instantly" because both realized they were allies in the cultural battle. When someone asked Decter how she could be so friendly with a "right-winger" like Schlafly, she replied, "It's easy—she's been doing my dirty work for years."[68] Feulner and Decter had gotten to know each other when she and her husband, Norman Podhoretz, who was editor of *Commentary* magazine, were invited by *Policy Review* editor John O'Sullivan to spend a day at Heritage, giving lectures and meeting its people.

Under O'Sullivan, *Policy Review* constantly challenged conservative minds with articles by George Gilder on the welfare crisis; Milton Friedman on the grassroots tax revolt; Walter Williams and Thomas Sowell on tuition tax credits; Winston S. Churchill II on the Soviet challenge to the West; novelist Kingsley Amis on a policy for the arts; and Midge Decter on affirmative action.

In the fall of 1982, Nobel Laureate Friedrich A. Hayek visited Heritage as a distinguished scholar and stated that "on the whole" he approved of the Reagan administration's economic policy. Regarding Reagan's tax policy, Hayek said that the idea of cutting taxes to produce higher revenues was right "in principle" but that he was "a little apprehensive" about the administration's scale of tax cuts. "I'm all for reduction of government expenditures," he explained, "but to anticipate it by reducing the rate of taxation before you have reduced expenditure is a very risky thing to do."[69]

Hayek also commented on his lifelong intellectual adversary, British economist John Maynard Keynes. "Keynes," he said, "was one of the most intelligent people I knew but he understood very little economics. He must not be blamed for his disciples. He knew the danger of inflation."[70]

A Special Relationship

There was no denying the close relationship between President Reagan and Heritage. In early 1981, Reagan declared there was "one group which gave us special substantive help we'll never forget ... The Heritage Foundation." But when the president and his administration warranted criticism, Heritage did not hesitate to deliver it, as with the publication of *The First Year*, an assessment of the Reagan presidency after one year in office. Edited by Richard N. Holwill, the study concluded that although headed in the right direction, the administration "should and could have accomplished more." The report's authors estimated that of two thousand recommendations made in *Mandate for Leadership*, about 1,270 specific suggestions—about 60 percent—had been implemented or initiated. The principal reason for the administration's "failure," Holwill wrote, was "personnel," a judgment that confirmed Ed Feulner's dictum that people lead policy.[71]

Responding to the modest grade from Heritage, President Reagan characteristically looked on the bright side. On February 8, 1982, he wrote Feulner a "Dear Ed" letter, saying, "Although you have been critical at times, the criticism has maintained a responsible tone.... I am reassured to be reminded of how much our friends expect of us. I ... look forward to working with you and the members of this team in pursuit of our common goals for a better America."[72]

Feulner appreciated Reagan's grace under pressure as well as his generous reference to the foundation as "the feisty new kid on the conservative block." But nine years after its founding and with an annual budget of over $7 million, Heritage was no longer new or a kid, but a major force in public policy in Washington and the nation. The ideas that Heritage and other conservative organizations had been promulgating for years had been nationally ratified by Reagan's presidential victory.

It was certainly pleasant to read in the *National Journal* that the foundation was "the marvel of the political establishment and the intellectual community." And it was gratifying to have the liberal *New Republic* cite Heritage as a model that the liberal establishment would do well to emulate.[73] But after fifteen years in Washington, Feulner was well aware how fleeting political influence was. How permanent a presence was Heritage?

Everyone at Heritage was deeply grateful for the generous support of Joseph Coors, Jack Eckerd, and the Noble Foundation, whose total gifts of just over $1 million had enabled the foundation to expand greatly its office space. But Feulner could not put out of his mind that Heritage was headquartered in a string of townhouses while the Brookings Institution had its own eight-story building, a visible symbol of its power and prestige. And he knew that William Baroody Jr., the new president of the American Enterprise Institute, had announced plans for a new AEI building. Despite all its accomplishments, Heritage was still regarded by many in Washington as a think tank in the making, dependent upon the Reagan administration for its success or failure. Feulner had an idea how to demonstrate that Heritage was here to stay, but it involved some risk and a lot of faith.

4

Coming of Age

The Heritage Foundation's first year, 1974, was clouded over by fallout from the Watergate scandal—Nixon's resignation, the massive defeat of conservative candidates for the House and the Senate, and the arrival in Washington of a brashly liberal freshman class of legislators. Many conservatives—notably William A. Rusher, a guiding force in the 1964 Republican nomination of Barry Goldwater—spoke openly of starting a new third party. Some even said that the Grand Old Party was headed for the ashheap of history. Early in that fateful year, Heritage could fit all eight of its employees into a couple of rented offices and ran on a minuscule budget of $250,000, almost all of it provided by the generosity of one person. As *USA Today* later commented, "Many of Washington's liberals derided [Heritage] as an inconsequential band of right-wingers."[1]

A decade later, President Ronald Reagan sat in the White House; Republicans controlled the Senate and kept the Democrats on their toes in the House; and conservative ideas, from supply-side economics to designation of the Soviets as an "Evil Empire," dominated the political agenda. Heritage had a staff of more than one hundred people—analysts, academics, and support personnel—an annual operating budget of more than $10.5 million, and financial support from 140,000 individuals and dozens of corporations and foundations. Remarked the *Washington Post*, "The impact of Heritage has been stunning."[2]

With the election in 1980 of President Reagan, the American conservative movement came of age, and, unsurprisingly, The Heritage Foundation began to experience growing pains.

Because of space limitations in the converted townhouses on Stanton Park, the foundation was renting more and more rooms in hotels and private clubs for its meetings. Researchers worked on different floors in different buildings. Public relations was in one building, the tiny library in another, and the president's office in still another. The Heritage offices at three different addresses resembled an institutional gerrymander. If the foundation wanted to host a luncheon, a lecture by a distinguished scholar, and private meetings with policymakers at the same time, it couldn't.

In late 1981, while Feulner was debating whether to bring plans for a new multi-million-dollar building before the board of trustees, he had breakfast with Senator John Warner (R-Va.), a veteran Washingtonian. Warner listened to Feulner outline the pros and cons and then said, "Ed, the buildings you have now are nice, but you need a major physical presence, like Brookings. Otherwise, you're just one more Washington think tank."[3]

Warner's counsel (and the reference to Brookings) decided Feulner, and at the next board meeting, he proposed the move and explained that there was a place available, an eight-story building at 214 Massachusetts Avenue, N.E., just three blocks from the Capitol. It had been the Annex of the Library of Congress, but had been unoccupied since the 1980 opening of the library's Madison Building.

The trustees' initial reaction, as Phil Truluck recalls, was, "You guys are policy experts—what do you know about real estate?" They asked Feulner and Truluck to come back with a specific plan, including purchase price, renovation costs, and means of financing. At the next meeting, Truluck, who would oversee the purchase and extensive renovation of the new headquarters, pointed out that a building with 65,000 square feet and a prime location on Capitol Hill wouldn't come along every day. And since this one contained double the space Heritage needed at the time, the foundation could, for the foreseeable future, rent out space to bring in some income. The estimated total cost was a little more than $9 million, almost equal to the foundation's annual budget. A limited partnership was proposed, consisting of six trustees who would put up $250,000 each toward the purchase of the building. The partners would then lease the building to Heritage, with the hope they would later donate it to the foundation. (Ironically, Reagan's 1986 tax reform bill would prevent such purchase-gift arrangements.)

It was, as Truluck says, "a very bold decision," made possible only because Joseph Coors, Richard Scaife, Thomas A. Roe, Arthur Spitzer, Lewis Lehrman, and Robert Krieble (and his wife Nancy) had confidence in what Heritage was doing and would yet do. Over the next twelve months, Phil Truluck and foundation controller Peter Pover oversaw the myriad contractors who transformed an aging, long-neglected library annex into a modern, up-to-date research and conference center. As evidence of Truluck's organizational skills, the foundation moved into its new head-quarters on schedule and without cost overruns in the summer of 1983. Just a decade after its birth, Heritage became a physical as well as an intellectual landmark in the nation's capital. In Pover's words, "We were here to stay."

At the Cutting Edge

A major component of Heritage's continuing intellectual impact was *Policy Review*. Editor Adam Meyerson (who succeeded John O'Sullivan in the summer of 1983) placed the foundation at the cutting edge of conservative thought and beyond with his imaginative coupling of authors and articles. A fall 1985 article by former Delaware Governor Pete du Pont, "Kamikaze Economics of Protectionism," was cited by Linda Chavez, director of the White House Office of Public Liaison, in briefing materials she prepared for President Reagan on the trade issue. "Can-Do Government" by William Kristol, in the winter 1985 *Policy Review*, demonstrated how three Reagan appointees made important changes in their agencies despite opposition from Congress, the news media, and the bureaucracy. Several hundred copies of the article were distributed to new appointees in the Reagan administration. Business executive J. Peter Grace called Dinesh D'Souza's article about the ignorance of Catholic bishops on economics, "The Bishops as Pawns," "one of the best treatises I have had the pleasure of reading." And in 1987, *Policy Review* published articles by presidential hopefuls Bob Dole, Jack Kemp, Pete du Pont, and television evangelist and businessman Pat Robertson, a relative unknown at the time.[4]

Heritage 10

During its tenth anniversary festivities in 1983, Heritage launched its first major fund-raising campaign, "Heritage 10—Funding the Conservative Decade," under the chairmanship of New York businessman and trustee Lewis Lehrman. Working closely with Lehrman were foundation treasurer John Von Kannon and fund-raising consultant Robert Russell. The campaign goal was $27.5 million, to be used for 1984 operating costs, help pay for the new building, and to establish a permanent endowment for the Asian Studies Center. By the end of 1983, Heritage had received pledges and contributions of nearly $10 million.

Lehrman, who nearly defeated Democrat Mario Cuomo for governor of New York in 1982, envisioned the 1980s as the "conservative decade," a time when conservative ideas and ideals would triumph in Washington. To that end, argued Lehrman, it was necessary to persuade those who decide policy in Washington and the country that the conservative way "is the right way, the American way."[5] President Reagan's landslide reelection victory in 1984 (he carried forty-nine states and received 525 electoral votes against the hapless Democratic nominee, former Vice President Walter F. Mondale) confirmed how much the political debate had changed since Heritage entered the scene just a decade earlier.

Washington policymakers no longer talked about containing the Soviet Union but about liberating the Soviet Empire. They no longer proposed new government welfare programs but new ways to liberate the underclass from welfare dependency. They no longer suggested new regulatory agencies but new methods to free American enterprise from government intervention.

The air was full of liberating ideas: enterprise zones in the inner cities, privatizing government services, choice in education, health-care vouchers, private-sector alternatives to Social Security, free trade zones, and SDI. Every one of these ideas had been born at or nurtured by Heritage. By mid-decade, Heritage was being described by *Forbes* magazine as "eclipsing much older, more established fixtures such as the Brookings Institution" and by *Time* as "the foremost of the new breed of advocacy tanks."[6]

Sometimes the foundation worked hard to puncture an old, unworkable idea—like national industrial policy. In February 1984, it published

A Blueprint for Jobs and Industrial Growth, edited by Senior Fellow Richard McKenzie, professor of economics at Clemson University. McKenzie's plan offered forty-three specific proposals for stimulating economic and industrial growth and employment without additional government spending. *Blueprint* was the result of a two-year study coordinated by McKenzie. Following its publication, industrial policy became a nonissue in the nation's capital—until Labor Secretary Robert Reich unearthed it, briefly, in the early Clinton years.

At the same time, Stuart Butler proposed a companion measure that would enable public housing tenants to become homeowners. The tenants' "Right to Buy" plan, adopted on an experimental basis by the Department of Housing and Urban Development in late 1984, was one of a continuing series of Heritage proposals on the privatization of public services. As Butler argued, "There is certainly no reason for the federal bureaucracy to have a monopoly on providing services to the public."[7] In the opinion of Heritage analysts, that included the "third rail" issue of American politics—Social Security.

The Third Rail

As President Reagan took office in 1980, Congress was still congratulating itself for having "solved" the Social Security crisis of the mid-1970s. In December 1977, Heritage analyst Peter J. Ferrara wrote, Congress enacted "the largest peacetime tax increase in U.S. history," designed to guarantee the financial soundness of the system "for the rest of this century and well into the next one."[8] Yet just four years later, the 1981 annual report of the Social Security Board of Trustees concluded that, by late 1982 or early 1983, the system would be unable to pay promised benefits.

The Reagan administration attempted to deal rationally with the problem by proposing a one-time, three-month delay in cost-of-living increases and a reduction of benefits for those who chose early retirement before age sixty-five. There was an immediate, near hysterical response by the powerful Social Security lobby. Reagan was accused of trying to "smash" the financial security of American retirees, and panicky congressional Republicans backed away quickly from the administration's proposals.[9]

A resigned administration appointed a national commission to devise a bailout scheme for Social Security and defuse the political crisis. The commission's proposals, released in January 1983, were predictable but swiftly adopted. They included an acceleration of payroll tax increases, an increase in payroll taxes on self-employed workers, federal taxation of formerly tax-exempt Social Security benefits, and termination of the right of state and local government employees to opt out of the system. Congress also added a gradual increase in the retirement age from sixty-five to sixty-seven. As Ferrara stated, the package only "tinkered with the basic structure of Social Security." Nearly everyone was hurt by the reforms, from the elderly whose benefits were effectively cut and taxed to workers whose FICA taxes were increased and whose promised benefits were reduced.[10]

Heritage concluded that a new compact between generations regarding Social Security and other entitlements was needed. The foundation published a series of studies about a private-sector retirement and healthcare system that would supplement and then partially replace the existing Social Security/medical benefits program. Developed for Heritage by former White House analyst Ferrara, the "privatized" system, built around expanded Individual Retirement Accounts (Super IRAs), would be gradually phased in. Wage earners would have the option of remaining in the Social Security program or enrolling in a private plan. Everyone would have to have either private or public coverage. Those electing to stay in Social Security would be guaranteed benefits through a Social Security bond.

When Barry Goldwater ran for president against Lyndon Johnson in 1964, he suggested that Social Security was in actuarial trouble and that a voluntary option ought to be considered. For this sensible suggestion, he was accused, by Republicans as well as Democrats, of trying to "destroy" Social Security.[11] A decade later, Heritage's suggestion of a partially privatized system was coolly received but not dismissed out of hand. By the mid-1990s, as the foundation approached its twenty-fifth anniversary, leaders of both major political parties were willing to concede that Social Security needed more fundamental reform than one more tax hike or an extension of the retirement age. The lesson was clear to Feulner and others at Heritage: when dealing with sacred cows like Social Security, patience and persistence are the twin pillars of success.

Sweating the Details

Despite his pledge in 1980 to balance the budget, President Reagan was unable to contain Washington's pro-spending propensities. He left the White House with the budget deficit about twice as high as when he was first elected. As Heritage analyst Stephen Moore wrote, "This explosion of national indebtedness stands as a conspicuous blemish on the Reagan economic record."[12]

The Reagan years taught Heritage that even the best rhetoric in the world is not enough to sustain the conservative revolution. Policymakers have to be specific about how they intend to downsize government, shift power from Washington to the states, and encourage individual and local community responsibility. One of Stuart Butler's favorite sayings is "We sweat the details." In early 1984, the foundation's domestic studies division released a major budget-cutting plan by analyst John M. Palffy. His proposals could have reduced the federal deficit by $119 billion in fiscal year 1985 without affecting services to the poor or weakening national defense.[13] The report was credited by OMB Director David Stockman with providing many of the money-saving ideas in the Reagan administration's 1986 budget. Congressman William Dannemeyer of California, chairman of the Republican Study Committee, called the report "must reading."[14]

But Heritage had just begun. Stuart Butler's 1985 book, *Privatizing Federal Spending: A Strategy to Eliminate the Deficit*, was widely reviewed and drew the attention of at least one high-ranking administration official. Just hours after James C. Miller was appointed director of the Office of Management and Budget, one of his top aides requested copies of all Heritage's privatization studies, and Butler was invited to brief high-level White House and budget officials on the potential of privatization. It was no coincidence that the administration's fiscal year 1987 budget plan contained several specific proposals to privatize federal programs.

When Conrail was "privatized" in early 1987 in a public stock offering, the stock-sale plan was remarkably similar to one proposed by Heritage analyst James Gattuso two years earlier. Stephen Moore, who put together an extensive privatization blueprint for the foundation, took a leave of absence that same year to become coordinator of research for President Reagan's Commission on Privatization. As the *Atlantic Monthly* put it, "Conservative thinking has liberal thinking outgunned.... In vigor, freshness, and appeal, market-oriented theories have surpassed government-oriented theories at nearly every turn."[15]

Winning the Cold War

On the foreign front, despite a new and reputedly more "liberal" Soviet leader Mikhail Gorbachev, the Cold War was still being waged in many different lands, including Nicaragua, Afghanistan, Angola, and Cambodia. As W. Bruce Weinrod, Heritage's director of foreign policy and defense studies, said, the Soviet Union and its assorted proxies were "clearly the source of much of the turmoil which threatens freedom and democratic government around the world."[16] Consequently, when Reagan traveled to Geneva in November 1985 for a "get acquainted" summit with Gorbachev, Heritage made certain that the president benefited from its analysts' best thinking. A copy of its fifty-four-page *Briefing Book* was personally handed to Reagan at a White House meeting of conservative leaders, including Feulner, two weeks before the U.S.-Soviet summit.

At Geneva, the president called on the Soviets to abandon their occupation of Afghanistan, stop subsidizing and training terrorists, rein in the Cubans and Nicaraguans, and obey all existing treaties, including the Anti-Ballistic Missile (ABM) treaty and the Helsinki Accords governing human rights. He also said flatly that the United States intended to move forward with research on strategic defense. And SDI was *not* negotiable. All of these points followed recommendations in the Heritage briefing book.

In an extraordinary recognition of the foundation's influence, Gorbachev brought up the Heritage report in the first ten minutes of his Geneva summit with Reagan, citing it as evidence of "right-wing pressure" on their talks. According to aides, the president countered that, yes, he did have the Heritage report, and he liked it.[17] Still fuming about Heritage, Gorbachev returned to Moscow where he told the Supreme Soviet that Reagan had stood fast on SDI because of "the 'mandate' given to the U.S. president by the forces of the American extreme right wing, represented by their ideological headquarters, The Heritage Foundation."[18] Heritage appreciated Gorbachev's acknowledgment of its influential role in international affairs, if not his precise wording.

Concerning other foreign fronts, the foundation published papers about Latin America (translated into Spanish for distribution abroad), NATO, and the Middle East. In the latter, adjunct scholar Daniel Pipes discussed Muslim fundamentalism and how religious fanaticism had become a driving force behind Middle Eastern events. Pipes' analysis anticipated the Algerian military's invalidation of the 1991 elections after the Islamic fundamentalists had won, as well as the continuing struggle between Islamic militants and the governments of Egypt and Turkey. As usual, the Asian Studies Center buzzed with activity, releasing a *Super-backgrounder* on U.S.-China relations just before President Reagan's trip to the People's Republic of China in April 1984 and a briefing book before the president's visit to Korea and Japan.

Cleaning Up the U.N.

Since 1982, Heritage had been monitoring the United Nations, believing that it was an important battleground in the Cold War. The foundation's United Nations Assessment Project helped the international body return, if marginally, to the high-minded purposes for which it was created. Even liberals conceded Heritage's impact. Congressman James Leach (R-Iowa) told a House Foreign Affairs subcommittee, "Few institutions in American history have played a more decisive role in American policy toward the United Nations than The Heritage Foundation."[19]

For example, when the United States withdrew in December 1984 from the U.N. Educational, Scientific and Cultural Organization (UNESCO), Heritage could take satisfaction that its recommendations had prevailed with the Reagan administration. The foundation's studies had found a persistent pattern of waste, corruption, cronyism, anti-Americanism, and anticapitalism in almost all of UNESCO's programs. UNESCO Director-General Amadou M'Bow had six official automobiles at his disposal in Paris and New York City. Millions of dollars evaporated on wasteful programs like a study of the epistemological foundation of economic theory. While M'Bow was busy collecting forty-two honorary degrees, three gold medals (from Czechoslovakia, East Germany, and Mongolia), and thirty-five decorations, the French government in 1982 expelled forty-seven Soviet spies—twelve of them employed by UNESCO.[20]

Since the United States had been providing one fourth of UNESCO's funds (about $50 million), Owen Harries, Heritage's John M. Olin Fellow in Political Economy and a former Australian ambassador to the U.N., concluded, in a December 1984 study called "UNESCO: Time to Leave," that it was not in the best interests of the American taxpayer or of American diplomats for the United States to remain in the organization.

But Heritage was not finished with the U.N. That same year, the foundation also published two book-length studies: *A World Without a U.N.* and *The U.S. and the U.N.: A Balance Sheet.* The foreword of the former work was written by Ambassador Charles M. Lichenstein, who had recently joined Heritage as a senior fellow. As Jeane Kirkpatrick's deputy at the United Nations in the early 1980s, Lichenstein had told the Soviet Union and other American critics, after a particularly long and acrimonious exchange, that they were free to move the U.N. headquarters to some other country. When they did so, said Lichenstein in a memorable line that was quoted around the world, "We will put no impediment in your way, and we will be at dockside bidding you a farewell as you set off into the sunset."[21]

Another major target of the foundation was the U.N. Conference on Trade and Development (UNCTAD). A Heritage study by economist Stanley J. Michalak Jr. concluded that, rather than fostering the economic growth of the developing world, UNCTAD was hindering it through the creation of "a new collectivist international economic order."[22] The critical study spurred UNCTAD's secretary general, Gamani Corea, to pay Heritage a personal visit. If he expected to dance a diplomatic minuet with Heritage analysts, he was mistaken; he encountered blunt criticism instead. Stories about Corea's "dressing down" at the foundation raced through the United Nations. Several months later, Corea resigned, his departure credited by observers to the confrontation at Heritage as well as the foundation's half-dozen pungent analyses. A new senior UNCTAD offical asked to meet with the staff of the U.N. Assessment Project and acknowledged that much of Heritage's criticism was correct. He stressed that he would "welcome" recommendations for improving the agency.[23]

Continuing the Revolution

Heritage had proved, with the publication of *Mandate for Leadership* immediately following Reagan's election as president, that the right book can significantly influence policymakers in Washington. Now Feulner and others wondered: Should Heritage try to repeat its *Mandate* success in 1984, with Reagan's reelection ensured? There was little debate: government was still too big—only the growth of domestic spending had been slowed—and the world was still a dangerous place—the Soviets and their allies were still active in Afghanistan, Angola, and Nicaragua. Who better than Heritage to continue showing how conservative ideas could be transformed into conservative policies and programs? Indeed, nearly everyone in Washington seemed to expect Heritage to produce another *Mandate*.

Accordingly, in early December 1984, the foundation published *Mandate for Leadership II: Continuing the Conservative Revolution*. Like its predecessor, it was a big book—26 chapters, 568 pages, 150 contributors, 1,300 recommendations—calculated to reform the federal government and strengthen U.S. defenses. Its editors were Stuart Butler; W. Bruce Weinrod, director of foreign policy and defense studies; and Michael Sanera, an assistant professor of political science at Northern Arizona University. It was immediately hailed by the *New York Times* as "one of the hottest tickets in town." *USA Today* called *Mandate II* "a new battle cry for recasting the U.S. government in a conservative image." And *Saturday Review* followed up: "if ideas really do have consequences, this may well be one of the most important books published in 1984."[24]

The media's enthusiasm was carefully kindled by a shrewd marketing campaign led by Herb Berkowitz and Hugh Newton that won the Silver Anvil Award of the Public Relations Society of America, the group's highest annual award.

One public relations challenge was the tendency of Washington journalists to treat book-length policy reports as "political stories, glossing over the policy recommendations." Such treatment would have defeated the central purpose of *Mandate II*—to stimulate public debate about specific federal policies and programs. In addition, research revealed that the Washington press corps was "overwhelmingly concerned with domestic and economic policy." Heritage, however, was highly concerned about

American foreign policy and national security, particularly U.S.-Soviet relations. A final challenge was the book's complexity, dealing as it did with
every cabinet department, the EPA, personnel policy, the budget, military
reform, and many other issues.[25]

Heritage followed a skillfully layered marketing strategy: (1) placing
generic stories about the forthcoming book with friendly columnists; (2)
leaking information to selected major media like the Associated Press,
United Press International, the *New York Times,* the *Washington Post,* and
the *Washington Times;* (3) holding targeted news briefings on national
security, foreign policy, and the general contents of the book; and (4)
scheduling private briefings for major news organizations and individuals, including the editorial boards of the *New York Times* and the *Washington Times* as well as conservative writers and columnists.

The strategy paid off handsomely: between November 18 and December 7, one or more different stories appeared every day but one in a major
news outlet. In a single issue, the *Post* carried four articles. Major pieces
were broadcast by PBS (MacNeil/Lehrer), CBS, CNN, and NBC. And
more than two hundred American and foreign journalists jammed Heritage's Lehrman Auditorium for the three major briefings. *Mandate II's*
most gratifying compliment came in January 1985 when President Reagan delivered his State of the Union address to Congress and the nation.
While it may be "a bit of exaggeration," remarked the *New York Times,* to
suggest that Reagan used *Mandate for Leadership II* as a model, many of the
proposals in the president's speech and the foundation's document "were
strikingly familiar."[26]

The similarities came as no real surprise to Feulner and other Heritage officials. Presidential Counselor Edwin Meese, who distributed copies
of the comprehensive report at the first post-election cabinet meeting,
later commented, "I know that [President Reagan] will personally use
Mandate II."[27]

A Long Way to Go

The president's reliance on the conservative ideas contained in the Heritage study reflected the significant shift in the American public's attitude
toward government. As Ed Feulner told the *National Journal,* by the second

Nixon administration in the early 1970s, "a very healthy skepticism" had developed about government's capabilities. In 1980, candidate Reagan was able to appeal to "a critical mass of public opinion" with his anti-government message. But, said the Heritage president, "we are still at the start of the power curve insofar as conservative ideas taking over. We've got a long way to go."[28]

So did President Reagan. Although his administration achieved much in its first term—as with its economic recovery program and defense buildup—it did not solve all the old problems and indeed failed to tackle some—such as the federal deficit and intrusive federal departments like Education—disappointing Heritage and other conservative organizations. After chalking up a series of dramatic budget victories in their first year and maintaining the policy initiative, Reagan officials, according to Stuart Butler, "appeared to lose their edge."[29]

There were several reasons for the slowdown. The federal bureaucracy, protective of its power, began to dig in and practice its well-honed delaying tactics. The Democratic opposition in Congress, led by seasoned House Speaker Tip O'Neill, organized more effectively. Worse, the staffs of Reagan officials kept urging them to put pragmatism before ideals. Then too, the complicated budget process allowed liberal legislators along the way to block White House proposals and whittle away at Reagan's early anti-spending victories. The resulting mounting federal deficits made the president's conservative supporters in Congress increasingly nervous.

While Reagan scored a remarkable political victory in 1984, Butler worried that the election masked "a disturbing loss of momentum and sense of direction" in governmental policymaking. He pointed out that the federal government had continued to grow from 1981–1984 and that the reforms introduced were "politically fragile and incomplete." The administration had to refocus its policy efforts in the second term or risk drifting into "mediocrity," thereby "betraying" the confidence of tens of millions of Reagan voters.[30] Butler's blunt words made one thing clear—Heritage was no one's sycophant, not even to a president who was so generous in his praise of it.

The administration's defense and foreign policy received a much higher rating from Heritage. Bruce Weinrod commended the consolidation of democratic institutions in El Salvador, the reversal of communist encroachment in Grenada, and the halting of more than a decade of Soviet expansion. But Weinrod cautioned the president to appoint those "who understand and are committed to his worldview."[31] Implicitly, Heritage was arguing that those in office who did not agree with Reagan ought to go. A dramatic application of this principle came six months later and involved one of the highest-ranking members of the Reagan administration.

Heritage vs. State

In July 1985, Burt Pines and three former Reagan administration ambassadors publicly called for the replacement of Secretary of State George P. Shultz because he was "undermining President Reagan's foreign policy." David B. Funderburk, ambassador to Romania from 1981 to 1985, described the State Department's friendly behavior toward communist Romania as "tragically wrong." Curtin Winsor, ambassador to Costa Rica from 1983 to 1985, criticized Shultz for opening direct talks with the Sandinista government of Nicaragua. For his part, Charles Lichenstein averred that career diplomats in the State Department were foiling Reagan policies they disliked by "outwaiting political appointees." Pines suggested that Shultz ought to be shifted from State to the Federal Reserve Board, thereby benefiting the country "both economically and in terms of foreign policy."[32]

Notoriously reluctant to fire anyone, Reagan did not make any move to replace Shultz, who had won the president's confidence by his willingness to be a team player—in sharp contrast to the ego-driven actions of his mercurial predecessor, Alexander Haig. Shultz, however, did ask Deputy Secretary of State John C. Whitehead, a conservative, to act as an informal liaison with the department's most persistent critics. A diplomat-in-residence program at Heritage was proposed, and Whitehead invited Heritage trustees and top executives to the State Department for a luncheon and discussions. At day's end, State's number two man said that "the differences were not quite as sharp and certainly not as personalized" as they had been. Feulner was more candid, remarking that while the meeting was "useful," there was not "any narrowing of differences."[33]

Shortly thereafter, a coldly unfriendly Shultz "jumped down" Phil Truluck's throat at a holiday party, charging that Heritage had called for his resignation and was sending him "ridiculous letters." Unshaken, Heritage continued to criticize wayward State Department bureaucrats. In February 1986, it released a study titled "Rhetoric vs. Reality: How the State Department Betrays the Reagan Vision." While not mentioning Shultz, the report, written by Benjamin Hart, accused State officials of "derailing and betraying" Reagan policies in Nicaragua, Angola, Cambodia, and Afghanistan. The same complaint had been made repeatedly by anticommunist organizations in those countries.

This time, Whitehead lost his temper and his perspective. On official State Department stationery, he wrote Heritage chairman Shelby Cullom Davis and vice chairman Robert Krieble, without sending copies to Feulner or any other foundation executive. In his letter, Whitehead accused the foundation of publishing " uninformed polemics and mischievous gossip" that were "an embarrassment" to President Reagan, Secretary of State Shultz, and "to me." He declared that the staff ought "to change what was being said" or "resign."[34]

They did neither, secure in the knowledge that they had their facts right and would receive full backing from the foundation's trustees. In his response to Whitehead, Krieble firmly defended Heritage's studies as "fair, authoritative, painstaking and, yes, hardhitting." Krieble pointed out that one public official who agreed with him about the value of the Heritage product was none other than Whitehead's ultimate boss, President Reagan. A Heritage spokesman said Whitehead had allowed his differences to degenerate "into a personal feud" and stressed that Heritage would continue to criticize or praise the State Department as warranted.[35]

The sharp dispute between the foundation and the State Department was revealing on several counts. It showed, first, that the foundation would not mitigate its criticism, no matter who or what was involved, if it believed that the criticism was justified; second, that the Heritage board of trustees, reflecting its confidence in Ed Feulner, would invariably support the decisions of the senior management, even in the face of strong outside pressure or criticism by conservatives; and third, that Heritage would stand firmly behind its analysts and their work. Although Ben Hart was not a foreign policy expert, his judgment about the pusillanimity and deceit of State bureaucrats was shared by many in Washington, including the future chairman of the Senate Foreign Relations Committee, Jesse Helms of North Carolina.

The Iran-Contra Scandal

The Iran-Contra scandal had its origins in two quite different but typical impulses of President Reagan: (1) to free the handful of American hostages held by terrorists in Lebanon, and (2) to support anticommunist rebels in Nicaragua, whose Marxist regime had become a serious threat to stability in Central America.

It was not global strategy or high politics but an emotional desire to help Americans held captive that led the president to approve the sale of arms to Iran. As Reagan biographer Lou Cannon put it, "Reagan was determined to get the hostages out, by whatever means possible." Indeed, the president became "so stubbornly committed to the trade of arms for hostages" that he could not be dissuaded from the policy even when new hostages were taken.[36]

In March 1987, as his administration struggled to contain a serious political crisis, a reluctant President Reagan conceded in a nationally televised address, "A few months ago I told the American people I did not trade arms for hostages. My heart and my best intentions still tell me that's true, but the facts and the evidence tell me it is not."[37]

Conservatives did their best to defend their favorite president. Heritage senior vice president Burton Yale Pines argued that the Reagan administration's goal of encouraging and developing influence with "moderate elements in Iran" was sensible and necessary. He conceded that although the president's policy did require that "we close an eye to our embargo on arms for Iran," it was justified by "the necessities of realpolitik." "Arms transfers," Pines said, were the "only negotiable currency for this kind of international transaction."[38]

While agreeing that the goal of forging a working relationship with Iran was "correct," James A. Phillips, Heritage's longtime analyst on the Middle East, blamed the administration for its "flawed" execution of policy. He was disturbed in particular by the mingling of the opening to Iran with "efforts to free American hostages in Lebanon." As a result, American antiterrorism policy "was undermined." And Iran concluded, correctly, that it could extract American concessions "without moderating its anti-American foreign policy and withdrawing its support of terrorism."[39]

In his memoir about the Reagan administration, Edwin Meese III asserts that when it became clear that the U.S. initiative to build ties with Iranian moderates was not succeeding, "it should have been dropped and Congress should have been notified of what had happened." Meese, attorney general at the time, did not defend "the protracted failure to disclose" but argued that it was "a policy error, not a crime."[40]

The public was unequivocal in its rejection of any arms for hostages deal. A December 1986 New York Times/CBS News poll recorded a drop in Reagan's approval rating from 67 to 46 percent, the sharpest one-month drop in presidential surveys since such polling began in 1936.[41]

The Contra controversy first erupted in March 1982 when Congress discovered that the CIA was involved in training anticommunist rebels in Nicaragua. Led by Democratic House Speaker Tip O'Neill, Congress passed, in the fall of 1982, the first Boland amendment, which prohibited funds "for the purpose of overthrowing the government of Nicaragua." As historian Richard Gid Powers points out, the administration argued that the goal of Contra funding was not to overthrow the Sandinista government but to persuade it to hold democratic elections (which it finally, though reluctantly, did in 1990).[42]

The funding continued until December 1984 when Congress strengthened the Boland amendment by denying any U.S. support at all, "directly or indirectly," to the Contras. Because the president wanted to keep helping what he called the Nicaraguan "freedom-fighters," administration lawyers decided that while Boland prohibited American agencies "engaged in intelligence activities" from operating in Nicaragua, the National Security Council was not an intelligence agency. So the administration shifted its Contra campaign from the CIA to the National Security Council under National Security Adviser John Poindexter and NSC staffer Oliver North.[43]

Apparently with CIA Director William Casey's approval, North illegally diverted funds from the Iranian arms sales to the Contras. Meese calls the fund diversion "a tremendous error that should never have been allowed to happen. That it did happen was a failure of the administration—for which it paid dearly."[44] According to Meese, the Iran-Contra affair taught the Reagan administration several lessons that were incorporated into policy:

1. Operations, especially covert operations, "should not be run out of the White House."
2. Clandestine operations, especially those entailing great risk, "should be reviewed frequently by the president and the National Security Council."
3. Good faith must be practiced by both the executive and the legislative branches to serve the national interest.
4. "The greatest threat" to constitutional government comes from a new congressionally established institution—"the independent counsel."[45]

Although Iran-Contra was nothing like Watergate and its pattern of official illegality and stonewalling, anticommunists "shuddered" to think what might have happened if President Reagan had been impeached or politically crippled. The Reagan Doctrine would have been abandoned, SDI would have become a negotiating chip, trade concessions would have been made to the tottering Soviet economy, and Eastern Europe would have been consigned to continuing Soviet domination. As Richard Gid Powers suggests, Gorbachev's *perestroika* might have succeeded, and the peoples of Poland, Hungary, Czechoslovakia, and East Germany might not have overturned their communist regimes in 1989.[46]

The Third Generation

Soon after the foundation moved into its new building on Massachusetts Avenue, senior officials noticed that many of those who attended Heritage lectures, seminars, and roundtable discussions were in their twenties. "There seem to be hundreds of young people," said Burt Pines at a senior management meeting, "who have come to town in the wake of the Reagan victory of 1980. We really ought to get to know them."[47] Shortly thereafter, Pines directed Ben Hart, himself a young conservative in his mid-twenties, to design a program that would attract the proliferating young conservatives in Washington.

In January 1984, the first meeting of the Third Generation was held at Heritage with Dinesh D'Souza, the twenty-three-year-old managing editor of *Policy Review*, as the speaker. D'Souza, a gifted writer whose articles were already appearing in the *New York Times,* the *Washington Post,* and the *Los Angeles Times,* led a discussion on how conservatives could gain more influence with the news media. D'Souza's talk was so well received that the group agreed to meet again in two weeks to hear Frank Cannon, at twenty-five the youngest congressional chief of staff. Cannon, who worked for Congressman Duncan Hunter (R-Calif.), suggested "How the Third Generation Can Win on Capitol Hill." Some sixty-five eager young conservatives attended the next meeting, featuring Amy Moritz, the twenty-five-year-old executive director of the National Center for Public Policy Research, which coordinated a variety of conservative efforts in Washington. Moritz's topic was "How to Mobilize the Third Generation." In response to the ballooning crowds, the Third Generation moved to the largest space in the Heritage building, the Louis Lehrman Auditorium on the ground floor.

Since then, on one evening a month, as many as one hundred members of the Third Generation have come together to discuss and debate the present and future of the conservative movement. They are traditionalists, libertarians, and neoconservatives, Old Right and New Right, Christians and Jews, black and white, but all agreeing, as Ben Hart puts it, that liberals should be "held liable" for the welfare programs that have trapped millions of Americans in poverty and for the accommodationist policies toward communism that have cost the lives of tens of millions around the world. Members of the Third Generation see free-market capitalism as "history's most successful economic system" and appreciate the vital role of America's religious traditions and institutions in maintaining a free and moral society.[48] After the formal meeting, they often move to a nearby restaurant to continue a usually spirited discussion. Phone numbers are exchanged, friendships are forged, and sometimes marriages are made.

The name "Third Generation" was chosen to reflect three eras in the development of the modern conservative movement in America. The First Generation was made up of the intellectual groundbreakers of the 1940s and 1950s, thinkers and philosophers like Friedrich A. Hayek, Richard Weaver, Russell Kirk, Robert Nisbet, Leo Strauss, and Whittaker Chambers. Special mention must be made of the seemingly tireless author, editor, commentator, and debater who more than any other individual popularized conservatism in America, William F. Buckley Jr. The First Generation shaped the conservative ideas which Barry Goldwater, managed by political pro F. Clifton White, offered in his principled run for the presidency in 1964.

The Second Generation comprised the organizers and activists of the 1960s and 1970s who raised money, mostly through direct mail, created political action committees, built think tanks, and ran candidates for public office. They included Richard Viguerie, Paul Weyrich, Edwin J. Feulner Jr., Howard Phillips, Morton Blackwell, M. Stanton Evans, Phyllis Schlafly, Terry Dolan, and Reed Larson. The Second Generation built the political and policy apparatus that helped carry Ronald Reagan into the White House in 1980.

Members of the Third Generation were described by the *Washington Post* as "revolutionaries" who sing a conservative antiphon to the themes of "patriotism, anti-Sovietism, and free enterprise." The *New York Times* called them "formidable ideologues and scathingly articulate."[49]

But sometimes young revolutionaries get carried away. The Wednesday evening after President Bush was defeated by Bill Clinton in November 1992, many at a Third Generation meeting laughed and applauded as someone carried in a rubber model of Bush's head—mouth open, eyes rolled back, neck bleeding—on a silver serving platter. Ed Feulner was not amused. He immediately sent a letter of apology to Bush that read in part, "Th[is] kind of behavior ... crosses the bounds of good taste and we will not tolerate it." The incident of Bush as John the Baptist is still mentioned to every incoming program director as the kind of "gag" that is beyond the Heritage pale.[50]

Rising (and risen) stars of the Third Generation include the aforementioned Dinesh D'Souza, author of the bestselling books *Illiberal Education* and *The End of Racism;* Ralph Reed, former executive director of the Christian Coalition; John Fund, editorial writer for the *Wall Street Journal;* John Barnes, editorial writer for the *New York Post;* Mona Charen, nationally syndicated columnist; Doug Bandow, senior fellow at the Cato Institute; California Republican Congressmen Dana Rohrabacher and Chris Cox; Paul Erickson, who managed Pat Buchanan's campaign against President Bush in the 1992 New Hampshire Republican primary, in which Buchanan received a remarkable 37 percent of the vote; Grover Norquist, president of Americans for Tax Reform and adviser to House Speaker Newt Gingrich; Leigh Ann Metzger, Washington representative of the Eagle Forum; Richard Vigilante, former issues editor of *National Review* and now associate publisher of Regnery Publishing; nationally syndicated columnist Cal Thomas; and Joseph Perkins, editorial writer for the *San Diego Union.*

Typical of the multitalented young people who work for Heritage is thirty-two-year-old Matthew Spalding, director of lectures and educational programs. Spalding oversees the Salvatori Fellows program, which brings young conservative academics to Heritage to study the ideas of the founders and their modern-day application. Over two hundred scholars from Harvard, the University of Chicago, Hillsdale College, Louisiana State University, and other academic centers have participated. "My role," explains Spalding, "is to make sure that the intellectual capital in conservative academics flows into Heritage and to make sure that our work flows out to them." [51] The coauthor of a new and much praised book about George Washington's Farewell Address, Spalding also runs a "Congress and the Constitution" program for congressional staffers that seeks to link constitutional thought to current policy issues. "Washington," says Spalding, a native Californian who received his Ph.D. from Claremont Graduate School, "is the atmosphere in which to make serious arguments about American society." [52]

At one Third Generation meeting, Russell Kirk listed seven principles that young conservatives should keep in mind as they sought to redeem America: belief in some transcendent order in the universe; opposition to "totalist ideology"; confidence in the American Constitution; maintenance of private property and a free economy; preference for state and local over central power; "a deep-rooted patriotism"; and a genuine preference "for the old and tried." [53]

Ronald Reagan put it well: "The greatest days of the conservative movement lie ahead.... This so-called 'Third Generation' of conservatives is extraordinarily well equipped—in terms of commitment, education, and professional experience—to promote the issues and values that are the bedrock of our movement." [54]

Let a Hundred Think Tanks Bloom

From its founding, Heritage was conscious that it was not just a Washington think tank but an essential part of a national conservative network that had been unimaginable a few short years earlier. Using the Resource Bank as a master Rolodex, the foundation was, by the mid-1980s, in constant communication with 1,200 scholars and more than 250 think tanks, public-interest law institutes, educational organizations, and other policy groups across the country. Thomas Atwood, Heritage director of coalition relations, explains that the Resource Bank serves three functions: it is "an information clearing house, a coalition builder, and a strategy forum."[55] Its annual spring meeting is a key event. In April 1988, for example, 130 representatives of over ninety public-policy groups, including twenty-five state think tanks, attended the Resource Bank's eleventh annual meeting in Chicago. Every one of these state organizations had received significant, tangible assistance from Heritage, including, in some cases, the names and addresses of the foundation's major donors in their states.

Early state policy groups included Chicago's Heartland Institute, founded in 1984, and Denver's Independence Institute, incorporated in 1985. Heartland quickly expanded, organizing affiliates in several other midwestern states, but has since streamlined its operations. Independence Institute founder John Andrews (now a vice president with TCI, one of the largest cable companies in America) says that his organization "nursed at Heritage's breast" but was careful to remain Coloradan. The institute combed the Resource Bank's *Annual Guide to Public Policy Experts* for the names of local professors to build "a board of leading Coloradans."[56]

Other state-level policy groups that have attended Heritage's conferences are New York's Empire Foundation for Policy Research, Michigan's Mackinac Center for Public Policy, North Carolina's John Locke Foundation, Washington State's Evergreen Freedom Foundation, and Arizona's Barry Goldwater Institute for Public Policy Research. James Peyser of the Pioneer Institute for Public Policy Research in Boston says that Heritage's openness and collegiality are "unique." John Andrews asks, "Who else would tell you the major donors in your state—and provide a printout of their names?" Byron Lamm, director of the State Policy Network, declares that Heritage deserves credit "not for inventing state think tanks but for being an invaluable agent of coordination."[57]

A key supporter of the State Policy Network from the beginning has been Heritage trustee Thomas Roe, who says simply, "I'm a grassroots person." He recalls that at a Heritage trustees' meeting in the mid-1980s, Robert Krieble declared, "The evil empire can be dissolved—I'm going to go out and help do it." Roe responded, "You capture the Soviet Union—I'm going to capture the states."[58] While Krieble underwrote the training of hundreds of people from behind the Iron Curtain on the techniques of electoral politics, Roe encouraged the formation of state think tanks in his native South Carolina (the South Carolina Policy Council) and across the country.

Increasingly, state think tanks are having an impact across state lines. A Heartland study criticizing plans to build a taxpayer-financed domed stadium in Chicago was cited by opponents of similar publicly funded plans in other cities. A popular Heartland innovation is the "Policy Fax," a compilation of think tank information which is sent to every state legislator in the country. Comments Heartland's Joseph Bast, "We've become a clearing house for state legislators for more than one hundred think tanks, including Heritage and Cato."[59]

As Terrence M. Scanlon, president of the Capital Research Center and past vice president of The Heritage Foundation, put it, "Heritage is a nurturer, especially of state think tanks, which will become more important with the downsizing of the federal government and the devolution of power to the states."[60]

No other Washington think tank attempts, let alone succeeds in carrying out, such a nurturing role—another instance of Heritage's indispensable role in the conservative movement.

More Serious Scholarship

In 1987, a gift of $510,000 from the Lynde and Harry Bradley Foundation of Milwaukee, one of the most creative conservative grant-giving institutions, enabled Heritage to launch yet another new program, the Bradley Resident Scholars. There had long been such programs at Brookings,

AEI, and other Washington think tanks, but this was a departure for Heritage, another sign of its maturation and its determination to extend its influence beyond the day's debate or headline. Michael S. Joyce, the far-sighted president of the Bradley Foundation, is convinced that because "the universities are becoming less and less important as centers of intellectual thought," independent institutions like Heritage "will flourish." He describes Heritage as the "flagship of the conservative intellectual movement."[61]

Under the Bradley plan, scholars are invited to spend up to one year at Heritage where they work on a major research project and familiarize themselves with Congress and other parts of the Washington policymaking community. The first year's crop included academicians like William Donohue (then chairman of the Department of Sociology at LaRoche College, Pittsburgh, and now head of the Catholic Civil Rights League), who exulted that his year in the nation's capital had made him "a stronger, more confident conservative. Pity the liberals!" Other prominent conservatives who also came to Washington under the Bradley program were Thomas West of the University of Dallas; Steven W. Mosher of Human Life International; Hadley Arkes of Amherst; Eugene Hickok, now Pennsylvania's secretary of education; Robert George of Princeton University; and a professor of journalism at the University of Texas at Austin whose book about compassion became a national bestseller.

Marvin Olasky, a devout Christian, had long been curious about the contemporary understanding of compassion, the desire to help those in need. The failures of the welfare state were obvious, he thought, but what were the alternatives? How had Americans combated poverty and other social problems in the eighteenth and nineteenth centuries before the creation of Social Security, Medicare, and other manifestations of the welfare state? Had Americans just been indifferent to the poor, Olasky wondered, until the New Deal?

Olasky was accepted for a Bradley Fellowship at Heritage. He spent the year from August 1989 to July 1990 in Washington, plowing through the stacks at the Library of Congress, giving an occasional lecture at Heritage (his Christmas meditation on compassion filled the Lehrman Auditorium), and working with Adam Meyerson on a *Policy Review* article. "He is the best editor I've ever had," says Olasky flatly. "He deserves special laud and honor." It was because Meyerson pushed him that "I came up with seven principles of effective compassion."[62]

The resulting article, "Beyond the Stingy Welfare State: What We Can Learn from the Compassion of the 19th Century," was reprinted all over America and led to the publication in 1992 of *The Tragedy of American Compassion* (which he wrote in one month with Rocky Balboa's "Eye of the Tiger" theme playing in the background). The book sold only a few thousand copies until William J. Bennett read it and recommended it to Newt Gingrich nearly two years later. Gingrich finally got around to reading *The Tragedy of American Compassion* over Christmas 1994, and he loved it. So much so that in his inaugural address as the Speaker of the House of Representatives, "Newt kept talking" about the book until he turned *The Tragedy of American Compassion* into a bestseller. "No one would have paid much attention to Newt in 1992," Olasky remarks, "but in 1994 they did. It all worked out very providentially."[63]

In 1996 Rabbi David G. Dalin joined the Bradley Fellows Program. An associate professor of American Jewish History at the University of Hartford, Dalin is writing a book on the clash between the principles of Jewish charity and the welfare state. Another Bradley Fellow, Jennifer E. Marshall, former research assistant to Charles Murray, is writing a book about the ways that churches can combat welfare dependency and poverty. Andrew Peyton Thomas, then assistant attorney general for Arizona, used his Bradley Fellowship to write *Disorder by Decree: Why Criminals' Rights and Judicial Wrongs Threaten American Democracy*. Also, research conducted by former Bradley Fellow John Hood led to the book *The Heroic Enterprise: Business and the Common Good.*

One of Ed Feulner's favorite intellectuals is Ernest van den Haag, a European leftist before World War II who emerged in the 1960s as one of America's most articulate defenders of conservative principles. As a Distinguished Scholar at Heritage, van den Haag has written about and debated such liberal icons as the welfare state, labor unions, militant feminism, and criminal rights. In a debate with Rev. Robert F. Drinan, S.J., of Georgetown University on "Human Rights and Foreign Policy," van den Haag used logic, sarcasm, and the apt quotation to demolish his opponent. When Father Drinan urged more international agreements, van den Haag pointed out that the U.N. Declaration of Human Rights and the Helsinki Accords were "subscribed to by the Soviet Union ... while its gulags flourished." While "we cannot be ... a world policeman," argued van den Haag, "we can be, as John Quincy Adams said, 'a friend of liberty everywhere, but the custodian only of our own.'"[64]

Another distinguished European intellectual who lectures at least once a year at Heritage is Erik von Kuehnelt-Leddihn, an Austrian Catholic who left his native land in the mid-1930s to teach first in England and then at a number of American institutions. He is, as conservative historian George Nash points out, historian, novelist, journalist, traveler, lecturer, and linguist, fluent in eight languages and with a reading knowledge of nineteen more. In his *Liberty or Equality,* Kuehnelt-Leddihn argued that Nazism was "neither a conservative nor a reactionary movement, but merely the synthesis of practically all ideas dominant in the last 160 years." It was, he said, the fulfillment, not the antithesis of the French Revolution.[65]

Throughout the 1980s, the pace quickened as Heritage became the hive of the conservative movement. A typical day in September 1986 could see the conclusion of a two-day meeting of Heritage Associates; a noon lecture in the packed Lehrman Auditorium at which Russell Kirk discussed "The Ten Most Important Conservative Books"; and a talk by Yitzhak Rabin, then Israeli defense minister. The foundation hosted over eighty public events that year, including a continuing series on the question, "What Does It Mean to Be a Conservative?" and lectures by freshman members of Congress.

The Woman of the Century

The Heritage Board of Trustees has had its share of stars—former Treasury Secretary William E. Simon, Pittsburgh philanthropist Richard Scaife, beer baron Joseph Coors, and chairman Jay Van Andel of the Amway Corporation, to name a few. But when Clare Boothe Luce became a Heritage trustee in 1985, the foundation took on a special luster. Luce had played a variety of public roles brilliantly—ambassador, playwright, editor, essayist, war correspondent, congresswoman, presidential adviser. She was charming, charismatic, and wonderfully quick-witted. Among her many sayings: "No good deed goes unpunished" and "Conservatives are liberals with children."[66]

During her all-too-brief two years on the board, she time and again contributed wit and wisdom to its proceedings. Invited to join many organizations when she moved to Washington in 1981, Luce turned down all but The Heritage Foundation, explaining, "Many things give me concern today, but Heritage gives me hope."[67] When she died in October 1987, Feulner, who had grown to know Luce well, felt her loss personally and deeply. "Among the women I've admired most," he says, "is Clare Boothe Luce, who broke through so many barriers in her life."[68] Reflecting their profound admiration for Luce's life and achievements, Heritage trustees named the foundation's highest public award after her. The first Clare Boothe Luce Award was given jointly to Ambassador Shelby Cullom Davis and Dr. Kathryn Davis in September 1991. And the first Clare Boothe Luce Lecture was delivered on that occasion by the Right Honorable Margaret Thatcher.

Breaking Out of the Poverty Trap

As Clare Boothe Luce knew from personal experience, change comes slowly in Washington, where bureaucrats, members of Congress, lobbyists, and even public-policy analysts prefer the status quo. Heritage is a rare exception and a paradox—a conservative institution committed to changing the way Washington works. A case in point is welfare reform, which the foundation singled out as a critical issue in need of the talents and thinking unique to Heritage.

From his first days at the foundation, Stuart Butler and other analysts had been building a body of scholarship and literature on alternative approaches to poverty problems. Their work was not armchair analysis. Researchers spent hour after hour with the welfare poor, garnering a better understanding of their problems and coming up with specific community-based solutions—some already in practice but unknown to most policymakers and ignored by antipoverty bureaucrats. One of their primary sources of information was Robert Woodson, the black founder and president of the National Center for Neighborhood Enterprise. Butler frequently quoted Woodson as saying that the "key to success in breaking the bleak cycle of poverty is the black family." The "vanishing" black family would soon reappear, Butler argued, if ideas like Woodson's family-to-family network of assistance were encouraged.[69]

In mid-1985, Heritage's development office secured special funding for an ongoing research effort from the Schultz Foundation of New Jersey, which has had a longtime interest in health and social welfare issues. Policy analyst Anna Kondratas was named Schultz Fellow in Health and Urban Affairs. Kondratas and Butler presented a paper that year on "The Future of the Welfare State: Beyond Welfarism" at a Ford Foundation conference. The paper brought together for the first time the data and analysis that served as the framework for *Out of the Poverty Trap*, Butler's and Kondratas's landmark book on welfare reform.

A large gift from Thomas and Shirley Roe of Greenville, South Carolina, endowed the Thomas A. Roe Institute for Economic Policy Studies at Heritage, which supported the final research and writing of the Butler-Kondratas book. Kondratas's ongoing work on hunger in America and urban poverty—published in a series of *Backgrounders*—drew so much attention that the Reagan administration recruited Kondratas for a top-ranking job in the Department of Agriculture. She was ultimately named administrator of the department's Food and Nutrition Service, which manages the national food stamp and other food-assistance programs. In the Bush administration, Kondratas moved to the Department of Housing and Urban Development where she served as assistant secretary for community planning and development under HUD Secretary Jack Kemp. Today, she is a senior associate at the Urban Institute in Washington, D.C.

Meanwhile, the wheels of welfare reform were grinding slowly and not very well. A series of Heritage papers critiqued the Reagan administration's catastrophic health-care plan as being too expensive for the elderly and inadequate to protect them against the costly long-term care that can easily bankrupt retired people. One paper argued that the major congressional welfare "reform" proposals only threw more money at the problems of the poor. Still another spelled out ways to rebuild the welfare system with workfare and other innovative programs. *Policy Review* played its part by publishing Stuart Butler's "A Conservative Vision of Welfare Reform" in the spring of 1987. The magazine hosted a special media briefing on the article, providing journalists with a preview of the major themes of *Out of the Poverty Trap*.

With the formal publication of the Butler-Kondratas book by the Free Press, Heritage was able to deliver copies to leading policymakers and

arrange briefings for key legislators and executive branch officials. A series of book excerpts was distributed to major daily newspapers, and the authors appeared on major TV and radio programs like ABC's "Good Morning America," the "Oprah Winfrey Show," National Public Radio's "All Things Considered," and "America's Black Forum."

What attracted such public attention was a comprehensive strategy for rebuilding the family that recommended: (1) reforming the tax code so that it does not hurt those who leave the welfare rolls; (2) eliminating or streamlining regulations that, for example, make it impossible for parents to work at home; (3) requiring parents on welfare to be responsible for the actions, including the sexual behavior, of their children; (4) adding a work component to every welfare program; and (5) making AFDC (Aid to Families with Dependent Children) a temporary program.[70]

Several of these recommendations were implemented in 1996 by the 104th Congress, which acted on President Bill Clinton's 1992 campaign promise to end welfare as America had known it for almost sixty years. At long last, as Butler and Kondratas wrote, Washington had awakened to the fact that it had badly erred when it decided that "decentralization, competition and pluralism were good for everything except fighting poverty, and that uniformity and central planning were bad for everyone except the poor."[71]

Steering the Elephant

Also published in 1987, but without so much fanfare, was *Steering the Elephant: How Washington Works* by Robert Rector and visiting fellow Michael Sanera—a blunt assessment of the successes and failures of the Reagan administration in implementing public policy. It should be required reading, columnist Donald Lambro wrote, "for anyone who contemplates accepting a political appointment in the executive branch, [and] for anyone who wants to understand how politics works in the nation's capital."[72] Its contributors included Jeane Kirkpatrick; Donald J. Devine, former director of the Office of Personnel Management; Thomas W. Pauken, ex-head of ACTION; and Morton C. Blackwell, a former special assistant to President Reagan. Kirkpatrick, one of the most influential American ambassadors to the United Nations since its founding in 1945, traced her

success to six key elements, beginning with the selection of a politically astute team committed to the president's policies and able "to guide the bureaucracy rather than be guided by it."[73]

In the concluding chapter, Rector and Sanera pointed out that, contrary to conservative hopes, President Reagan had not cut government spending. In fact, it had risen slightly, from 22 percent to about 24 percent of GNP, during his first six years in office. But the change in priorities was "significant," with defense spending increasing from 5 to 6.5 percent of GNP, which enabled the president to deal with the Soviet Union from strength. Even so, they added, far from being the "largest military spending increase in U.S. history," as liberal critics often charged, the Reagan defense buildup, measured in constant dollars, was "about half the size of Eisenhower's peacetime military increases."[74] That suggested, ironically, that Eisenhower himself may have been responsible, at least in part, for the creation of the "military-industrial complex" about which he warned America in one of his last presidential speeches.

Successful presidencies, Rector and Sanera stated, set the stage for "long-term change by altering public perceptions." Here too they gave Reagan no better than a passing grade. Although "the great communicator" did make a good case for a stronger military defense in a hostile world, he and his administration failed to stress, for example, that reducing government was not just an "unpleasant necessity" but "a positive investment in America's future," an investment that would make all Americans more prosperous.[75] Rector and Sanera went on to say that in public education, "there is no middle ground between offense and defense," and the Reagan administration had too often been on the defensive.

A fundamental political transformation such as Reaganauts were trying to bring about, Rector and Sanera asserted, could not be effected in only six or eight years. Both incremental and cumulative change had to last for two decades or longer. The importance of the Reagan administration, therefore, "will be determined as much by its impact on the attitudes that the American public carry into the twenty-first century as by its impact on budget, legislation, regulation, and administration in the 1980s." Then and only then, said the authors, would we be able to say whether there had been a real "Reagan Revolution."[76]

After Reagan, Who?

In the fall of 1987, Ed Feulner and other Heritage officials were con-
templating a Washington without Reagan well before Senator Bob Dole
remarked at a meeting of the President's Club that, while "we don't know
who's going to be in the Oval Office in January 1989, we know it's not
going to be Ronald Reagan."[77] Heritage decided it was time to return to
its congressional roots and help move policy in a conservative direction
through the legislative branch. Several experienced people were added
to the foundation's congressional liaison office, including the redoubtable
Kate O'Beirne, who would make a lasting impression on Heritage. At the
same time, while continuing to publish short papers on the issues of the
day the foundation focused more on selected major themes like welfare
reform and free trade.

And there would be more big books. In 1988, for example, Heritage,
in cooperation with Paul Weyrich's Free Congress Foundation, published
Issues '88: A Conservative Platform for America, a three-volume, 633-page policy outline for candidates seeking federal office in the fall. The Platform
Committee at the Republican National Convention that summer relied
on *Issues '88* to write more than three dozen foreign and domestic policy
planks.[78] With the Claremont Institute, Heritage co-published *The Imperial Congress: Crisis in the Separation of Powers,* edited by Gordon S. Jones and
John A. Marini. (The crisis had resulted from a decades-long dominance
of Congress by liberals in love with pork-barrel politics.) Then, in December, Heritage released its third manual for an incoming administration,
Mandate for Leadership III: Policy Strategies for the 1990s, edited by Charles
Heatherly and Burt Pines. Like its predecessors, *Mandate III* was large
(953 pages, 37 chapters, 400 contributors) and unambiguously conservative: the federal government should be the last not the first resort to solve
societal problems, and America was duty-bound to resist communism and
expand freedom around the world.

But its emphasis was different. As Ed Feulner said in the foreword,
"The first two *Mandates* diagnosed the federal government's afflictions,
e.g., obesity and arthritis, and prescribed the appropriate therapies, e.g.,
deregulation and reduced spending." *Mandate III* outlined in detail how
to administer the therapies and "retrain the patient" by managing the

federal bureaucracy. Indeed, the *Christian Science Monitor* said it was "as comprehensive as the Yellow Pages." Congressman Thomas D. DeLay of Texas, who would serve as House Majority Whip in the historic 104th Congress, called *Mandate III* "cover-to-cover good government."[79]

Along with all the policy prescriptions, Heatherly raised a key political question in the very first chapter: "If Ronald Reagan and his 'Reaganauts' could only *slow down* the growth of federal spending, not reverse it or eliminate wasteful programs, what hope is there for any other conservative president who wants to challenge the entrenched orthodoxies of the modern liberal welfare state?" The answer, suggested Heatherly, was a "politics of governance" that would seek control of the policy apparatus "at both ends of Pennsylvania Avenue," i.e., the White House and Congress.[80] Such a strategy would require a commitment to *party government* as distinct from "government by personality." It would mean uniting a political party around principles that would constrain "the economic interests and passions" that motivate most human endeavor. The strategy, wrote Heatherly, would promote party alignment and produce a debate between the two parties focused on principle and not merely a partisan political agenda. "Each of the two major parties would vie for control of the White House *and* Congress." The almost certain result would be a renewed interest in politics as citizens realized that the results of elections would make a true difference in their lives.[81]

The suggestion that any party other than the Democrats might control the House of Representatives seemed outlandish in January 1989. The Republican majority in the Senate between 1981 and 1986 was dismissed by many analysts as a deviation from the liberal political norm. Divided government seemed to be preferred by the American electorate. And classical realignment was deemed most unlikely, despite the consecutive presidential victories of Reagan and George Bush in 1980, 1984, and 1988. The remarkable elections of 1994, still in the offing, would force the reconsideration of many things, including the argument that a national realignment such as had occurred after the Civil War and during the Great Depression was indeed possible.

The conservative political victories of the 1980s did not, of course, just happen. They flowed from the increasingly sharp public perception of conservative ideas articulated and promoted, in large part, by The

Heritage Foundation. As Ed Feulner pointed out in his foreword to *Mandate III:*

> What history will find remarkable about the 1980s is how far and fast we've advanced. In many ways, the dreadful 1970s have been repealed. We've taken what, ten years ago, was called unthinkable and shown that it's *workable*—when given a chance. Just as the New Deal revolution of the 1930s laid the foundation for the Great Society of the 1960s, the intellectual battles we've won over the last decade have established the premises for formulating public policy well into the next century.[82]

5

The Perfect vs. the Good

Fifty years ago, six famous but very different writers—Arthur Koestler, Richard Wright, Ignazio Silone, Stephen Spender, André Gide, and Louis Fischer—explained why they had become communists and then anticommunists in *The God That Failed*. The one common link among these uncommon intellectuals was that all of them chose communism because they had lost faith in Western democracy. And they all subsequently rejected communism because they learned that "peace" and "freedom" were used only as catchwords by communists and that the very things for which they had joined the Communist Party, such as peace and freedom, were those most endangered by the party.

In 1989, millions of East Germans, Poles, Hungarians, Czechs, Slovaks, Romanians, Chinese, and other nationalities declared, in their streets and in their parliaments, that communism was a fraud and a failure and that they preferred Western democracy and economic freedom. Without the glue of Marxist-Leninist ideology, the communist facade of righteousness and authority collapsed, and the people's desire to determine their own future, dammed up for more than forty years, burst forth.

The State of Conservatism

Ed Feulner was in a triumphant mood over the events of 1989. In an essay on the "state of conservatism," he proclaimed that "1989 was the most

103

significant year in the most important decade since World War II." The victory over communism, he declared, belonged to American conservatives, specifically Ronald Reagan, who not only had strengthened America's defenses during his presidency but had stopped winking at "Soviet adventurism." Even Reagan's deregulation of oil prices helped "turn the tide against the Soviets" by triggering a worldwide price drop that cut sharply into Moscow's hard currency earnings from oil exports and made it more difficult for the Soviets to match the American military buildup.[1]

As a result of communism's collapse, Feulner argued, conservatives had "a chance like none other since the New Deal to reshape the political landscape." In the 1980s, conservatives popularized their principles of limited government, individual liberty, and free enterprise. In the 1990s, said Feulner, "our goal must be to translate these principles into policy." To do so, conservatives had to stop merely "adjusting to liberal initiatives" and start pushing their own policies and programs more aggressively. Otherwise, warned Feulner, what Ed Meese called the "tin-cup syndrome" would continue, turning America from "a nation of entrepreneurs into a nation of lobbyists" who poured into Washington to beg Congress for money.[2]

Conservatives, Feulner assured, were up to the task. He pointed out that in recent years, four conservative economists—F. A. Hayek, Milton Friedman, George Stigler, and James Buchanan—had received Nobel Prizes. Younger intellectuals like Charles Murray, Stuart Butler, George Gilder, Daniel Pipes, Kim Holmes, and Richard McKenzie had helped "reshape the way America thinks." And there was a growing conservative public-interest law movement, dozens of lively conservative journals on college campuses, and an increasing interest among mainstream publishers in conservative books and ideas.

Conservatives had spent the last forty-five years, Feulner went on, "preventing the Left from dismantling the barricades against Soviet communism." Now they had to do battle on the domestic front. Many were already engaged. Butler, Anna Kondratas, and Jack Kemp, for example, had proposed "a conservative war on poverty," and columnist Warren Brookes was predicting that the environment would be "the great battleground of the 1990s." The fight against drugs and the sorry decline of the public schools were two other critical issues that demanded quick attention.[3]

Ending on a characteristically optimistic note, Feulner predicted that if conservatives put their principles into practice, the 1990s would be remembered as "a decade of freedom" and of "unprecedented opportunity" for every American.[4]

A Promising Beginning

Relations between The Heritage Foundation and the Bush administration began on a friendly note. After all, Vice President George Bush had spoken at the 1983 dedication of the new Heritage building. "To paraphrase Archimedes," he had remarked, "give me a place to stand and a lever strong enough and I can move the world. Well, The Heritage Foundation has been that place, and their lever has been the truth. And so far, you have been real world movers."[5] It was natural that when he faced political pressure to ban imported assault rifles, President Bush would call Ed Feulner for his opinion. Subsequently, when the president was asked at a news conference what he was going to do about assault rifles and drug-related crime, he suggested that the correspondent read "that very intelligent, thoughtful paper from Ed Feulner's group over at Heritage."[6]

Shortly thereafter, in late 1989, President Bush went to Malta for his first summit meeting with Soviet Premier Mikhail Gorbachev. Before leaving Washington, the president told the Executive Committee of Heritage's President's Club (supporters who donate a minimum of $2,500 annually) that he was looking forward to seeing the foundation's summit recommendations. At a private Camp David meeting, Ed Feulner personally handed the president Heritage's analysis, written by Leon Aron and Jay Kosminsky, which urged him to take a firm line with the Soviet leader.

Throughout 1989 and into 1990, Heritage stuck to its conservative principles but resolved to be flexible in its tactics. As Burt Pines put it, "We are pragmatic conservatives." In explaining the foundation's common-sense approach to problems, Feulner liked to paraphase Milton Friedman: "Don't let the perfect be the enemy of the good."[7]

In its pursuit of the good, Heritage offered a comprehensive national health-care plan that would guarantee affordable medical care to all Americans. The plan, developed by Stuart Butler and health-care policy analyst Edmund Haislmaier, was detailed in a 127–page study, *A National*

Health System for America. It proposed that the existing employer-provided health insurance system be replaced by a new system, based on tax credits, in which most Americans would pay directly for routine medical needs and buy their own health insurance to protect against the cost of major illnesses.

Most American workers received health and hospitalization insurance as an employee benefit. Although this clearly amounted to additional income, it was not treated as income; the employee paid no taxes on the benefit. "This tax policy," said the Heritage study, "encourages Americans to think that their health care is paid for by someone else ... they lack the normal incentives to question the need for care or the prices charged for it.[8] The Heritage plan proposed individual tax credits to enable the employee to purchase the kind of health insurance he wanted.

"Americans would still receive the same total tax relief for their health expenses," explained Butler. "The difference is that under our plan that assistance would be up-front [and to the employee], instead of through the current back-door mechanism of employer-provided insurance."[9] The government would continue to pay for medical care and health insurance for those citizens who couldn't afford them. Among Heritage's proposals were "Health Care Savings Accounts," which would be used by young working Americans to buy insurance and medical care.

"Unless conservatives respond to the challenge to devise an alternative national health system," the Heritage study warned, "the United States will likely move toward the kind of nationalized health-care system used in Britain, Sweden, and Canada, where costs are controlled by rationing and there often are long waiting lines for routine medical services."[10]

Following the release of the foundation proposal, Butler and Haislmaier were asked to brief Health and Human Services Secretary Louis Sullivan as well as a number of senators, congressmen, and their legislative assistants. Even OMB Director Richard Darman, no friend of Heritage, instructed his staff to read the Butler-Haislmaier study.[11]

Another Butler proposal—changing federal policy to allow tenants to own and manage public housing—became a reality for families in Washington, D.C., and St. Louis. The 464–unit Kenilworth-Parkside housing project in northeast Washington was turned over to a tenant association for $1. And a housing project in St. Louis was transferred to tenants there.

The Heritage Foundation Board of Trustees in December 1995.

Forrest Rettgers, an executive with the National Association of Manufacturers, was the first chairman from 1973 to late 1974.

The Honorable Ben B. Blackburn, a four-term congressman, was chairman of the board from 1975 to 1982.

The Honorable Frank Shakespeare, former ambassador to the Vatican, was chairman of the board from 1982 to mid-1985.

The Honorable Shelby Cullom Davis, former U.S. ambassador to Switzerland, was chairman of the board from 1985 until early 1992.

Dr. David Brown, an orthopedic surgeon, has been chairman of the board of trustees since April 1992.

Frank Walton, Heritage president from 1975 to 1977, at the 1980 dedication of the Coors and Noble Buildings on Stanton Park.

Ribbon-cutting at the new building. From left Joseph Coors, Ed Noble, Board Chairman Ben Blackburn, and President Edwin J. Feulner.

Leadership, scholarship, and creativity describe the Heritage senior management team. Of the eight-person team shown here in 1982, five are still with Heritage. Leading the way are Phil Truluck, executive vice president, left, and Ed Feulner.

Trustees Joseph Coors, right, and the late Dr. Robert H. Krieble in the early 1980s.

Former trustees Robert F. Dee, left, and Lewis Lehrman, at a board meeting in the early 1980s.

National Review *editor John O'Sullivan, center,* was Policy Review *editor from 1979 to 1983. He is flanked by Adam Meyerson, current editor, and Heritage president Ed Feulner.*

The Heritage building under construction in 1982.

The "new" Heritage building after a 1996 facelift.

Trustee Midge Decter cuts the ribbon for the new Heritage building in 1983, as fellow board members and Vice President George Bush look on.

A 1983 lecture panel featured, left to right, Dr. Russell Kirk, Wall Street Journal editor Robert Bartley, Rep. Newt Gingrich, and neoconservative scholar Dr. Irving Kristol.

In early 1981 Edwin Meese III, Ronald Reagan Fellow in Public Policy and then counselor to the president, publicly endorsed Heritage's landmark study, Mandate for Leadership.

Free-market economics meets free-market politics at the Heritage Tenth Anniversary dinner. Nobel Laureate Milton Friedman and his wife Rose with President Ronald Reagan and Ed Feulner.

October 3, 1983, was a landmark day for Heritage as it dedicated a new building, and celebrated its Tenth Anniversary with President Ronald Reagan and 1,500 guests.

Among 1,000 guests honoring Senator Barry Goldwater in 1985 were Vice President George Bush, Clare Boothe Luce, board chairman Shelby Cullom Davis, and Ed Feulner.

Economist, columnist and educator Dr. Walter Williams with Elaine Chao, now a Heritage Distinguished Fellow.

In 1989 Polish Solidarity leader Lech Walesa visited Heritage and, with Phil Truluck, enjoyed the gift of a Heritage tie.

Ed Feulner, Vice President Herb Berkowitz, and PR Counsel Hugh Newton discuss the communications program that introduced Mandate for Leadership II.

Butler first proposed the idea in a Heritage *Backgrounder* in 1984 and worked closely with the chief sponsor of the law allowing such conversions—former Congressman Jack Kemp of New York, who had become Secretary of Housing and Urban Development for President Bush.

Heritage's tenant-homeowner proposal demonstrated that helping the poor did not conflict with conservative principles, that indeed, it was conservative principles that provided the most effective and long-lasting help for the poor. "While liberals talk endlessly about their concern for the poor," wrote Butler, "the public housing tenants of Washington, St. Louis and many other cities know better. They know it was liberals who either sat on the sidelines or actively opposed this example of economic empowerment for the poor—and they know it was conservatives who stood by them when they wanted to become independent homeowners."[12] At least one prominent liberal agreed. Black leader Jesse Jackson admitted, "What this group has done—allowing people to manage where they live and in effect turning projects into condominiums—is right and sound."[13]

Heritage's influence on Washington was evident in many other ways, large and small. In its 1990 budget proposal, the Bush administration offered six of the ten budget reforms contained in *Mandate for Leadership III*. And for the first time in decades, the president submitted a federal budget without the "current services" baseline method of estimating spending. This was no mere matter of juggling figures. Under the old method, *projections* were used as the baseline for computing federal spending. Thus, if the administration in 1989 projected that 1990 spending for a program would be at a certain level, the actual spending would be called a "cut" unless it met or exceeded that amount, *even if the actual dollar amount exceeded the previous year's level.* It was precisely by the use of such deceptive accounting devices, wherein an increase is described as a decrease, that politicians and bureaucrats had been able to keep raising government spending.

In the area of child care, Heritage's Robert Rector continued to have a major impact on Capitol Hill and downtown. Four different family tax-relief bills, based in large part on Rector's work, were introduced in the House of Representatives. A White House policy statement on child care echoed the language of *Backgrounder* papers written by Rector. When Bush's child-care policy was criticized by liberals, Rector suggested that the president visit a black daycare center and explain how the liberal Act for Better Childcare (ABC) bill would deny funding to such centers. Bush subsequently held a news conference in a black church-run daycare center. A White House official told Rector at a White House meeting, "I've read all your materials on families and child care. I can't tell you how crucial your research has been on this issue, but then I guess everyone tells you that."[14]

In the course of the child-care debate, Rector did things he had not done before as a Heritage analyst but discovered he had to do if he wanted to have a legislative impact. One, he and other conservatives, not the liberal opposition, framed the debate. "Our theme was that the American family is over-taxed and should be allowed to keep more of its income." Two, at the request of a member of Congress, he helped write legislation. "After a while, I could rip out a draft amendment in a couple of hours." Three, he did a lot of original research, creating, for example, a data base about the American family. "It was the first time Heritage did that." Four, he worked closely with conservative groups like the Family Research Council, Eagle Forum, and Concerned Women of America. "When Jim Dobson went on the air and talked about the child-care bill, the congressional switchboards were frozen for days." And five, he constantly monitored the progress of the bill, closely watching for any Republican defections. "The battle of public policy never stops." As a result of the child-care campaign, says Rector, conservatives were able to "mainstream" the voucher principle.[15]

When the ABC was introduced in 1987, "it was a moving freight train," recalled Kate O'Beirne, then deputy director of domestic policy studies. "There was no way anyone dreamed that there wouldn't be a federal child-care scheme in place within a year."[16] ABC was derailed, essentially, by Robert Rector, whose hands-on research style became the model for every Heritage analyst.

Democracy vs. Communism

On the foreign policy front, confirmation of the abject failure of communism in China came in June 1989 when armed units of the People's

Liberation Army massacred hundreds of Chinese, most of them students, who had been holding pro-democracy demonstrations in Beijing's Tiananmen Square. Rarely before had communism's inherent fear of a popular movement been so graphically revealed.

That same month, Vice President Dan Quayle picked Heritage to make a tough anticommunist speech. Appearing at a forum of Heritage's Asian Studies Center, Quayle urged Congress to increase American aid to the noncommunist guerrillas in Cambodia and prevent the communist Khmer Rouge from returning to power. He drew a sharp contrast between the steady development of democracy in the Republic of China on Taiwan and the brutal suppression of peaceful demonstrations in the People's Republic of China. The vice president stated that it was the "duty" of the United States to denounce "the violence and reprisals against those who have called for democracy" in mainland China. And he condemned the "Orwellian inversion of truth" being spread by the communist regime about the executions and other bloody events in and around Tiananmen Square.[17]

Assessing the Congress

In March, consistent with its renewed emphasis on the people's branch of government, Heritage began the U.S. Congress Assessment Project. "Congress has developed a tendency to usurp power that belongs to the president," explained Phil Truluck, while failing to "fulfill its duties.... Congressional reform is long overdue."[18] The project was headed by the foundation's director of special projects, Mark Liedl, and evolved from the sharply critical book, *The Imperial Congress,* that Heritage had published in cooperation with the Claremont Institute. The assessment began with the creation of a comprehensive database on the size and growth of congressional staff, the committee and subcommittee structure, Congress's rules, and how they have changed over the years. At the same time, Heritage continued to work with members from both parties to reestablish Congress's "proper constitutional role as a law-making body."[19]

Along these lines, Congressman Richard K. Armey of Texas, who would become House Majority Leader in the 104th Congress, declared that his own *Policy Review* article about closing obsolete military bases (for savings of $700 million a year) "was crucial in getting my bill passed." Without the public forum of *Policy Review,* Armey asserted, "the base closing legislation would never have been placed on the congressional agenda, let alone passed into law."[20] Armey was not alone in acknowledging Heritage's usefulness. A top aide of Senator Malcolm Wallop (R-Wyo.) told Heritage's Senate liaison Meg Hunt "how valuable" the foundation's monthly newsletter, *USSR Monitor,* was. The senator frequently used material from the publication in his speeches and statements about developments in the Soviet Union.[21] And in November, policy analyst James Phillips was personally invited by Senator Joseph I. Lieberman (D-Conn.) to join a congressional study group on terrorism. Attending the first meeting, chaired by Senator Lieberman, were Senator John Glenn (D-Ohio), Senator Charles Grassley (R-Iowa), and several experts on terrorism and low-intensity warfare. Phillips outlined for the group "the continuing threat from Iran."[22]

Later that year, at a meeting of congressional supporters of the Strategic Defense Initiative, one assistant remarked, "What we really need now is a good pithy article summarizing all the best recent arguments for SDI." Congressman Jon Kyl (R-Ariz.), now a U.S. senator, explained, "That article already exists. It's by the vice president and it's in the latest issue of *Policy Review.*" Vice President Quayle, who was present, was described as pleased by the recognition. No less pleased was Adam Meyerson, who had asked Quayle to write "SDI and Its Enemies" for *Policy Review.*[23]

Policy Review was an important conservative journal under its first two editors, Robert Schuettinger and John O'Sullivan, but achieved must-read status in Washington under its third editor. Meyerson was part professional journalist (his writing skills were honed at the *Wall Street Journal*), part academic (he attended Yale University and Harvard Business School), and part neoconservative (who has now dropped the "neo"). He stresses that Ed Feulner has always wanted *Policy Review* to be "independent"— that is, "to advance conservatism" through the open debate of controversial issues. When Meyerson published an article by Charles Kesler of the Claremont Institute in the summer of 1990 against term limits—an idea strongly favored by Heritage—he "never heard a word" from Feulner, Meyerson says.[24]

During the Meyerson years, *Policy Review* has been at the cutting edge of conservative ideas, ranging from Ralph Reed's "constructive criticism" of the Christian Right to several articles about black America and black conservatism (*not* an oxymoron, Meyerson insists) to an outline of "conservative environmentalism" by R. J. Smith. Reed argued that the pro-family movement "must speak to the concerns of average voters in the areas of taxes, crime, government waste, health care, and financial security." According to political journalists Dan Balz and Ronald Brownstein, the Reed article was a "turning point" for the conservative Christian movement.[25] Corroboration of Meyerson's sharp eye for popular issues has come from *Reader's Digest* (U.S. circulation, over 16 million), which has reprinted more than ten of *Policy Review*'s articles in the past decade. Meyerson explained that one of his goals is "to make *Policy Review* the conscience of conservatism—a place where conservatives think about what they have done right and what they've done wrong."[26]

Encouraging Academic Excellence

The late Henry Salvatori was one of California's most prominent conservatives, responsible among other things, for persuading Ronald Reagan to run for governor in 1966. Long interested in the American founding, Salvatori made a $1 million, five-year grant to The Heritage Foundation in 1991 to underwrite the Salvatori Center for Academic Leadership. In 1995, the California conservative permanently endowed the center, whose name was changed to the Salvatori Center for the Appreciation of the Founding Fathers.

Each year, the center appoints twenty-five young academics in the social sciences and the humanities as Henry Salvatori Fellows. The fellows become members of Heritage's network of conservative scholars and participate in a Washington seminar on the "Foundations of American Liberty." While in the nation's capital, they also meet with policymakers and examine the history and present workings of Congress, the executive branch, and the courts. In addition, an annual Salvatori Prize for American Citizenship, totaling $25,000, is given to an outstanding American citizen who has helped his community solve problems that government has been unable or unwilling to solve.

The 1996 recipient was Conna Craig, president of the Institute for Children, which develops practical steps to help foster children find permanent families. Thanks to adoption reforms prepared with the help of the Institute for Children and implemented by Governor William Weld, 1,102 foster children were adopted in Massachusetts in 1995, nearly double the figure of 599 in 1992. Craig described her recommendations for foster care and adoption reform in "What I Need Is a Mom: The Welfare State Denies Homes to Thousands of Foster Children," first published in *Policy Review* in the summer of 1995 and then reprinted in *Reader's Digest.*

Good Neighbors and Free Trade

Heritage's efforts over the years to focus Washington's attention on the importance of Mexico reached critical mass in 1989. A new spirit of cooperation between the United States and its neighbor to the south resulted in agreements on Mexico's skyrocketing debt and promises by President Carlos Salinas de Gortari to curtail drug trafficking and illegal immigration. The foundation established its Mexico Project in 1987 with a grant of $125,000 for three years from the J. Howard Pew Freedom Trust of Philadelphia. The project, along with Latin American trade and security, was the primary thrust of Heritage's Institute for Hemispheric Development, which was also financially supported by prominent California businessman Arthur Spitzer. A major aim of the hemispheric institute from the beginning was to create a common market between the United States, Mexico, and the rest of Latin America, building on the suggestion (first made by presidential candidate Ronald Reagan in 1980) of a North American free trade zone. Heritage's unwavering support for a North American common market would put it at odds with Patrick J. Buchanan and other paleoconservatives in the 1990s.

"The 2,000–mile shared border between the United States and Mexico," said Kim Holmes, the foundation's director of foreign and defense policy, "makes Mexico a natural partner in trying to bring economic prosperity and democracy to the region."[27] Holmes was among a small group of opinion leaders invited to a private Blair House luncheon with Mexico's President Salinas during his October 1989 visit to Washington.

Preserving the Reagan Legacy

With a $1 million grant from the Grover M. Hermann Foundation of Chicago and another $1.5 million raised by an endowment committee headed by Ambassador Holland H. (Holly) Coors, The Heritage Foundation established the Ronald Reagan Chair in Public Policy in the early spring of 1989. It was the only Reagan chair in the United States formally approved by the former president, a fitting honor for the foundation which had been so closely identified with Reagan.

A year later, former Attorney General Edwin Meese III was named the Ronald Reagan Fellow in Public Policy, a position he occupies to this day. Speaking at the seminar that announced Meese's appointment, President Reagan warmly endorsed the selection of his longtime friend and colleague and praised the foundation's many contributions to his administration. "You [were] an invaluable resource on key issues," Reagan said, "such as tax cuts, reducing government spending, SDI, supporting freedom in Grenada, Nicaragua, Eastern Europe—whenever I needed Heritage, you were there."[28] Conceding that he might sound "a little mystical," the seventy-nine-year-old statesman repeated one of his favorite themes: Americans "were pre-ordained to carry the torch of freedom for the whole world. One of the places that torch has burned most brightly has been at The Heritage Foundation, as it always will."[29]

In a formal address entitled "The Reagan Legacy," Ed Meese began by saying that "perhaps more than any other organization in Washington," The Heritage Foundation was instrumental in developing that legacy. *Mandate for Leadership I,* for example, was "the only document that the president asked every cabinet member to read. It was distributed literally on the first day of the administration." Meese pointed out that Heritage contributed people as well as ideas. And it always maintained "its intellectual integrity," thereby serving as "a valuable critic" when government policy headed in the wrong direction.[30]

Rather than talk about the record economic expansion at home or the "triumph of democracy" around the world, Meese chose to stress the former president's spiritual legacy, starting with how he "restored the confidence of a nation which had been badly shattered." Reagan, to begin with, restored Americans' faith "in the vital credos of personal, political, and economic liberty."

Second, Meese continued, he provided perspective about our values and our history, defining the principles of the Reagan Revolution as "limited government, individual liberty, free enterprise, and peace through strength."[31] (It is not coincidence that these same principles are part of the mission statement of The Heritage Foundation.)

Third, Reagan provided a vision of "where America was going, where it should go, and how to get there." One part of that vision was a defense against intercontinental ballistic missiles—SDI. Another part was lower taxes so that "people could make more of their own choices about how to use their wealth." Still another part of the Reagan vision, offered in Westminster in 1982, was that "the march of freedom and democracy . . . will leave Marxism-Leninism on the ashheap of history."[32]

Turning to domestic issues, Meese recognized "the constant cry for new taxes" in Washington, D.C., but he urged policymakers to abide by the tested Reagan principle that "tax cuts and decreased federal spending are the only way to cope with the problems of the budget." The new Ronald Reagan Fellow concluded by assuring the audience that Heritage would lead the way in the effort "to preserve, protect, and perpetuate the Reagan Legacy."[33]

The commitment was not made idly by Meese or The Heritage Foundation. It meant that the foundation was prepared to challenge anyone who ignored or impaired the legacy, including a sitting president.

Flip-Flops and Betrayals

Hell hath no fury like a conservative betrayed. Shortly after George Bush was elected president, Ed Feulner publicly urged skeptical conservatives to give the new chief executive the benefit of the doubt, commenting, "Being against George Bush when he's wrong is one thing. Being against him because he's 'not one of us' is something else." Feulner was referring to populist conservatives like Richard A. Viguerie, who castigated Bush for being a card-carrying member of the GOP establishment and for describing Reagan's supply-side economics, while vying with him for the 1980 GOP presidential nomination, as "voodoo economics."[34]

In a December 1989 article for the Sunday *Washington Post*, subtitled "Bush Can Do for the Right What Reagan Couldn't," Feulner pointed out that Bush had presented himself "as an uncompromising conservative" during the presidential campaign and ought to be taken at his word. Feulner characterized Bush's endorsement of "a caring conservatism that will make America a kinder, gentler nation" as "not without intellectual substance," despite its implication that his predecessor, Ronald Reagan, had promoted an "uncaring" conservatism. After proposing several specific policy approaches to issues like the environment and health care and urging the frequent use of the veto, Feulner concluded that the direction of the Bush administration depended upon its chief executive: "Does the conservative George Bush I have known for the last twenty years really want to fight for the principles he believes in?"[35] It was clear from the friendly tone of his article that Feulner believed that Bush would be a principled president.

The Heritage Foundation worked closely with the Bush administration through 1989 and into 1990, when technocrats in the White House and Democrats on Capitol Hill began pressuring Bush to do something about the stagnant economy (growing by barely 2 percent) and the rising deficits (estimated at $160 billion). For liberals, the solution was obvious: raise taxes. At first, conservatives disregarded the liberal voices. Such a decision would be bad policy and worse politics, reversing Bush's famous campaign utterance, "Read my lips: no new taxes." But the liberals kept up the pressure for a tax increase, and to its consternation Heritage came to realize that Bush was considering just such a potentially disastrous move.

In May, Daniel J. Mitchell, then the foundation's John M. Olin Senior Fellow in political economy, warned that new taxes would "slow economic growth and could lead to a recession." He argued that the primary cause of the deficit was not lack of tax revenue but "runaway government spending." Citing the Congressional Budget Office, he pointed out that federal tax receipts had doubled over the last decade—from $517 billion in 1980 to an estimated $1.067 trillion in 1990. Later that month, at a Heritage panel discussion, four economists stated that the budget deficit problem was deliberately being "hyped" to stampede voters into accepting an unnecessary tax hike. There was no *deficit* crisis, they asserted, only a *political* crisis for big spenders seeking more funds for their expensive programs.[36]

But the warnings of The Heritage Foundation and other conservatives on and off Capitol Hill were to no avail. President Bush caved in and agreed to make a deficit-cutting deal with the Democratic Congress which included some "tax revenue increases." Heritage's reaction was swift and sharp: "If George Bush had pardoned Willie Horton, or burned Old Glory on the lawn of the White House," wrote Daniel Mitchell caustically, "it would hardly have rivaled the flip-flop he has committed on taxes."[37]

In his 1990 annual look at the state of conservatism, Feulner accused President Bush of "retreating" on one of conservatism's first principles— low taxes. "We know Ronald Reagan," Heritage's president said flatly, "and George Bush has shown he is not Ronald Reagan." Phil Truluck called George Bush's surrender in the 1990 tax battle "a betrayal of the conservative movement." Feulner was no less blunt in his assessment a year later, stating that the United States was a "Ship of State without a helmsman" and Bush a "president without purpose."[38] Burt Pines later remarked that George Bush could have been "our Harry S. Truman," codifying the Reagan legacy as Truman did FDR's New Deal. Instead, Bush did almost "everything he could, in the most crass and oedipal way, to undermine the Reagan Revolution."[39]

Building a Counter-Establishment

Although conceding that much of the public-policy agenda was still being dictated by the Washington power elite, Feulner insisted that liberalism was nevertheless "a dying creed with little popular support." The problem was that conservatism lacked a national leader because of George Bush's unwillingness or inability to articulate a conservative vision. How, then, could conservatives make sure that their message was not "sullied" by a "visionless White House" or an extremist like David Duke? The answer, Feulner said, was to renew and redouble efforts to build "an effective counter-establishment to replace the existing order," one that remained grounded "in solid, traditional American principles."[40]

This process was well under way, always aided and abetted by The Heritage Foundation. Not only in Washington but in some twenty-five states, conservative research organizations offered policymakers alternatives to the tax-and-spend-and-regulate policies that had led the United States into a recession. These state think tanks strengthened the American federalism which Alexis de Tocqueville praised so highly in *Democracy in America* and which Russell Kirk saw as the most effective counterweight to what he called "the behemoth state."[41]

Despite the plethora of liberal daily newspapers, conservatives—led by William F. Buckley Jr., George Will, Patrick J. Buchanan, Tony Snow, Thomas Sowell, Walter Williams, William A. Rusher, Cal Thomas, Mona Charen, and many others—dominated the field of newspaper commentary. Unlike television, talk radio was very nearly the exclusive province of conservatives, with Rush Limbaugh capturing millions of listeners and Paul Harvey and Jim Dobson, among many others, drawing millions more.

Whereas in the 1950s there was only a handful of conservative policy journals (most prominently, *National Review*), there were now dozens, including *Policy Review, The National Interest, Commentary, The Public Interest, Reason, Chronicles, The American Spectator,* and *The American Enterprise*. The most important journal of all, according to Feulner, was the magazine that "the intellectual establishment most loves to hate: *Reader's Digest,* which has done more to popularize conservative ideas than any other publication in the world."[42]

Because of Ronald Reagan *and* George Bush, continued Feulner, conservatives were a strong force in the federal judiciary. The family values coalition, led by Focus on the Family and the Family Research Council, was displaying its muscle power in Washington and at the grassroots. There were even signs that conservatives were beginning to loosen the grip of the Left on the African-American and Hispanic communities with the emergence of J. A. Parker's Lincoln Institute and Robert Woodson's National Center for Neighborhood Enterprise. Feulner also noted the continuing growth of "a centrist faction within the Democratic Party, which for three decades has been hostile to conservative ideas."[43]

However, too many components necessary for a true counterestablishment were still missing, and as a result, the balance of power in Washington "still lists heavily toward the left." Congress led Feulner's list of disappointments: In it, he said, were many conservatives but "too little conservative leadership." Yet the ever-resilient Feulner refused to be discouraged. The failings of conservatives, he insisted, were not ideological but institutional. And thus the task of conservatives was to work even harder to build up the institutional base, "with or without George Bush and the Republican Party."[44]

Here Feulner was stating a simple truth about conservatives like him-

self and organizations like The Heritage Foundation: they were committed to ideas rather than to any political party. They were conservative first
and then Republican or Democratic or both, depending upon the issue
and the policy. Grover M. Hermann Fellow Scott Hodge believes that with
Bush's 1990 budget "deal," The Heritage Foundation truly "matured as a
leader in the conservative movement." Rather than invariably support the
Republican approach, says Hodge, "we became the loyal opposition, looking for ways to redefine the conservative agenda."[45]

Determining the Public Agenda

During the 1980s and early 1990s, Heritage was at the top of its game,
popularizing ideas that helped change the way that Washington policymakers and other Americans looked at government. Those ideas included
cutting taxes to stimulate economic growth; bringing federal spending
under strict control; building a strategic defense shield to defend America
and its allies against missile attack; pushing for parental choice in education; privatizing government activities and programs; reforming "the
imperial Congress"; and urging an antipoverty program based on less government intervention and more individual empowerment.

As Ed Feulner put it, the question should not be "Where are we going?"
but "What can we do to ensure that we get where we want to go?" Heritage believed, and still believes, that the great majority of Americans want
a destiny based on the "ideals of freedom and democracy and a belief in
the remarkable potential of the individual"—words uttered by former
President Ronald Reagan at the foundation's annual board meeting in
1990.[46]

With a president whose vision was increasingly out of focus, Heritage
concentrated more and more on Congress, where it helped conservatives
like Dick Armey and Tom DeLay stand their ground on taxes. The House
Republican Conference, for example, overwhelmingly passed a resolution opposing any new taxes over the vehement objections of the Bush
White House. Supporters relied heavily on Heritage papers analyzing federal spending trends and the likely recessionary effects of tax increases.
Following Bush's abandonment of his "no new taxes" pledge, Heritage
formed a Budget Reform Working Group, which among other things pro-

duced a proposal that became known as the "four percent solution." Analyst Scott Hodge showed that the federal budget could be balanced without new taxes simply by limiting spending increases to 4 percent a year. Several members of Congress straightway incorporated the plan in alternative budget proposals. Reflecting the influence of analyst Robert Rector, Congressman Frank Wolf (R-Va.) and Senator Bill Bradley (D-N.J.) made extensive use of Heritage research in their proposals to provide tax relief for families with children.

Meanwhile, abroad, Iraq invaded neighboring Kuwait. The government relations staff, headed by Kate O'Beirne, immediately went to work and provided Congress with policy guidance. On the House floor, Congressmen Duncan Hunter and Wally Herger of California distributed copies of Heritage's first paper dealing with the invasion: "How to Stop Iraq's Saddam Hussein." According to Frank Staar, chief of the *Baltimore Sun*'s Washington bureau, Heritage's studies "laid much of the groundwork for Bush administration thinking" about what constituted American interests in a world where the Soviet Union was no longer able to project its military strength in conflicts around the world.[47] In a *New York Times* essay, Christopher Gacek, the foundation's Jay Kingham Fellow, warned that the United States and its allies should not stop short of removing Saddam from power, an admonition that has haunted American presidents ever since.

Back home, the foundation's plan for health-care reform in America emerged in 1991 as one of the three options seriously considered by Washington policymakers. Under the Heritage approach, consumers would shop for health coverage as they do for other goods and services, making "providers" like hospitals and physicians compete for their business. But the foundation plan would have had little impact on the debate without aggressive, Heritage-style marketing. As Thomas Sowell, author and Hoover Institution Fellow, put it, "Heritage is unique among think tanks. ... As fast as various organizations and movements on the Left can create hysteria over some issue, Heritage can shoot it down in flames with facts and figures. They must work through the night."[48] Writing in *The New Republic,* liberal commentator Michael Kinsley praised Heritage for producing "the simplest, most promising, and in important ways, most progressive ideas for health care reform."

"There is no free lunch at The Heritage Foundation," *National Review* wrote about the foundation's health-care plan. "By getting individuals to pay medical bills themselves, we might just end the insane overuse that has brought the system to its knees."[49] Critics, however, pointed to what they saw as significant flaws in the Heritage plan. First, the plan assumed that all Americans were sophisticated enough to compete in the market for the best insurance. But, as the *Los Angeles Times* said, millions of Americans have been "the victims of scams and swindles" in the life insurance business. Second, a free market might not lead to major cost savings. As long as insurance covered the cost of serious illness, patients and physicians would have "an incentive to use the newest—and most expensive—medical technology. Only government regulations, asserted critics, could restrain the growth of such high-priced technology."[50] As we shall see in the next chapter, Heritage had ready answers for all of its critics.

Joining the Cultural War

In the fall of 1991, at the urging of Richard Larry of the Sarah Scaife Foundation and Michael Joyce of the Lynde and Harry Bradley Foundation, The Heritage Foundation formally entered America's culture wars and named former Secretary of Education William J. Bennett as its Distinguished Fellow in Cultural Policy Studies. At a private New York City meeting in 1990, Larry had sharply questioned the foundation's downplaying of cultural issues. "Don't you understand everything is deteriorating," he reportedly asked Heritage senior management, "and the rest of your stuff doesn't mean anything if the culture deteriorates?"[51] Larry, a strong supporter of The Heritage Foundation for many years, had particularly in mind the disintegration of the family, an issue which became a major Heritage concern.

In his first Heritage lecture, entitled "The War Over Culture in Education," Bennett argued that the major reason why American education had deteriorated was that "our schools were systematically, culturally deconstructed." By whom? By the education establishment, a frequent Bennett target during his tenure as Education secretary. He infuriated the National Education Association and similar groups by insisting that public schools did not belong to the teachers but to the American people. After suggesting how American schools might be "reconstructed," starting with the creation of a safe and orderly environment, Bennett quoted commentator Midge Decter that "a culture war is a war to the death ... [because] it is a battle about matters of the spirit."[52] The following year, Heritage produced eight major cultural studies on topics ranging from "the fraud of multiculturalism" to "America's ailing families."[53]

Russell Kirk pointed out that multiculturalism was far from invincible. When a secret ballot of the faculty at the University of Texas was conducted, a majority declared their opposition to a proposed multicultural program. As a consequence, the university president resigned. Kirk commented, "a little more courage on the part of college administrators and professors would undo this anti-cultural tyranny."[54]

Heritage hit the cultural jackpot in March 1993 with the release, along with Empower America and the Free Congress Foundation, of one of the most popular studies in its history—"The Index of Leading Cultural Indicators." In just 22 graph-filled pages, the Index documented how crime, illegitimacy, divorce, teenage suicide, drug use, and fourteen other social indicators had become measurably worse over the last thirty years. In his introduction, Bennett argued that many things could be done to "encourage cultural renewal," starting with a government that heeded the old injunction "Do no harm." He urged lawmakers to ask themselves basic questions such as: "Will this legislation support or undermine families?" and "Will it encourage individual responsibility or dependency?" He proposed a "reform-minded and thoughtful legislative social agenda" that included "a reversal of the destructive incentives of the welfare system," an increase in the personal dependent exemption from $2,300 to $7,000, removal of major obstacles to adoption, and enforcement of laws requiring fathers to take responsibility for their children.[55]

So hungry were Americans for information about what was happening to their families that forty-eight hours after Bennett aired his findings on the Rush Limbaugh radio program, 73,000 people called Heritage to request copies of the landmark study. The next year, the "Index" was published as a book by Simon and Schuster. In a special acknowledgment, Bennett thanked Heritage and "especially its president, Edwin J. Feulner Jr.," for their "encouragement, assistance, and cooperation in the preparation and publication of the original "Index of Leading Cultural Indicators. "The remarkable impact of the cultural index study led to William

Bennett's bestseller, *The Book of Virtues,* and its several offspring, including the PBS animated series "Adventures in the Book of Virtues."

There were also important changes in 1992 in the foundation's board of trustees. Shelby Cullom Davis, who had served as a trustee since 1979 and chairman since 1985, retired and was elected chairman emeritus. The new chairman was David R. Brown, M.D., a distinguished orthopedic surgeon and Noble Foundation trustee, who has provided steady, sure board leadership ever since. The new vice chairman, one of Heritage's earliest supporters, was Richard M. Scaife, philanthropist and publisher-owner of the Greensburg, Pennsylvania, *Tribune-Review.*

At almost the same time, Senior Vice President Burton Yale Pines resigned, and the board of trustees rewarded the service of two senior Heritage managers, electing Stuart M. Butler vice president and director of domestic and economic studies, and Kim R. Holmes vice president and director of foreign and defense policy studies.

Operating in the Post-Cold War World

As Heritage's Kim Holmes and Thomas G. Moore, deputy director of foreign policy and defense studies, have written, the fall of the Soviet Union and the disintegration of the Warsaw Pact ended communist threats to American and allied security, but also unleashed nationalist and other forces contained by forty-five years of the Cold War. America finds herself in an era marked by the global spread of ballistic missiles, nuclear, chemical, and biological weapons, and other high-tech weapons among potential enemies. While the threat of thermonuclear war has receded, if not disappeared, the possibility of nuclear proliferation, terrorism, and ethnic conflict has increased. A "Fortress America" strategy in our interconnected world is not possible. "The North Koreas, Iraqs, and Irans," Holmes and Moore assert, "not to mention the positive demands of trade and commerce, would not allow it." The only prudent course for America is to use all possible components of national power and influence to "shape a world friendly to America's interests and values."[56]

The Bush administration's failed attempt to construct a New World Order led Heritage, starting in the fall of 1991, to draw up a blueprint for a new foreign policy, described by one national columnist as "a strategy to guide America safely into the twenty-first century." In *Making the World Safe for America* (published in April 1992), Kim Holmes and other foundation analysts described the major threats that the United States is likely to face in the future—such as nuclear proliferation among hostile Third World dictatorships—and carefully defined the primary interests that U.S. foreign policy ought to serve, especially those warranting the use of military force. "We needed," explains Holmes, "a practical alternative to the disengagement being proposed by conservatives like Patrick Buchanan and the vague multilateralism of liberals like Bill Clinton."[57]

The 32-page blueprint was followed in 1993 by an even more comprehensive 84-page study, *A Safe and Prosperous America,* which in turn defined American geopolitical interests in the absence of a Soviet threat and offered a prioritized strategy for American intervention around the world. The study's central thesis was that the United States should step in only when its vital interests were at stake and defined those interests as: protecting American territory, sea lanes, and airspace; preventing a major power from controlling Europe, East Asia, or the Persian Gulf; ensuring U.S. access to world resources; expanding free trade throughout the world; and protecting Americans against threats to their lives and well-being.[58]

In keeping with its generally *realpolitik* tone, the Heritage paper rejected the calls of neoconservatives like Joshua Muravchik and Ben Wattenberg to export democracy around the world.[59]

As Russell Kirk put it in a Heritage lecture, a conservative foreign policy should be neither interventionist nor isolationist but "prudent." Its objective should not be the triumph everywhere of "America's name and manners" but the preservation of "the true national interest and acceptance of the diversity of economic and political institutions throughout the world."[60]

The Heritage blueprint identified nuclear proliferation in countries such as North Korea as the leading threat to U.S. interests, a threat that increasingly became a reality as 1993 ended. The number two threat was the possible breakdown of democracy in Russia, which almost occurred when President Boris Yeltsin and the communist-dominated parliament settled their differences with tanks and guns. Widely praised on Capitol Hill (Senator Malcolm Wallop said it "should be the foundation on which other attempts to forge a post-Cold War strategy should be built") and in leading military publications like the *Armed Forces Journal International*, the blueprint became required reading at the U.S. Naval Academy and other colleges and universities.[61] The editor of *Foreign Affairs* termed it "one of the best such analyses I have seen in a long time."[62]

Consistent with its principles of enlightened nationalism, *A Safe and Prosperous America* emphasized that the United States should not allow its armed forces to be used as proxies for every far-flung conflict the United Nations favored, should not condition its decision to take military action on U.N. approval, and should not, under any circumstances, place U.S. forces under U.N. command. (In its first year, the Clinton administration managed to violate all three of these core concepts of the Heritage study.)

In a foreword, Ed Feulner insisted that promoting "American national interests" was not amoral or selfish but rather "a moral act required by the Constitution." Furthermore, American freedom and democracy "are beacons to the rest of the world; they serve as models which other countries wish to emulate." The survival of America, therefore, advances "the cause of freedom and democracy around the world." At the same time, he argued that the United States should take "moral stands" on foreign policy issues but without becoming "the world's policeman." Supporting humanitarian causes should be an "act of charity," not the fulfillment of a fundamental goal of American strategy or purpose. A humanitarian act, Feulner concluded, "is something Americans may choose to do, not something they must do."[63] Feulner's common-sense approach made all the more sense after the debacle in Somalia where "mission creep" produced the unnecessary deaths of eighteen American servicemen.

Bottoms Up and Out

"The Clinton administration does take national interests into account when formulating foreign policy," remarked Lawrence Di Rita, then deputy director of foreign and defense policy studies, at a Heritage briefing. "The trouble is they are frequently the interests of other nations."[64] Another problem with the Clinton administration, the foundation discovered, was its tendency to fund inadequately the nation's defense needs.

In studies published during 1993, Heritage found the administration's "Bottom-Up Review" of military requirements in the 1990s "haphazard," its downsizing plans "damaging" to America's defense industrial base, and its frequent use of U.S. forces for noncombat missions "ill-considered."[65] Just before he announced his resignation as Secretary of Defense, Les Aspin admitted that the Department of Defense could not meet its own goals and commitments without an additional $50 to $70 billion.

The following March, Heritage senior defense analyst Baker Spring revealed that the Clinton administration had underfunded its own defense plan by a five-year total of $100 billion. Spring quoted General Gordon R. Sullivan, army chief of staff: "Smaller is not better. Better is better."[66] The White House and the Pentagon immediately dismissed the foundation's findings, but the General Accounting Office (GAO), Congress's auditing arm, undertook a cross-examination of Clinton's defense plan and the Pentagon's budget. To the extreme embarrassment of the administration, GAO found that Heritage had been too conservative in its estimate—the shortfall was closer to $150 billion.[67]

After the GOP takeover of Congress in 1994—which placed longtime friends of Heritage, Senator Strom Thurmond and Congressman Floyd Spence, both of South Carolina, at the head of the Senate and House Armed Services committees—the administration reversed direction and acknowledged that the defense budget would have to be increased to maintain military readiness.

To help the president find the necessary money, Heritage identified billions of dollars in "non-defense pork" that had been buried in the defense budget, including $161 million for small business "innovative research," $50 million for assistance to local educational agencies, $40 million for the Civilian Community Corps, and $9 million for World Cup USA.[68] Analyst John Luddy pointed out that one disturbing result of such misguided spending was that the first army brigade sent to Kuwait in October 1993 had platoon leaders who had never trained with their troops in the field, platoons that had never been evaluated in a live-fire training exercise, and tank crews that had not completed vital crew drills. "If the president and Congress are serious about meeting critical training, maintenance, and equipment shortfalls," wrote Luddy, "they can start by taking a hard look at Pentagon money now being spent on medical research, the Summer Olympics, and research on electric vehicles."[69]

In other foreign policy areas, the Asian Studies Center launched an

American Trader Initiative, seeking to encourage political cooperation and social liberalization through America's commercial ties with Asia. As with earlier editions, the 1993 *U.S. and Asia Statistical Handbook* earned widespread praise as an authoritative reference work.

In yet another part of the world, the Institute for Hemispheric Development played a critical role in the debate on the North American Free Trade Agreement (NAFTA) signed by President Bush, Mexican President Carlos Salinas de Gortari, and Canadian Prime Minister Brian Mulroney on December 17, 1992. With overwhelming Republican support led by Minority Leader Newt Gingrich and over the objections of key Democrats like House Majority Leader Richard Gephardt, the House of Representatives approved NAFTA in November 1993 by a vote of 234–200. Republicans backed the free trade plan 132–43 while Democrats opposed it 156–102.[70]

One of Heritage's most influential NAFTA papers was a state-by-state survey (compiled by analyst Doug Seay) which revealed that forty-two governors, Democratic and Republican, liberal and conservative, strongly favored the agreement because it would create thousands of new jobs and strengthen the economy of their states. The foundation followed up by inviting Governors Tommy Thompson of Wisconsin and Kirk Fordice of Mississippi to Washington to explain to policymakers how global economic development would promote jobs within the states. President Clinton and International Trade Representative Mickey Kantor both cited Heritage in their hard-fought campaign to persuade Congress to approve NAFTA. "President Clinton said the governors' support was key," recalls Kim Holmes.[71]

The Moscow Connection

Throughout the 1980s, Heritage had been frequently and sharply criticized by the Kremlin. One Soviet publication declared that the foundation was the "ideological headquarters" of American "reactionary circles." Another described Heritage as the "brain center" of "U.S. ultra right-wing circles." Hardliners in Politboro meetings regularly cited the foundation's policy recommendations and argued that Moscow should do exactly the opposite.[72] But as communism faded and disappeared, Russian reformers increasingly turned to Heritage for advice and assistance on how to chart a new course for their nation. While liberals in America continued to extol the virtues of Mikhail Gorbachev, Heritage analysts focused on Boris Yeltsin, the ex-communist turned reform populist. The foundation invited Yeltsin's top economic advisers to attend a privatization workshop in June 1991. Yeltsin, who met with President Bush the same week, told Heritage trustee J. William Middendorf II that the Heritage seminar was the most important part of his delegation's visit to Washington, D.C., and remarked gratefully, "The Russian republic is in good hands with Heritage."[73] A leading Moscow analyst told the *Washington Post* the following spring that American liberals had been "reluctant and slow to recognize that power was shifting. The Heritage Foundation was in Moscow 18 months ago trying to work with Boris Yeltsin. Brookings wasn't."[74]

Heritage formalized its efforts to help Russia stay on a democratic course by opening an office in Moscow in November 1992 and putting Jeffrey Gayner, the foundation's veteran counselor for international affairs, in charge. Reform leaders in Russia and the Newly Independent States (NIS) constantly asked the foundation staff for research and advice on how to make the transition to free markets and a democratic government. Heritage's place of honor among Russia's reformers was summed up by former Deputy Prime Minister Yegor Gaidar during a Washington visit: "We remember that Heritage supported us long before it was fashionable to do so in the West."[75] Evidence of Heritage's influence could be found in the most unexpected areas. During one trip to the region of the Ural Mountains, hundreds of miles from the capital, the Moscow office staff discovered excerpts of Heritage studies in a 50,000-circulation newspaper read by the area's emerging businessmen. Dimitri Karaulov, co-chairman of the Russian Republican Party, put it succinctly: "Heritage's ideas are the guiding light" for Russian reformers.[76]

Why Communism Ended

No less an authority than Margaret Thatcher, three-time prime minister of Great Britain, agreed that the ideas of The Heritage Foundation and other conservative institutions were responsible in a significant way for bringing down the Soviet empire. Delivering the first Clare Boothe Luce

Lecture in September 1991, Thatcher attributed the final raising of the Iron Curtain to three factors: an alliance of free peoples; the "ideas of liberty, free enterprise, private property, and democracy"; and the Russian, Czech, Hungarian, Polish, and other peoples in the enemy camp. "All we had to do," she said, "was to tell the truth ... that the system under which they lived was wicked, brutal, and founded on force."[77]

The power of truth and of ideas prevailed, Thatcher declared, and will always prevail as "the ruins of Marxist communism in Eastern Europe and the Soviet Union testify most eloquently." But, she added, ideas alone will not suffice. "They will get nowhere without politicians of courage who are prepared to fight to implement them." Thatcher recalled a dinner given by a British think tank at which it was stated that the ideas and influence of intellectuals really ruled the world. "I was forced to remind them," she said, "that although it is the cock that may crow, it is the hen who lays the egg."[78]

She singled out one political leader in particular for his indispensable role: "Ronald Reagan won the Cold War without firing a shot." He had a little help, of course, but, Thatcher insisted, "that imperishable achievement will be seen by history as belonging primarily to him."[79]

Looking back at the twentieth century, "the totalitarian century," pockmarked by collectivism, mass murder, wars, tension, and fleeing refugees, Thatcher expressed the hope that the coming century would in fact be the "American Century," a time when people everywhere would turn to what have become American ideas—"ideas of liberty, democracy, free markets, free trade, and limited government."[80]

In his opening remarks, Ed Feulner also looked back to the early 1970s when Heritage was newly founded and government was seen as "the solution to every national problem." During those dark years, the nation's defense was "inadequate" and the economy was being "strangled" by antigrowth regulations, policies which reflected the *zeitgeist* of the time. Policymakers truly believed, said Feulner, that these "old statist ideas would bring peace and prosperity. They did not see that there was a better way."[81]

With the initial help of a handful of entrepreneurs like Joseph Coors, Richard Scaife, and the Noble family, and the continuing support of tens of thousands of individuals, Heritage was able to change "the policy landscape in Washington." "We have made conservative ideas not merely respectable," Feulner declared, "we have seen them become mainstream."[82]

The Heritage president then sounded a note of caution, quoting F. A. Hayek to the effect that in order to win political battles, "you must be ever-vigilant in the war of ideas." Although liberalism was "an old decaying order," Feulner pledged that Heritage would not relax its vigilance but would stick to its time-tested strategy: begin with a principle, apply it to a particular situation, draw up a blueprint for its implementation, and then market it to "our target audiences." "This," said Feulner, "is how we conduct warfare in the battle of ideas ... and why Heritage has become a permanent fixture in the policymaking process in Washington."[83]

Heritage may have become a permanent institution, but much of Washington is temporary and even fleeting. As Margaret Thatcher was speaking and Ambassador Shelby Cullom Davis and Dr. Kathryn Davis were jointly receiving the first Clare Boothe Luce Award, President Bush, in the wake of the spectacular American-led victory in the Persian Gulf War, was a heavy favorite to win reelection, Newt Gingrich was amusing pundits and Democrats with his detailed plans for a Republican takeover of Congress, and a feisty New Democrat named Bill Clinton was insisting he could win the Democratic nomination for president and capture the White House.

6

New Democrats

Never before in modern politics had a president seeking reelection gone more quickly from sure thing to long shot. In the spring of 1990, shortly after America's *blitzkrieg* and victory in the Persian Gulf War, President Bush and his aides, wallowing in his popularity, were so confident about 1992 that they almost thought they needn't file for reelection.

In less than eighteen months, the president watched, appalled, as his approval ratings plummeted nearly 60 points—from over 90 percent to the mid-30s prior to the Republican convention in July. The central reason for the public's runaway dissatisfaction was the faltering economy. Median household income in 1991 fell 3.5 percent. Only about one million new jobs were created during the first three-and-a-half years of the Bush presidency—the worst record of any administration since World War II. And unemployment hit 7.7 percent, the highest since the 1982–1983 recession.

The public was unforgiving. When the federal government failed to provide emergency relief quickly in the wake of Hurricane Andrew, a Gallup Poll showed that Americans, by 57–35 percent, thought that President Bush cared more for the suffering of victims in Iraq and Bosnia than those in Florida and Louisiana.

In one sense, Bush was a victim of what has been called the Churchill Syndrome, coined by political scientists to describe the shocking defeat of the British prime minister in the 1945 elections after he had guided his country to victory over the Nazis in World War II. Like Churchill, Bush was being told by an inward-looking electorate: "You're a wonderful global leader, but you don't understand our problems here at home."

Confronted by a superb campaigner in Bill Clinton, a united Democratic Party, and a well-financed third-party nominee, billionaire Ross Perot, whose balance-the-budget-now message appealed strongly to Republicans, Bush went down to decisive defeat in November 1992. He received only 38 percent of the popular vote, half a point less than Barry Goldwater totaled in his humiliating 1964 loss to Lyndon B. Johnson. Exit polls revealed that the overriding reason for the collapse of the broad-based coalition that had won the last three presidential elections for Republicans was Bush's reneging on his no-new-taxes pledge. That not only destroyed his credibility, particularly on taxes and spending, but helped prolong the recession—laying Clinton's major issue in his lap.

Clinton ran as a "different kind of Democrat," as a founder of the moderate Democratic Leadership Council, not the liberal successor to George McGovern. He spoke in favor of a balanced-budget amendment, federal deregulation, free trade with Mexico, the line-item veto, the death penalty, getting tough with China over its brutal violations of human rights, and intervening in the war in former Yugoslavia. These were issues that, in the words of conservative Congressman Vin Weber (R-Minn.), "Ronald Reagan would probably have been running on if he ran in 1992."[1] And they were issues about which The Heritage Foundation had published extensively.

President-elect Clinton insisted that he was a New Democrat who sought a "third way" between the Big Government of liberal Democrats and the No Government of ultra-conservative Republicans. His "third way" would foster community, encourage opportunity, and demand responsibility. One of Clinton's most applauded lines during the campaign was his pledge to "end welfare as we know it." Whatever his original intentions, however, the new president immediately encountered and surrendered to Democratic liberals who had their own ideas about the best balance between government and society.

The State of Conservatism 1993

As Ed Feulner asked in his annual look at conservatism in January 1993, "Who would ever have thought that a Republican president closely identified with the Reagan revolution would be defeated by a Democratic challenger campaigning against him from the right?" Candidate Clinton even quoted Heritage studies, like the one which reported that the Bush administration had "increased regulation on the private sector more than anyone in the last twenty years." "Conservatism didn't cost Bush the election," wrote Feulner. "It was his failure to press ahead with the low-taxes, 'get-government-off-our-backs' agenda of his predecessor."[2] Along with Clinton's shrewd strategy of riding the wave of America's antigovernment mood.

Heritage's president was quick to acknowledge that America owed George Bush a "great debt of gratitude" for his lifetime of service to the country, bringing dignity to the Oval Office, standing firm on judicial appointments, and steering the Persian Gulf War so skillfully. But on the twin issues most important to the majority of Americans—taxes and spending—"he stumbled badly." Perhaps worse, in his campaign Bush failed to convince the electorate that he knew what he wanted to do in a second term. He proved, said Feulner, that "a 'leader' without a cause is a leader without a following."[3]

As to the future, added Feulner, the beliefs that motivated the Reagan Revolution—individual freedom, limited government, competitive enterprise, and peace through strength—lived on. President Clinton had a choice: to embrace conservative ideas or to give in to the liberal demands of the special interests that had dominated the Democratic Party for so long. An administration bent on "real change," said Feulner, would undertake the following:

- Tackle the budget deficit by restraining government spending. Over the years, Heritage had uncovered wasteful programs totaling tens of billions of dollars.
- "Empower" poor and middle-income families by, for example, giving them school-choice vouchers. "Why not promote competition in education," Feulner asked, "by giving poor . . . families the same choices as the rich and famous enjoy?"

- Champion tax relief, not tax increases. In 1948, the typical American family of four paid the federal government 2 to 3 percent of its income in taxes. In 1992, it paid 24 percent with another 8 to 10 percent going to state and local governments.
- Reduce "the regulatory burden" on American business and society. In 1970, the *Federal Register,* the encyclopedia of government rules and regulations, was a formidable 20,036 pages long. In 1992, it had more than tripled in size to an elephantine 67,716 pages.
- Solve the national health-care problem in a way that "won't make matters worse." During the campaign, Clinton had embraced a concept known as "managed competition" along with what he called "global budgeting," a political euphemism for rationing. A better way, Feulner argued, was the Heritage Consumer Choice Health Plan, based on consumer choice and market competition.[4]

Turning to the conservative movement, the Heritage president reported that its philosophy remained "prescient, clear, and unchanged." The major domestic enemy was "the bureaucratic state" with its "insatiable appetite for our money and our obedience." The conservative alternative was, is, and will ever be "free men, free minds, and free markets." Internationally, conservatives rejected "both isolationism and crusaderism" but not "internationalism." America, Feulner insisted, "must remain engaged in the world."[5]

Warming to his theme, the foundation's president said that what the conservative movement needed was a "set of practical objectives." With the Cold War won and essentially over (although China remained communist and potentially dangerous), a domestic war remained to be fought, a war against government. The objective was clear: "to halt any further encroachment on our freedoms and regain freedoms previously lost." And the only realistic way to roll back "the Leviathan state," Feulner insisted, was through "realistic, practical alternatives." It was not enough, as Bill Buckley did with the launching of *National Review* in 1955, to stand athwart history yelling "Stop!" We must remember, said Feulner, that "the bottom line in everything we say and do is people." Instead of merely condemning welfare dependency, for example, conservatives had to make the case for the "strategy we call empowerment."[6]

And finally, the movement required people and institutions with "determination and a clarity of purpose." Feulner identified a major reason for the conservative failure in Washington: its disconnection from the grassroots—"too many conservatives have become creatures of the same Beltway culture we so readily condemn."[7] That criticism could not pertain to The Heritage Foundation, which had been reaching out to the grassroots through the Resource Bank, its media and direct-mail programs, and other mechanisms for nearly twenty years. In April, the fifteenth annual Resource Bank meeting, organized by Thomas Atwood under the theme "Ideas Have Consequences: A Conservative Battleplan for the 1990s," attracted a record three hundred participants representing 105 organizations.

Ed Feulner speculated that in the wake of Bush's defeat and the continuing Democratic dominance of Congress, "the Republican Party may be in worse shape" than at any time in the last twenty-five years, because so many voters were wondering "What, if anything, [the GOP] stands for."

Many conservatives were worried. They wondered whether conservatism was the progressivism of the late twentieth century—fated to fade away as other idea-based movements in American politics had. And too, how important had the personal magnetism of Ronald Reagan been to the success of conservatism?

The always optimistic Feulner had ready answers. He pointed to a new generation of Republicans, "rich in talent, firm in its convictions, and determined to put the GOP back on course." He mentioned William Bennett, John Engler, Phil Gramm, Jack Kemp, and Tommy Thompson. Although he had been dropping by Heritage since his arrival in Washington in 1979, Newt Gingrich was not on the list. Neither was another frequent Heritage visitor, Bob Dole, nor commentator-presidential hopeful Pat Buchahan.[8] Feulner would later make up for these oversights with a spectacular prediction about the outcome of the 1994 elections, anticipating that historic Republican victory.

Looking back over the Reagan and Bush years, the Heritage president noted that several important lessons had been learned. One, "there are no permanent victories in Washington." Two, "there are no permanent defeats in Washington either." Three, "most Americans remain committed to the low-taxes, pro-growth, limited-government message of contemporary conservatism."

But, Feulner lamented, while the rhetoric of politics "remains mostly conservative," the activities of Washington "remain mostly liberal." The solution lay in a "reinvigorated conservative movement" doing a better job of "holding the political system accountable for the damage it does."[9]

Heritage resolved to regain the policy momentum which had slowed drastically during the often frustrating Bush years. One senior foundation manager, for example, derisively described the Bush administration's efforts in the inner city as "the Skirmish on Poverty."[10] Among the initiatives suggested by Heritage had been drug programs, tenant management in public housing, choice in education, and enterprise zones. Although the Bush administration blamed congressional Democrats for lack of action on these measures, many conservatives insisted that the principal problem lay inside the White House.

Reasons for the inaction included the president's clear preference for foreign policy and the consistent opposition to urban initiatives from the administration's big three in domestic policy—Richard G. Darman (head of the Office of Management and Budget); Treasury Secretary Nicholas F. Brady; and White House Chief of Staff John H. Sununu. There was also a White House fear that the Democratic Congress would transform the proposals into billion-dollar bureaucratic programs. Also, many Republicans could not see any "political payoff" from inner-city programs.[11]

"Formally," recalled Stuart Butler, "the [urban initiatives] became Bush policy. But always in the White House there was nitpicking, cutting down, not giving any real support on the Hill, not spending any political capital, and not framing any kind of policy or political confrontation with the Democrats."[12]

For the Clinton administration, Heritage adopted a two-part strategy: first, attack explicitly the welfare system, pointing out its many weaknesses and failures; and second, address a bottom-line concern of almost every American, the breakdown of the family.

The foundation unleashed policy analyst Robert Rector against welfare. One result was Rector's startling finding that government had spent over $5 trillion since the War on Poverty was launched in the mid-sixties, but had had comparatively little impact on the level of poverty in America. With regard to the family, Heritage proposed a number of measures calculated to strengthen and rebuild the institution broadly acknowledged to be the cornerstone of every society.

The Heritage strategy, designed by Stuart Butler and his team, moved the whole locus of the welfare debate, particularly in the 104th Congress, rapidly to the right. "Our position prevailed," says Butler.[13] But first came a gargantuan issue, health care, which was absorbing a breathtaking one seventh of our national economy.

Clinton's "New Deal" for Health Care

During the 1992 presidential campaign, Bill Clinton frequently mentioned the urgent need for health-care reform but offered few specific proposals. In January 1993, he declared his support for a comprehensive overhaul of the nation's health-care system and, surrendering to hubris, promised to send the Democratic 103rd Congress a proposal within ninety days. In fact, it was not until eight months later that Clinton at last submitted legislation.

To meet his ambitious goal, President Clinton announced that his wife, Hillary Rodham Clinton, would chair a health-care task force of cabinet officers and White House staffers to draft the administration's historic measure. The White House also set up fifteen working groups on different health-care topics that included congressional staffers and experts from federal agencies and across the country with public- and/or private-sector backgrounds. The Task Force was instructed to build a system that would resolve two contradictory ends: expand health care for all Americans—about 38 million people were uninsured—and reduce the rapidly rising rate of health-care spending.

In that spring of 1993, everyone agreed that the health-care system was running wild. Costs had rocketed. The money spent on U.S. health care had reached an astonishing $832 billion the previous year, one seventh of the economy. The total annual cost of health care was projected to rise to an astounding $1.6 trillion by the year 2000. Most Americans— some 74 percent according to a Wall Street Journal-NBC poll—felt strongly that an overhaul was needed.[14] But there were sharp differences about the kind and cost of the cure. Some called for a single-payer plan (like Canada's), under which the federal government would pay the health-care bills of all Americans. Others (including Heritage) recommended using tax credits to encourage consumers to buy their own health insurance on the open market.

In September 1993, President Clinton delivered a nationally televised address to Congress on "Health Security," the most important and controversial initiative of his presidency. He asked legislators and citizens to work with him to give "every American health security—health care that's always there, health care that can never be taken away."[15] A core element of the Clinton plan would force nearly every American to join a "health alliance," a quasi-governmental entity that would buy health insurance for everyone in a region. The alliance would have the power to negotiate doctors' fees, limit the plans that consumers could subscribe to (i.e., limit health-care services), and monitor the plans' performance.

Clinton's blueprint to change the nation's approach to health care was widely compared to the revolutionary New Deal policies of President Franklin D. Roosevelt. Like Roosevelt's sweeping programs of the 1930s, Clinton's proposed health-care reform, affecting 14 percent of the nation's economy, would "touch every American."[16] But unlike the 1930s, the America of the 1990s was skeptical about government. There was no strong support, even among congressional Democrats, for a gigantic, expensive new government program. And the Clinton design aimed to pay for itself without a broad-based tax, in sharp contrast to previous Democratic social programs, like Social Security and Medicare, which were at least meant to be financed by payroll taxes.

The very title of Clinton's proposal, "Health Security," recalled the Social Security Act of 1935. The president's reference to a "Health Security Card" that every American would receive if his "reforms" were enacted was an obvious variation on the Social Security card found in every citizen's pocket. As one Harvard social scientist put it, Clinton's invocation of Social Security "symbolized a faith that problems shared by a majority of Americans could be effectively addressed through a comprehensive initiative of the federal government."[17]

But this liberal shibboleth collided with the realities of experience and a new conservative age. One year later, on September 26, 1994, Senate Majority Leader George Mitchell abandoned his efforts to pass the Clinton health-care legislation, lamely blaming Republicans and special interests for blocking the bill (which was never voted on by either house). Senate Republican leader Bob Dole retorted that the fault lay with Democrats, who controlled both houses but "never had the votes for any reform plan."[18]

How could so timely and broadly supported an idea die so ignominious a death? There were several reasons why Health Security did not join Social Security as another pillar of our entitlement society. In the words of one journal, Clinton's proposal "suffered from being too sweeping and too difficult to explain to the public and to lawmakers."[19] Big business had initially pushed for reform, but later concluded that the Clinton plan would exact new taxes and even more regulations. Small business was concerned from the beginning that the costs of providing health insurance for employees would eliminate jobs and cut into profits needed to survive and grow.

Further, the Clinton administration and the Democratic leadership in Congress did very little to create bipartisan support for health-care reform until it was too late. "There were bipartisan bills around," said one political scientist, "but [Democratic leaders] rejected them out of habit and the feeling that they couldn't trust enough Republicans to come on board. They've gotten out of the habit of bipartisanship, and they paid for it."[20] Throughout, the White House kept insisting that the one principle it would not surrender was universal coverage, but it never explained satisfactorily how such coverage would be paid for.

The confidential, even secretive, operations of Hillary Clinton's Task Force, which conspicuously excluded Republicans and conservatives, elicited strong negative reactions, including a suit by the Association of American Physicians and Surgeons to make the group's meetings and records public. The health alliances at the core of the Clinton program were, moreover, attacked as bureaucratic, restrictive, and enormously susceptible to the expansion of federal power. A bumper sticker captured the public's skepticism:

National Health Care?
- The compassion of the IRS!
- The efficiency of the post office!
- All at Pentagon prices![21]

The Heritage Alternative

Since 1989, Stuart Butler, Edmund Haislmaier, and other Heritage representatives had been crisscrossing the country talking about health-care reform and describing the contents of the Heritage Consumer Choice Health Plan. It was a true comprehensive alternative to the liberal plan for a government-financed and -controlled health-care system. As Butler says, "there was no conservative proposal until we came along. In fact, conservatives had angered many Americans by only slowing the introduction of liberal programs without offering a responsible alternative."[22]

The Heritage plan would allow workers to purchase their own health insurance policies or pay directly for their health care, using the money their employers currently spent on premiums as a supplement to their own resources. In addition, employees would receive federal tax credits to ease family health expenses in place of the tax benefits now available for employer-sponsored coverage. At a minimum, the insurance policy would have to cover so-called catastrophic expenses. The tax credits—a central element of the Heritage plan—would be based on family size and medical expenses as a proportion of income, so that all families could afford decent coverage. The credits could also be used for contributions to a medical savings account.

All workers would have equal access to health-care coverage because the new tax code would treat the self-employed plumber the same as the Fortune 500 CEO. Families would choose and own their own insurance and, if they wished, medical savings accounts, rather than face tax penalties, as they do today, if they do not enroll in their employer's plan. As Ed Feulner said, employees would "shop wisely for health benefits since they would be paying for them."[23]

While the Heritage plan was favorably received by many conservatives and even a few on the left, it was dismissed by leading members of the liberal establishment. A typical comment was that of the *New York Times,* which argued that consumer-choice plans relied "on individuals to buy their own coverage. But complexity of insurance plans makes comparison shopping virtually impossible by anyone other than an experienced professional."[24]

Heritage responded to such elitist criticism by citing a consumer-oriented system that already existed and did work for more than nine million people—

the 32-year-old Federal Employees Health Benefits Program (FEHBP). It was Robert E. Moffit, the foundation's deputy director of domestic policy studies, who integrated FEHBP into the Heritage plan. As a federal employee during the Reagan administration, Moffit had benefited from its generous provisions. The program gave consumers a wide choice of health plans and advice on how to choose among rival plans. It promoted intense competition among health insurance carriers. It controlled costs and provided excellent benefits. And those enrolled (including the president, members of his cabinet and members of Congress) were quite satisfied with the system.

The FEHBP was the second key element of the Heritage plan. It provided a working example of consumer choice that significantly strengthened the foundation's approach to reform. Heritage could, and did, say reasonably, "What is available for Congress and its employees should be made available to every American family."[25]

Under the Heritage proposal, Butler explained in *Policy Review*, Americans would receive tax credits or vouchers to help them buy "the health plan of their choice," and they would be able to keep the same plan "no matter how often they changed jobs."[26] The overriding concern of people, Butler reported, was that at some time in the future—perhaps because of a change in jobs or a rapid rise in insurance rates—they might not be "able to afford or otherwise obtain access to the quality of care they count on today." Conservatives, he argued, could not just say that uninsurance was "an overstated problem." Every middle-class American, conservative or liberal, "knows a relative or neighbor who has faced financial disaster because they lacked adequate insurance. No one wants to be next."[27]

In the area of health care, Butler continued, people wanted "an 800-pound gorilla to represent their interests against the insurance companies and the hospitals." Which is why the Heritage plan concentrated on enabling Americans to turn to a labor union, a church, or a similar powerful organization "to bargain with health-care providers and to construct a family plan."[28]

Such an organization was the Federal Employees Health Benefits Program, which allows almost four hundred private insurance carriers to compete for the business of congressmen and their staffs along with about nine million federal employees, retirees, and dependents.[29] Individuals and families choose the benefits and insurance plans they want at the price they are willing to pay. Federal workers and retirees in any area can choose from among at least a dozen different plans.

Each year, the government contributes a set dollar amount to each individual or family for the purchase of a private insurance plan of their choice. If they choose a more expensive plan with more generous benefits, they pay directly for those benefits. If they pick a less expensive plan with less generous benefits, they pocket the savings. All of the plans include catastrophic coverage.

The federal government sets basic ground rules for competition among private insurers and ensures that the private companies meet fiscal solvency, consumer protection, and basic benefit requirements. FEHBP isn't perfect, but it provides wide choice, excellent cost control, good information for making choices, and portability.[30]

At the same time, Heritage admitted, its consumer choice plan did include some government regulation and was not 100 percent market-oriented. It let consumers choose, but from among government-approved insurance plans. Butler believed that new kinds of group plans would emerge from fraternal organizations, churches, unions, and other groups that could negotiate more effectively with an insurance company than an individual could. Haislmaier explained that the Heritage health-care proposal was constructed to achieve as much market-oriented reform as possible and to be adopted by Congress and the public.[31] Such a pragmatic approach was consistent with Ed Feulner's borrowed dictum not to let the perfect be the enemy of the good.

Conservative columnist James Jackson Kilpatrick described the foundation's health-care recommendations as "conservatively radical." Noting that the key element in the Heritage proposal was "the marketplace," Kilpatrick pointed out that both insurance carriers and health-care providers would be obliged to compete for the business of consumers. On the other side of the political spectrum, liberal commentator Michael Kinsley, writing in *The New Republic,* said that "Washington's leading right-wing think tank has produced the simplest, most promising, and, in important ways, most progressive idea for health care reform." Heritage would require all Americans, he wrote, to prove they have health insurance (just as almost all states require auto insurance), but no family "would have to pay more than 10 percent of its income on health care."[32]

In so doing, Kinsley argued, Heritage accepted the principle that society has a duty "to guarantee everybody affordable access to decent health
care.... If you're looking for universal health care protection," he concluded provocatively, "and at least a shot at cost control, the Heritage plan
looks pretty good. If you're looking for an excuse to expand the government, look elsewhere."[33]

Even before Kinsley approvingly characterized the Heritage plan as
"beyond socialism," some conservatives, led by John Goodman of the
National Center for Policy Analysis and analysts at the Cato Institute, had
questioned the foundation's approach. Goodman believed that ordinary
Americans were capable of shopping around in the medical marketplace
without any guidance from Washington and that government policy should
encourage self-insurance through Medical Savings Accounts (MSAs) or
Medisave. But unlike the Heritage plan, nobody would be required to
obtain any insurance coverage—a family could opt to be uninsured. And
the tax breaks would be available only for medical savings accounts (families would buy catastrophic coverage with their MSA funds).

In *Patient Power: Solving America's Health Care Crisis,* Goodman and coauthor Gerald Musgrave proposed that families receive funds to buy health
care through tax credits. But, unlike the Heritage plan, families would
not be required to purchase any particular amount of insurance. Instead,
they could choose a mix of insurance coverage, out-of-pocket payment,
and savings in tax-free MSAs. Goodman and Musgrave credited Jesse Hix-
son, a researcher at the American Medical Association, with the concept
of Medisave accounts, but they expanded the idea to address mounting
problems like Medicare, Medicaid, and the state and local regulation of
medicine and hospitals they have generated.[34]

Goodman argued that the Heritage plan would discourage self-insurance by locking in third-party payment for health care. And by endors-
ing so much government action, it stood exposed as being *too* political.
"The liberals [defending managed competition]," argued Goodman, "can
point to their plan and say that 'even the conservative Heritage Foundation says government must intervene' in many areas."[35]

Some of the foundation's strongest admirers, like Michael Joyce of
the Bradley Foundation and John Fund of the *Wall Street Journal,* believe
that Heritage "misjudged" the health-care debate and proposed too statist

a plan. Fund describes the foundation as "spectacularly wrong."[36] Libertarian John Hood, in his turn, has suggested that both the tax credits of Heritage *and* the Medical Savings Accounts of the National Center for Policy Analysis should be adopted. And indeed, legislation passed in August 1996 did establish a trial Medical Savings Account program. But because of liberal opposition in the Senate, led by Edward Kennedy (D-Mass.), the program was entangled in so much regulatory red tape that, as Ed Feulner says, "failure is almost certainly assured."[37]

Butler responds to the criticism by saying, "Other institutions may insist on 100 percent or nothing at all and will sometimes disagree with us. I say that if a proposal moves policy in a conservative direction, go for it." Regarding health-care reform, he asserts, "Conservatives were steadily losing a yard at a time. We could keep on losing ground or put forward a real alternative that contained real risk."[38]

He notes, too, that those who thought MSAs were a "magic bullet" seem to have given away the store. The legislation creating a very modest MSA program, he points out, also enacted features that these critics found unacceptable in the Heritage plan—such as insurance regulation—as well as insurance mandates and heavy fines on doctors.[39]

When the estimated savings of the Heritage plan were challenged, the foundation pointed out that they were the calculations of Lewin/ICF, a leading health-care econometrics firm, often described as the "Vatican" of health statistics. Lewin/ICF's imprimatur was the third key element, after tax credits and the FEHBP model, of the Heritage consumer choice proposal.

A Prescription for Big Government

Whatever the differences among conservatives about the right way to reform health care, they were united about the wrong way—President Clinton's "Health Security" plan. As a Heritage *Special Report* put it, what made the Clinton health plan so "dangerous" was that it relied on the rhetoric of "security, open markets, and free choice." But "the devil is in the details," said the report, which added up to one simple proposition: the plan was "actually the largest power grab made by the federal government ... since the New Deal."[40]

The Heritage analyst who provided the shocking details about the Clinton administration's attempt to control one seventh of the national economy was Robert E. Moffit, deputy director of domestic studies. Moffit, who has a Ph.D. and a Philadelphia cop father, is one of the few people in America who have read every word of Clinton's 1,342-page health-care reform plan. When the plan was formally presented to Congress in mid- November 1993, Moffit went home with a copy and, away from telephone calls and other office interruptions, started reading.

"I got up at 6 AM," he remembers, "had my first cup of black coffee, and made notes on my yellow pads until midnight. My wife brought me sandwiches when I got hungry. At the end of six days, I called Stuart [Butler] and said, 'They will never pass this.' "[41]

Well aware of how much was at stake—the course of the nation's economy, the future of the Clinton presidency, and the reputation of the foundation—Moffit was scrupulously careful in his 37-page analysis, "A Guide to the Clinton Health Plan." Giving "the administration the benefit of the doubt where I could," Moffit's devastating conclusions were never once challenged as misrepresenting the president's proposal in any way. In fact, as Harvard professor Theda Skocpol later conceded, the themes developed in the Moffit analysis "became staples in stepped-up nationwide attacks on the Health Security plan."[42]

The Heritage guide termed the Clinton plan "a massive top-down, bureaucratic command-and-control system" which would govern "virtually every aspect of the delivery and the financing of health care services" of Americans. It would mean either increased taxes or reduced care; not even sympathetic Democrats could say how much the Clinton approach would cost. The guide was particularly critical of the National Health Board, whose cost-containment decisions—including the pricing of insurance premiums and the enforcement of public and private spending limits—would not be subject to either judicial or administrative review. "Whatever may have been the intention of its framers," Moffit said, "the Clinton plan will eventually herd every aspect of private-sector medicine under the government's umbrella, and punish those that resist."[43]

The same day the guide was released, Heritage officials held a news conference on Capitol Hill with Senators Bob Dole, Trent Lott, Don Nickles, and other Republican leaders to discuss the Clinton proposal and alternatives such as the Consumer Choice Health Security Act of 1993, based on the Heritage plan. Newt Gingrich and Dick Armey were House cosponsors of the legislation. At the same time, the foundation hired David Winston, an experienced statistician, to calculate the financial impact of Clinton's "Health Security" on various groups. The strong positive reaction of Congress and the media to Winston's revealing data reinforced a foundation decision to do more primary research.

The foundation conducted a multiple-front publicity campaign. It encouraged its experts to testify before congressional committees, set up dozens of radio-TV interviews for its analysts, ran advertisements in selected publications, and informed its supporters through direct mail exactly what Clintonian "Health Security" would mean. One report began starkly:

> We all know socialism when we see it: The Berlin Wall. The Kremlin. Castro's Cuba. Red China. But what does it sound like? Try these: Standard Benefits Package. National Health Board. Regional Alliances. Managed Competition. Gatekeepers. Price Controls. These are the sounds of the Clinton health plan—and of socialized medicine.[44]

During the summer of 1994, as Congress considered options to the mortally wounded Clinton Health Security Act, Heritage worked early and late, publishing, during one three-week period in August, twelve major studies detailing the flaws in various health-care proposals. The foundation kept pushing hard for its "consumer choice" plan, trumpeting in one widely published ad: "Hillary Rodham Clinton Has It. George Stephanopoulos Has It. Donna Shalala and All Cabinet Members Have It. Ted Kennedy Has It. So Why Can't All Americans Have What They Have?"[45] "It" was the consumer-based Federal Employees Health Benefits Program, on which the Heritage health-care plan was based.

Ironically, most major sponsors of reform legislation, including President Clinton and Senator Kennedy, began to claim kinship to FEHBP. At a presidential news conference, Clinton claimed, "I have always thought that we ought to allow every American to buy into the Federal Employees Health Insurance" plan. As students of the Clinton presidency will not be surprised to learn, that was not an accurate assertion. In the original draft of the Clinton health plan, FEHBP was to be phased out and all federal personnel compelled to join regional alliances. A later draft called for the eventual abolition of FEHBP *after* the alliances were up and running. There was even a possibility that federal workers might not have to join the system at all if the results were not satisfactory. Why? Because government employees like postal workers have more political influence "than ordinary Americans."[46]

Only the Heritage plan, based on the principles of individual choice and market competition, truly followed the FEHBP model. The Heritage approach was ultimately supported by twenty-five senators (just five fewer than the Clinton plan had) and twenty-five congressmen, several state medical societies, a national association of nursing homes, and many major newspapers, magazines, and columnists. More than seven hundred doctors became personal advocates of the consumer-choice plan as members of The Heritage Foundation Physician's Council. Under the able chairmanship of Heritage trustee Dr. David R. Brown, the council has stayed active because as surely as there are winter colds and spring allergies, health-care reform will remain an issue that will not go away until it has been resolved. Heritage remains convinced that consumer choice must be at the center of any meaningful reform.

For her part, First Lady Hillary Rodham Clinton revealed how little her statist position had changed during a visit to Estonia in July 1996. She told reporters that government regulation of the U.S. health care system is needed and will happen eventually. Referring to the 1993 "reform" that was rejected by Congress and the American people, Mrs. Clinton insisted, "I think that basic model is still the right model."[47]

Towers of Babble

As it celebrated its twentieth anniversary in December 1993, Heritage could look back on its recent record with some satisfaction: That year's annual budget was just under $23 million (up from $20.1 million the previous year); *Policy Review* had an all-time-high circulation of 23,000; Heritage analysts had appeared on nearly eight hundred major radio programs and close to three hundred television news and public affairs shows; the foundation had sponsored major lectures by such prominent American and foreign public figures as Czech Prime Minister Vaclav Klaus, U.S.

Marine Corps Commandant General Carl E. Mundy Jr., Senator Phil Gramm (R-Tex.), Wisconsin Governor Tommy Thompson, Russell Kirk, William Bennett, and Jack Kemp; and Heritage had distributed more than 2.3 million paperback copies of *The Ruling Class,* Eric Felten's book on congressional reform. Rather than replay its late-1970s role as a member of the "loyal opposition" to President Carter, Heritage now stood at the core of the national policy debate.

The Economist pointed to a key reason for the foundation's central position: the think tank had replaced the university (which had become a "tower of babble") as the primary producer of new ideas. "In the 1960s," the prestigious British journal wrote, "it looked as if universities would establish a monopoly over the life of the mind, providing policies for politicians, sinecures for writers, ideas for journalists, and breakthroughs for industrialists. The 1980s changed all that. Governments in search of advice looked to think-tanks such as the Institute of Economic Affairs in Britain and The Heritage Foundation in the United States, rather than to Oxford or Harvard."[48]

The accuracy of this observation was borne out later that year when the freshman class of the historic 104th Republican Congress chose Heritage rather than Harvard to receive its orientation on how Washington works. A veteran House Republican, Henry Hyde of Illinois, summed up the foundation's place: "Heritage is the most influential of all the think tanks. Its work is scholarly, accurate, realistic.... If we relied on you before the Clinton election, you can imagine how we rely on you now. There are others, but Heritage is indispensable."[49]

Putting Families First

When President Clinton challenged critics in early 1993 to produce a better budget plan, the foundation did just that. Under the direction of Scott Hodge and Robert Rector, it issued a *Backgrounder,* "Putting Families First: A Deficit Reduction and Tax Relief Strategy." The strategy was based on three common-sense principles: families deserve to keep most of the money they earn; the private sector, not government, creates jobs; and spending money we don't have is the path to economic ruin. The study proposed limiting the annual growth in federal spending to 2 percent per year, thus wiping out the deficit in less than eight years.

Hodge's and Rector's plan offered American families much-needed tax relief in the form of a $500-per-child tax credit, fulfilling the president's own campaign promise of a middle-class tax cut. When Ohio Congressman John Kasich and other GOP leaders introduced the Heritage budget, Donald Lambro, the *Washington Times'* national political correspondent, praised it as one that "finally breaks free of the GOP's antigrowth, austerity policies of the 1990s and joins budget-cutting with pro-growth, pro-family tax cuts." Conservatives were not the only ones who liked the Heritage approach. Writing in the *Washington Post,* James Fallows, then Washington editor of *The Atlantic* (now editor of *U.S. News & World Report*), said that Heritage was "the only opponent of Clinton's plan to survive ... with its reputation enhanced. ..." He described the Heritage budget as "a real and relatively honest plan, one against which Clinton's should be compared."[50]

Legislative success on Capitol Hill requires months, even years of painstaking policy analysis, articulate spokesmen, creative public relations, and the right political dynamics. All these factors combined in the spring of 1993 *almost* to produce a significant victory for conservatives in the budget battle.

Here is how Heritage and its allies came so close in their effort to put families first.

On January 20, Scott Hodge issued "A Guide to the Families First Bills," outlining the various legislative options. Shortly thereafter, the House Republican leadership informed President Clinton that family tax relief would be included in their budget.

On February 2, Hodge and Mike Franc, then the foundation's House liaison, were invited to meet with the House sponsors of "Putting Families First" to discuss the upcoming budget debate. Congressman Vin Weber of Minnesota, a top conservative strategist, wrote in *National Review* that the Putting Families First plan was "the only major legislation proposed since President Clinton came to office which directly challenges the basic tenets of Clintonomics."

On February 24, Congressman John Kasich of Ohio called Hodge at home to ask for his help in designing an alternative budget based on Putting Families First. Within three days, Hodge and Robert Rector, along with House Budget Committee staffers, were working through the weekend to find spending cuts that would pay for a $500-per-child tax credit. They started with a list of $300 billion in possible reductions prepared by the Heritage staff.[51]

On March 4, Heritage distributed a memorandum from Hodge and Franc outlining the results of a foundation-commissioned survey: Americans favored family tax relief 3 to 1—even if it meant cuts in entitlement spending. The *Washington Post* ritualistically attacked the Kasich family tax-relief budget but had to concede its honesty: the authors "haven't fudged; they clarify a set of choices that too many past Republican budgets have obscured."[52]

The foundation immediately released two papers by Hodge and Rector that described the total value of the family tax credit in each congressional district, Democratic and Republican. Such a district-by-district breakdown had never been attempted before by any Washington think tank or, for that matter, by any government department or agency. The figures showed that, regardless of the *Washington Post*'s arguments, the tax credits benefited constituents in GOP and marginal Democratic districts, giving natural allies reason to unite behind the measure. Heritage distributed targeted releases to local newspapers and other media in each congressional district. The result was an avalanche of news stories around the country which helped swell grassroots support for the family tax credit. On March 10, for example, the Christian Coalition and other pro-family groups blanketed House offices with phone calls supporting the Kasich budget and the $500 tax credit.

The House then began floor debate on the widely divergent Clinton and Kasich budgets. Worried Democratic leaders held an emergency whip meeting and pleaded with their members not to vote for the Kasich proposal, while a rattled White House lobbied hard against the Republican alternative. Throughout the day-long debate, Heritage charts and statistics were used repeatedly by House Republicans. Kasich told Hodge that Democrats privately admitted they didn't know how to attack his plan. Meanwhile, the Republican staff of the Senate Budget Committee decided to include a $500 tax credit as the core of their alternative budget in the Senate.

On March 11, after intense pressure by the Democratic leadership, the Kasich budget was defeated by a vote of 245 to 165. But seven

Democrats voted for the Kasich bill, and it received "a higher vote than any House Republican alternative budget in the last twelve years."[53]

Conservatives were euphoric over the Putting Families First strategy. Although defeated, the Kasich plan put liberals on the defensive and gave conservatives in Congress and across the country a potent new tax and budget weapon. When Dick Armey and Newt Gingrich crafted the 1994 Contract with America, which sparked the Republican capture of Congress that fall, pledge number five was to submit the American Dream Restoration Act, which promised "a $500-per-child tax credit."[54]

Ending the Welfare State As We Know It

In the spring of 1994, President Clinton having done almost nothing to redeem his campaign pledge on welfare, Heritage senior analyst Robert Rector proposed a comprehensive reform of the federal welfare system that would end government subsidization of "self-destructive behavior" and reinforce "moral and cultural renewal." It was not just another paper but the culmination of years of thought and study by the veteran expert on welfare and family issues. Rector's seminal study, running 28 pages and 10,000 words, would serve as a model for future work in the area of cultural policy studies by Patrick Fagan and other Heritage analysts.[55]

Rector pointed out that more than ten thousand days—dating back to the mid-sixties—had passed since President Lyndon B. Johnson told the nation that "the days of the dole are numbered." Now, nearly thirty years later, the War on Poverty had cost American taxpayers more than $4.9 trillion (repeat, *trillion*) on antipoverty programs, about $305 billion in the last year alone. But instead of eliminating poverty, the Heritage analyst reported, the welfare system had actually "bribe[d] individuals into behavior—such as not marrying and having children out of wedlock—which is self-defeating to the individual, a tragic handicap for children, and ... increasingly a threat to society."[56]

What was needed, Rector insisted, was "a complete reversal of existing policies." A true welfare reform strategy would be based on three principles: promoting individual responsibility by requiring welfare recipients to give something in return for benefits; controlling welfare costs; and dramatically reducing the illegitimate birth rate by increasing the marriage rate. These principles were embodied in pledge number three of the 1994 Contract with America—the Personal Responsibility Act.[57] Specific reforms proposed by Rector included establishing "serious workfare," denying additional payments to mothers who had more children while on welfare, and putting a 3.5 percent cap on welfare spending growth.

All these ideas were included in the welfare reform legislation of 1996, which won Rector's praise as "historic ... the largest change in welfare since the early days of the War on Poverty." The Heritage analyst, frequently consulted by members of Congress as they wrote the bill, pointed out that the growth of welfare spending would be slowed, albeit by a 4.5 percent growth limit rather than the 3.5 percent recommended by Heritage. Illegitimacy would be reduced by three provisions, including extra funding to states that lowered the number of illegimate births without increasing abortions. And a specified percentage of AFDC recipients would be required to take private-sector jobs or to perform "community service work in exchange for benefits."[58]

It was the extraordinary, sustained impact of Robert Rector on welfare reform, Scott Hodge on government spending and the budget, and Daniel Mitchell on tax reform and economic growth that led one observer to dub them "the Untouchables."[59] Like their counterparts in the 1930s who sought to wipe out the corruptive influence of organized crime, the Heritage trio of policy analysts was committed to eliminating the corruptive influence of organized government on the individual, the family, and the community. Their increasingly original research and that of other analysts such as William Beach and Patrick Fagan, along with the foundation's finely honed marketing skills, enabled The Heritage Foundation to become, by the mid-1990s, a first-hand dealer in ideas that resonated across the country and around the world.[60]

Calculating Economic Freedom

No better example of Heritage original research can be found than its *Index of Economic Freedom*. It was Milton Friedman who first suggested— to Canada's Fraser Institute in the 1980s—that a country's economic freedom and growth ought to be measured. A few years later, investment adviser and Heritage trustee J. William Middendorf II urged the foundation to undertake the monitoring of economic freedom around the world. And then in the late 1980s, Edward L. Hudgins, then director of Heritage's Center for International Economic Growth, devised a set of criteria for members of Congress to judge how economically free different countries were and how they had prospered as a result of their freedom.

The analysis was initially intended to help Congress determine which nations should and should not receive U.S. foreign aid. Congressmen and ordinary citizens had long been vexed at seeing American assistance squandered by Third World countries. A paradox emerged: those nations that appeared to need U.S. help the most deserved it the least. Why? Because their government-controlled economies grossly misused the money. In the developing world, Heritage research suggested, the key to economic prosperity was not foreign aid but economic freedom. It was an idea that Ed Feulner had heard Professor Peter Bauer (later Lord Bauer of Clare Market) discuss at length at the London School of Economics in the 1960s. Feulner and Kim Holmes agreed that a comparative study of economic freedom around the world could "lay to rest once and for all doubts about whether economic freedom is integral to economic development."[61]

The first *Index of Economic Freedom*—coauthored by policy analyst Bryan T. Johnson and Thomas P. Sheehy, the Jay Kingham Fellow in International Regulatory Affairs—was published in early 1995. William Simon, former secretary of the Treasury and a Heritage trustee, predicted that the *Index* could be "the most important publication" ever issued by the foundation, even surpassing the various *Mandate for Leadership* reports that had helped guide the Reagan administration during the 1980s.[62]

For the first time in economic analysis, the *Index* examined the economies of 101 countries in ten essential areas: trade policy, taxation policy, government intervention in the economy, monetary policy, capital flow and foreign investment, banking policy, wage and price controls, property rights, regulation, and the black market. Each country's performance in each area was given a numerical score from 1 to 5 and totaled, with the lower the score, the better the economy. Tied for first place were Hong Kong and Singapore, with the United States ranking fourth. Only forty-three countries were found to have free or "mostly free" economies, while fifty had "mostly unfree," and eight had repressive economies.[63]

Washington Post columnist James K. Glassman noted the consistently high ratings of the smaller Asian countries. Hong Kong, Singapore, Taiwan, South Korea, Malaysia, and Thailand all ranked in the top twenty, and all featured low government spending and regulation, stable money, and strong property rights.[64] Other *Index* revelations included a number twelve ranking for the Czech Republic, well ahead of Hungary (32nd), often touted as the former communist nation most hospitable to business. Ireland, not generally known as a bastion of capitalism, ranked sixteenth, ahead of France (18th), Italy (20th), and Sweden (24th).

Johnson and Sheehy expanded the second edition of the *Index* (published in early 1996) to 364 pages, adding forty-one countries to their survey as well as a chapter on freedom and foreign investment. Hong Kong still led the free enterprise pack, but the United States dropped to seventh place. The authors explained that as countries became wealthier, they added welfare and other social programs that caused them to slip down "the scale of economic freedom," Hong Kong being a conspicuous exception.[65] Johnson and Sheehy also compiled a list of twenty-four countries—led by Botswana, Indonesia, Israel, Panama, and Portugal—that were becoming more economically free.

The *Index* has been used by conservative members of Congress, like Chairman Robert Livingston of the House Appropriations Committee, to produce at least one major legislative change. U.S. foreign aid was reduced significantly from $20 billion in fiscal year 1994 to less than $12 billion in fiscal year 1996. That $12 billion included $5 billion in assistance to Egypt and Israel, a sacrosanct commitment given the tense Middle East.[66]

Already cited in many popular and scholarly publications in the United States and abroad, the *Index* is ensured an even greater impact in the future. As the result of a series of discussions between the foundation's Herb Berkowitz and officials of the *Wall Street Journal,* the 1997 edition is titled *The Heritage Foundation/Wall Street Journal Index of Economic Freedom.*

Of the ten highest ranking countries in the 1996 edition, four received a worse score in the 1997 edition, five remained the same, and only one was better. These results substantiated a basic contention of the *Index:* "wealthy and economically free countries tend to reintroduce restrictions on economic freedom over time."[67]

The 1997 *Index,* reviewing the economies of 150 countries, found that

Nobel Laureate Friedrich Hayek, one of the 20th century's foremost economists, visited the U.S. in 1983 as a Heritage Distinguished Scholar.

Issues '88 *is introduced by Paul Weyrich, Heritage's first president, and Ed Feulner.*

Frank Shakespeare, Dr. Walter Judd, and William F. Buckley Jr., left to right, at the 1987 dedication of The Lawrence Fertig Boardroom.

CIA Director Bill Casey at Heritage in 1989 with Heritage trustee Clare Boothe Luce.

Heritage trustees and key foreign policy staffers in front of the Berlin Wall in 1990.

Former Prime Minister Margaret Thatcher presented the first Clare Boothe Luce Award to Ambassador Shelby Cullom Davis and Dr. Kathryn Davis at a 1991 dinner.

Now retired Vice President for Administration and Finance Peter E. S. Pover with Ambassador Holly Coors.

"Talk Radio" at Heritage in 1993: Kate O'Beirne, a former Heritage vice president and now Washington editor of National Review, *with former Senator Bob Dole, host Armstrong Williams, and Senator Orrin Hatch.*

Czech Premier Vaclav Klaus, a free-market advocate, speaking at Heritage in 1993.

Heritage trustee Jay and wife Betty Van Andel with Ed Feulner at the May 1992 dedication of the Van Andel Center.

Senate Foreign Relations Committee Chairman Jesse Helms delivered the 1996 B. C. Lee Lecture and met Jay Y. Lee, grandson of the founder of the Samsung Group. Making the introduction are Heritage Distinguished Fellow Richard Allen, right, and Ed Feulner.

Former Vice President Dan Quayle with Heritage foreign policy analysts Tom Moore, left, and Ariel Cohen.

House Majority Leader Dick Armey explains economic policy and family income to a standing-room-only Lehrman Auditorium audience in 1996.

Senate Majority Leader Bob Dole and House Speaker Newt Gingrich help launch Town Hall, the conservative Internet site, in 1995 with, from left, Ed Feulner, Ed Capano of National Review, *and Phil Truluck.*

Jeb Bush, son of the former president and a Florida business leader, joined the board of trustees in late 1995.

Discussing activities at the state level are, from left, Vice President Lew Gayner, Bob Moffit, Karen Miller, and Tom Atwood.

Longtime Heritage Distinguished Fellow Jack Kemp was Senator Bob Dole's running mate in the 1996 presidential campaign.

Heritage trustee Dick Wells and wife Marion meet House Speaker Newt Gingrich.

a narrow majority of the world's economies remained economically unfree. Seventy-two were free or mostly free (up from sixty-five the previous year) and seventy-eight were mostly unfree or repressed (slightly up from seventy-seven in 1996). Most of the world's freest economies were in North America and Europe, with the exception of the Asian "tigers" like Hong Kong, which again led the world in economic freedom. Still, as the *Detroit News* editorialized, "economic freedom is on the march in nearly every corner of the globe. Deregulation has replaced statism, much less Marxism, as the intellectual model of choice."[68]

Because of Hong Kong's first place standing, the two publishers formally released the 1997 *Index of Economic Freedom* at a news conference in the British colony, which reverted to mainland China in July 1997. The reaction of Fred Armentrout, publications director of the American Chamber of Commerce in Hong Kong, was typical: "The *Index* is now on everybody's calendar here."[69] It remains to be seen whether Hong Kong will remain Number One under Chinese Communist rule, particularly after the passing of paramount leader Deng Xiao-ping.

In a new chapter, George Melloan, international deputy editor of the *Wall Street Journal*, showed how the *Index* would be useful in "country risk analysis." Risk specialists can use the Heritage-Journal survey to single out those countries whose economic freedom makes them attractive investment opportunities.

Echoing conservative economists from Adam Smith to Milton Friedman—and a basic belief of The Heritage Foundation—Ed Feulner summed up the *Index*'s findings: "To be free is to grow and prosper."[70]

7

... And Newt Republicans

The story of the historic 1994 elections began more than a year earlier when House Minority Leader Robert Michel of Illinois announced that he would retire at the end of that Congress. Within a week, Newt Gingrich, who ranked second in the party as Republican Whip, had obtained the support of a majority of House Republicans to succeed Michel as party leader.

Gingrich, who had been talking about a Republican Congress since coming to Washington in 1979, immediately began reshaping the party in the House and crafting a campaign strategy to nationalize House races. The centerpiece of Gingrich's strategy was an event to be held on the steps of the U.S. Capitol at which Republican candidates, challengers as well as incumbents, would pledge to support "a unified party platform." Gingrich asked Congressman Dick Armey of Texas, chairman of the Republican Conference, to assemble task forces to develop different parts of the platform. The task forces relied on the advice of conservative public policy groups like The Heritage Foundation and on the guidance of polls and surveys supervised by Frank Luntz, a brash young pollster who had worked for third-party presidential aspirant Ross Perot in 1992.[1] As former college professors and intellectuals, Gingrich and Armey instinctively turned to congenial think tanks to help them draft their political platform.

More than three hundred Republican congressional candidates signed the Contract with America in September 1994, pledging to bring ten specific bills (which would balance the budget, cut taxes, reduce regulations, and pass a line-item veto) to the House floor for a vote within the first one hundred days of a Republican House. Flustered Democrats, with President Clinton leading the way, immediately attacked the contract and, by giving it nationwide publicity, fell into Gingrich's trap. Although many voters did not know all the details of the contract, they did realize they had "a clear choice" between politics-as-usual and a new and seemingly more open and responsive way.[2]

The 1994 elections were in fact a referendum—Reagan's limited government policies of the 1980s (clearly reflected in the Contract with America) versus Clinton's expanded government policies of the 1990s (represented most tellingly by his rash attempt to bureaucratize the nation's health-care system). The electorate decisively rejected Clinton and the Democrats.

After losing the presidency in 1992, Republicans came roaring back in 1994 to capture the U.S. House of Representatives for the first time in forty years, take back control of the U.S. Senate after an interim of eight years, and wind up with twenty-nine governors, representing 70 percent of the country's population. Not one Republican seeking reelection lost in the Senate, the House, or a state capital. Newt Gingrich was the new (and euphoric) Speaker of the House, Bob Dole, once again the Senate Majority Leader. Both men had been frequent visitors to Heritage over the years. Ed Feulner remembers Gingrich at a brown-bag luncheon in 1979, talking about the coming impact of computers in the home: "He was really a visionary."[3] It had been logical that Heritage should ask the fiery reformer from Georgia to write the foreword for its 1988 look at Congress.

In *The Imperial Congress,* co-published by The Heritage Foundation and the Claremont Institute, Gingrich declared: "Every citizen should be concerned about the arrogance and corruption of the present-day Congress. At stake is the liberty of the American public. We must reform Congress to make it truly representative once again."[4]

One week after the remarkable 1994 Republican victory, Newt Gingrich gave his first major address as the future House Speaker at the largest President's Club meeting in The Heritage Foundation's history. "Heritage,"

Gingrich said generously, "is without question the most wide-reaching conservative organization in the country in the war of ideas, and one which has had a tremendous impact not just in Washington, but literally across the planet."[5]

Heritage had been feeding ideas to present and future members of Congress throughout 1994, beginning in May with a first-of-its-kind briefing book for congressional candidates. Conceived by Kate O'Beirne, cleared by the foundation's legal counsel, and edited by Peter J. Ferrara, *Issues '94* analyzed key national issues from federal spending and taxes to foreign policy and congressional reform. Post-election interviews proved that dozens of candidates constantly used the 296-page book. Fred Thompson, elected to the U.S. Senate from Tennessee that year, liked to open *Issues '94* and read from it to reporters. Successful congressional challenger Ron Lewis of Kentucky wrote that "Heritage provided the best, most accurate facts and figures that I used in my campaign. They were right on target every time."[6]

Shutting Out Harvard

The conservative character of the 1994 Republican sweep was confirmed when the liberal Kennedy School of Government at Harvard University canceled its orientation conference for new members of Congress for the first time since it had launched the program in 1972. The reason was simple: seventy-three of the eighty-six newcomers were not only Republican but "terminally conservative" and uninterested in flying to Boston at government expense to hear John Kenneth Galbraith and other liberal dinosaurs pontificate about the virtues of Keynesian economics and other statist shibboleths. A headline in the *Boston Globe* lamented, "New Republican order dims Harvard's star."[7]

Instead, about sixty new members traveled to Baltimore to attend a three-day orientation meeting cosponsored by the Heritage Foundation and Empower America. Kate O'Beirne had suggested the idea of a conservative school for freshman congressmen in 1992 as a direct challenge to the long-running Harvard program, which had official standing with the House and received government funding. "We asked ourselves," explained O'Beirne, "why shouldn't we compete?"[8] The 1992 meeting, cosponsored by Heritage, the Free Congress Foundation, and the Family Research Council, was held in Annapolis, Maryland, and attracted about thirty new Republicans. (Democratic House Speaker Thomas Foley reportedly told the handful of Democrats who expressed an interest in attending to forget it or they would not get preferred committee assignments.)[9] Encouraged by the enthusiastic response, Heritage prepared for a much larger turnout for the 1994 meeting. The foundation's optimism was spurred by its president, Ed Feulner, who boldly—and presciently—predicted in September 1994 that Republicans would pick up fifty seats in the House and regain control of the Senate. "Some people thought I was nuts," he recalls.[10]

At the Lord Baltimore Hotel, the new members heard Ralph Reed of the Christian Coalition, former Education Secretary William J. Bennett, former HUD Secretary Jack Kemp, social scientist Charles Murray, atomic physicist Edward Teller, talkmeister Rush Limbaugh, and other conservative panelists and speakers from the Hudson Institute, the Hoover Institution, and the Cato Institute. "Just think," joked Vin Weber, a former Minnesota congressman and codirector of Empower America, "if you were at Harvard you could be listening to Michael Dukakis." There was a roar of laughter from the Republican rookies.[11]

Limbaugh was presented a "Majority Makers" pin, the emblem of the new members. "My interest in politics was partially fueled by people like Rush Limbaugh," said Congressman-elect Jon Christensen (R-Nebr.). "Tonight it is a real opportunity for me to say thank you."[12] In his remarks, a surprisingly humble Limbaugh insisted that radio hosts like himself "only validate what's in people's hearts and minds already.... I'm in awe of you," he told the freshmen-elect. "You are the ones who took the risks. You are the ones who ran for office. I'm just a media guy."[13]

Ed Feulner told the incoming members to consider The Heritage Foundation their "weapons factory" in the battle over ideas. "As you begin to fill your staff," he said, "think of Heritage as a resource," adding that the foundation could and would provide witnesses for hearings, "translate your ideas into legislation," and even supply "experts" for town hall meetings back home.[14]

Congressman Martin R. Hoke (R-Ohio), who attended both the Heritage and Harvard programs in 1992, characterized the courses at Harvard as "eggheady" and "somewhat condescending." In contrast, the

Heritage sessions were "much more nuts and bolts, practically oriented toward the implications of policy decisions on people's lives."[15] It was clear which approach Hoke, and the congressmen-elect who came to Baltimore in 1994, preferred.

Not content to rest on its laurels, in mid-December Heritage released a 130-page guide for new members of Congress, with policy recommendations on everything from budget cutting to national defense. Coeditors Stuart Butler and Kim Holmes explained that the members' guide was based on the "ideological" nature of the 1994 elections. The American people, they asserted, wanted (1) "A more limited federal government," with control of resources returned to the states and the people; (2) "A thorough overhaul of the way Congress functions"; and (3) "Radical changes in programs that have failed," like welfare and crime control.[16]

As usual, the foundation's analysts did not pull their programmatic punches. "Pork-buster" Scott Hodge urged lawmakers not to allow themselves to be talked out of a balanced-budget amendment by those who "will challenge conservatives to name the specific budget cuts before a vote has even taken place." The amendment, he insisted, was not a *list* of cuts but a *rule* for developing budgets and limiting the behavior of government. Once such a limit was imposed by state ratification, Hodge said, "it is up to Congress to change its budget rules and make spending decisions to comply with the amendment."[17]

Overhauling the House

The House of Representatives of the 104th Congress demonstrated that it was a different kind of House by staying in continuous session for fourteen and a half hours on its first day of business, January 4, 1995. When the final gavel sounded, the House had adopted a far-ranging series of new rules calculated to produce a more efficient and open national legislature. Of fifteen reforms, thirteen were recommended by The Heritage Foundation, going back as far as Gordon Jones's 1988 *The Imperial Congress*.

Those reforms included: requiring a supermajority for tax increases; cutting committee staff by one third and eliminating three full committees and twenty-five subcommittees; limiting the terms of committee chairmen and the Speaker; and opening all committee meetings (unless classified) to the public and the news media. Observers had recently compared the House committee structure to "a feudal system" in which competing chairmen exercised excessive and arbitrary authority. GOP reforms like term limits for chairmen were designed to curb that power.

By creating a Congress, wrote David Mason, in which there are "few hiding places" and even fewer excuses for failing to "advance an advertised agenda," the Contract with America might prove to be a more important reform than any of its specific provisions.[18]

Rolling Back and Rebuilding

As the *New York Times* wrote, these were "heady days" for Heritage and other conservative institutions in Washington. For the first time in decades, they could work with a congressional majority "to change the role of the federal government."[19] In April 1995, the foundation published *Rolling Back Government: A Budget Plan to Rebuild America,* which proposed to eliminate nine cabinet departments, overhaul Medicare, cut taxes by $152 billion, and shift many federal responsibilities to the states and the private sector. According to editor Scott Hodge, the proposals would save nearly $800 billion and balance the federal budget by the year 2000—a good two years earlier than the deadline later designated by Congress and President Clinton in their historic agreement to balance the budget.

Rolling Back Government used strategies and ideas developed by Heritage over the years but never implemented, not even during the halcyon Reagan era. "With the arrival of the Republican Congress," said Stuart Butler, "the momentum's come back to us. The Contract with America was an important step, but we see it as transitional." As usual, Butler explained, Heritage was trying "to push the envelope while staying within the envelope."[20]

Commenting on the Heritage analysis, management expert Peter Drucker wrote that "'really re-inventing government' will remain the central and urgent political 'hot button' in the United States—and in all developed countries—for years to come."[21]

The emboldened foundation then buckled its belt and took on one of the most sacred cows in Washington—federal farm policy. In his 1964 presidential campaign, Barry Goldwater had been pilloried by Democrats

and the media for even suggesting the gradual elimination of farm subsidies. Thirty-one years later, Heritage released *Freeing America's Farmers:
The Heritage Plan for Rural Prosperity* by John Frydenlund, with significant
help from senior fellow David Winston and policy analyst John Barry. The
analysis showed that ending agricultural subsidies and related programs
(initiated during the Great Depression of the 1930s) would help American farmers compete more efficiently in the world market and would
boost the economy of rural America by $35 billion over five years.

The study included 10 pages of charts showing the state-by-state impact
of the foundation's reform proposal on net income. Senators and congressmen referred frequently to *Freeing America's Farmers* in the ensuing
debate which culminated, in March 1996, in the Freedom to Farm Act, a
market-based system under which crop subsidies would cease by 2002.
"For the first time in more than six decades," Frydenlund said, "farmers
will grow for the market, not for the government."[22]

Telecommunications Unbound

When Alexander Graham Bell patented the telephone on March 7, 1876,
Heritage analyst Adam D. Thierer has pointed out, few Americans, including Bell himself, realized how vital the telephone would become to our
nation. Western Union, the leading telegraph company of the time,
declined to buy the Bell patents for a modest $100,000, believing the new
machine was just a novelty. But the impact of the telephone on American
business and society has been revolutionary, almost eliminating time and
distance and uniting a diverse people and an immense nation.

Now, according to Thierer, we are on the verge of a new era in telecommunications that will end what he calls "regulatory apartheid." In late
1995, after two years of hearings and legislative debate (heavily influenced
by Thierer's research), Congress passed and President Clinton signed a
new law that will afford consumers as much choice in telecommunications as "in cereals, detergents, automobiles or other products."[23]

Specifically, the reform legislation allows the so-called Baby Bells to
offer long-distance telephone service; ends the Baby Bells' monopoly on
local telephone service; lets phone companies compete with cable providers
in the area of video services; and allows utility companies to enter the

communications business. But the act fails to deregulate the important wireless sector of the telecommunications industry—things like cellular, broadcast, and satellite services—and it does not eliminate a subsidy system that artificially raises the cost of telephone services.

Washington nevertheless accepted the obvious lesson of six decades of telecommunications regulation: "Heavy-handed, centrally planned, bureaucratic regulatory micromanagement is no substitute for open markets and consumer choice."[24]

1.2 Billion Operations a Second

Heritage's research capabilities have been significantly enhanced with the 1995 addition of a highly sophisticated supercomputer—a Viper 1000 capable of analyzing economic and social databases as fast as the Office of Management and Budget and the Congressional Budget Office. The Viper 1000 can process data at the phenomenal speed of 1.2 billion operations per second, about one thousand times faster than the typical Pentium chip computer. As a result, Heritage analysts were able to tabulate the costs of Clinton's proposed increases in income and gasoline taxes for every state, county, and congressional district in the country. They were also able to show how much additional disposable income families in each state, county, and congressional district would have under Heritage's alternative budget plan.

With Ed Feulner's enthusiastic support, Olin Fellow William Beach and Heritage Fellow David Winston began overseeing the foundation's next logical step in information-building—the creation of a free-market econometric model for the United States, something that does not currently exist. The building of the computer equipment and the databases is a three-year, multi-million-dollar project. If the foundation is successful—and Beach admits that it's an open question—Heritage will be able to operate, in Stuart Butler's words, as "the CBO of the conservative movement."[25] Already, such congressional leaders as House Majority Leader Dick Armey and Senator Spencer Abraham of Michigan are asking Heritage for econometric analysis of legislation.

Feulner's commitment to high tech led him in 1996 to hire Grace-Marie Arnett as the foundation's vice president for information marketing. One of

Arnett's first ideas was a series of two-sided, colored, 3 x 9-inch cards that summarize Heritage papers on taxes, welfare reform, health care, and other issues in short, punchy sentences. The cards, says Arnett, have been "wildly successful" with members of Congress and their staffers. House Speaker Newt Gingrich held one up on CNN's "Larry King Live" and quoted from it.[26]

Another technique is the "minibook," which is a condensation of a popular Heritage study or book that is given free to Heritage supporters and friends. Titles include *The Flat Tax: Freedom, Fairness, Jobs and Growth* by Daniel Mitchell (400,000 copies); *Strangled by Red Tape: The Heritage Foundation Collection of Regulatory Horror Stories* (400,000 copies); *The Ruling Class: Inside the Imperial Congress* by Eric Felten (2.3 million copies); and *Issues '96: A Pocket Guide to Election Issues* (350,000 copies).

New electronic products will be developed for what Arnett calls "the digital age." And there will be increased use of market research and focus groups by polling specialists like the Wirthlin Group. Amid all the innovations the foundation is not neglecting its most important audience — Congress. Executive summaries of selected Heritage studies are sent every week to members of Congress to trigger comment and action.[27]

Another significant personnel change in 1996 was the naming of Elaine Chao, outgoing president of United Way of America and director of the Peace Corps under President Bush, as a Distinguished Fellow. Chao was appointed United Way president in 1992 when the charity was in the midst of a financial and ethical crisis. She soon restored public trust by instituting new financial and management controls and other reforms. "This wasn't affirmative action," says Ed Feulner. "Elaine shares our views and our perspective. She is a tremendous asset for Heritage."[28]

A $5.4 Trillion Failure

"To understand what Republicans are trying to do about welfare, don't look to Newt Gingrich. Watch Robert Rector." So counseled the *Wall Street Journal*.[29] Throughout 1995, Heritage's senior analyst on welfare and family policy not only was in the middle of the contentious issue of welfare reform but frequently drew up the legislative battle plans for conservatives.

While liberals offered only nominal changes in the complex mix of seventy-seven overlapping federal welfare programs, Heritage recommended sweeping changes, many of them developed by Rector and his colleague, Patrick Fagan, the William H. G. FitzGerald Fellow in Family and Cultural Issues. The reforms were based in large part on the pioneering study *America's Failed $5.4 Trillion War on Poverty*, written by Rector with William F. Lauber. To dramatize just how astronomical, how galactic five-and-a-half trillion dollars is, Rector and Lauber pointed out that "for $5.4 trillion one could purchase every factory, all the manufacturing equipment, and every office building in the U.S." But that was not all. "With the leftover funds, one could go on to purchase every airline, every railroad, every trucking firm, the entire commercial maritime fleet, every telephone, television, and radio company, every power company, every hotel, and every retail and wholesale store in the entire nation."[30]

And yet, despite the $5.4 trillion that had poured out of Washington since 1965, low-income families had disintegrated, illegitimacy had soared, and crime in the inner city had multiplied. Changes recommended by Heritage included: limiting the length of time a family can be on welfare; requiring young teenage mothers to live with their families rather than setting up government-subsidized households of their own; returning primary responsibility for public assistance to state and local governments through "block grants"; and ending the entitlement, Aid to Families with Dependent Children, the federal government's largest and most demoralizing welfare program. The last proposal was accepted by Congress and President Clinton in their welfare reform compromise of August 1996.

At the same time, Patrick Fagan and Denis Doyle, senior fellow in education, were addressing the moral implications of the nation's failed urban policy. Working with Republican Congressmen J. C. Watts of Oklahoma and James Talent of Missouri, Fagan, Doyle, and Rector helped develop the American Community Renewal Act. The legislation was intended to encourage charitable giving and increase education scholarships in the inner city while eliminating federal restrictions against funding faith-based drug- and alcohol-abuse programs.

The positive role of religion in society was convincingly documented in 1996 by Fagan's widely quoted study, "Why Religion Matters: The Impact of Religious Practice on Social Stability" (the studiously secular *Washington Post* devoted a full page to it).[31] Pointing to almost 100 social science studies, some going back more than twenty years, Fagan declared, "the time is ripe for a deeper dialogue on the contributions of religion to the welfare of the nation." The studies were in agreement that regular religious practice produced healthier, happier, more stable individuals and families. Fagan concluded that "Congress and the courts have crowded religion out of the public square. It is time to bring it back."[32]

Applied Tocqueville

In the first hundred days of the Republican 104th Congress, Heritage analysts testified more than a hundred times on Capitol Hill, held more than a hundred briefings for members of Congress, and granted hundreds of radio, television, and newspaper interviews. Heritage people were almost as much in demand as the Beatles on their first American tour. A glorious and bloodless revolution seemed to be at hand, with historian-revolutionary Newt Gingrich essaying the combined roles of James Madison, Vladimir Lenin, Alvin Toffler, Peter Drucker, and Alexis de Tocqueville. It was the best of times for conservatives since the election of Ronald Reagan in 1980, and maybe even better.

While Heritage experts were showing how electoral promises and slogans could be transformed into viable bills and resolutions, Adam Meyerson, vice president for educational affairs, was quietly preparing a new look and a new mission for *Policy Review*, one that inevitably affected its parent, The Heritage Foundation.

For all its emphasis on the quick response and modern methods of marketing, Heritage remains an institution of ideas, of conservative principles—free enterprise, limited government, individual freedom, traditional American values, and a strong national defense. But with the Cold War won and communism no longer a clear and present danger, the question obtrudes: how do you unite the disparate elements of the conservative movement in furtherance of those principles? After months of discussion with Ed Feulner and other senior Heritage managers and conservatives across the country, Adam Meyerson concluded that the best possible unifying mission for the movement was the restoration of American citizenship. That meant rebuilding the institutions of civil society: families, neighborhoods, religious institutions, schools, civic associations, businesses, and local governments. In the words of Heritage trustee and author Midge Decter, there had to be an emphasis on "what is right and wrong in our nation."

"Sixty years of liberalism," Meyerson wrote in an open letter to *Policy Review* readers, "have left America's social fabric in tatters."[33]

Meyerson described the magazine's new mission as "Applied Tocqueville," in honor of the mid-nineteenth-century French aristocrat Alexis de Tocqueville, whose *Democracy in America* is one of the most quoted books among modern conservatives. An admiring Tocqueville traced America's socio-economic-political success to its limited national government, active citizen involvement in local government, strong families, imaginative entrepreneurs, and countless voluntary associations. *Policy Review*, Meyerson promised, would present "the success stories of institutions and civic leaders today who are carrying on this tradition."[34]

The phrase "American citizenship," he explained, combined *freedom* and *responsibility*, the two central themes of modern conservatism. Both are essential for the good society. "Freedom without responsibility cannot endure," he wrote; and "responsibility without freedom cannot create." Given the perilous state of American culture, he argued, the restoration of American citizenship was "essential" to the nation and the conservative movement. Such a cause, he said, would appeal to all conservatives—libertarians, religious conservatives, "growth-and-opportunity conservatives," and nationalists.[35]

A "major influence" on Meyerson's thinking was Michael Joyce, president of the Bradley Foundation, who in December 1992 articulated his vision for conservatism in the next generation:

> Americans are eager to seize control of their daily lives again— to make critical life choices for themselves, based on their own common sense and folk wisdom—to assume once again the status of proud, independent, self-governing citizens intended for them by the Founders.[36]

There was also a practical reason for *Policy Review*'s new mission. When the magazine was launched in 1977, there was no *Weekly Standard*, no *Washington Times*, no talk radio, and *The American Spectator* had a circulation of 20,000. But by 1996, there was serious intellectual competition everywhere. "We could no longer be a thought leader," says Meyerson, "as a generalist publication." With the end of the Cold War, an article by anti-communist UNITA leader Jonas Savimbi wasn't the model for the future, but an article about McDonald's "as the best job producer" in America was. By emphasizing "the private sector and local solutions to problems," *Policy Review* would demonstrate that conservative ideas can make a difference anywhere in America.[37]

Accepting the counsel of Midge Decter and others not to make too dramatic a change, *Policy Review* retained its name but added a new subtitle, *The Journal of American Citizenship*. It also increased its frequency to six times a year, redesigned its cover, and added special features like "Profiles in Citizenship" and "Town Square."

As an example of what the federal government could do to encourage a rebirth of civil society, the journal published an article by Senator Daniel J. Coats (R-Ind.), who described the package of nineteen bills he had introduced under his ambitious "Project for American Renewal." The centerpiece and symbol was the Comprehensive Charity Reform Act, which would allow individuals to donate $500 of their tax liability to private antipoverty organizations. The measure, explained Coats, would take about 1.5 percent of current federal spending—about $25 billion—and "provide it directly to [private] institutions actually winning their war on poverty, armed with spiritual vitality, tough love, and true compassion." Because government had helped undermine civil society—by, for example, replacing fathers with welfare checks and dismissing religious volunteers as "amateurs"—it should now atone by taking the side of people and institutions that "are rebuilding their own communities."[38]

The End of Big Government?

Following President Clinton's dramatic declaration in his 1996 State of the Union message that "the era of big government is over," Ed Feulner surprised many in the conservative movement by not echoing *The Weekly Standard*, which trumpeted, "WE WIN." Normally among the first to accentuate the positive, Heritage's president described Clinton's admission as, yes, "a victory" but not a "surrender" in the war of ideas. He pointed out, for example, that Clinton's first request to the returning Congress was for $8 billion in new federal spending in the current fiscal year.[39]

At the same time, Feulner disagreed with those conservatives who lamented that the 104th Congress had so far failed to pass term limits, a balanced-budget amendment, entitlement reform, and an end to the National Endowment for the Arts, the Legal Services Corporation, or the Department of Commerce. "We have made real progress," he insisted. "The American people and the tide of history remain on our side." But, inasmuch as it took sixty years to build "the liberal dynasty in this country," he said, it cannot be undone "in a year."[40]

As he frequently does in his annual State of Conservatism analysis, Ed Feulner provided a historical background on the conservative movement. In the 1950s, he pointed out, conservatism was "an intellectual movement," with Friedrich A. Hayek, Russell Kirk, Milton Friedman, William F. Buckley, and others leading the way. In the 1960s, Barry Goldwater and then Ronald Reagan made conservatism "a political movement." He called Reagan's 1964 televised speech for Goldwater "a defining moment" for American conservatives.[41]

Conservatism's next step was to become "a governing movement," beginning with Reagan's two terms as president and gaining momentum in 1994 when the liberal "stranglehold" on Congress was sundered. But legislative governance, Feulner acknowledged, was not easy. Besides, most conservatives had been "backbenchers" for so long, they did not know how to govern. Mistakes had been made. "Perhaps," said Feulner, "too much was attempted. Perhaps compromise was dismissed too easily in the fervent desire for real change. Perhaps the message became too unfocused and thus susceptible to redefinition by the special interests and the media."[42]

The Heritage president was clearly referring to the government shutdowns that occurred in late 1995 and early 1996 when Republican leaders in Congress underestimated President Clinton's determination to stand firm in the battle over the 1995 budget; the multi-million-dollar advertising campaign of the AFL-CIO which helped mislead many Americans, especially senior citizens, into believing that Republicans wanted to "cut" Medicare; and the failure of the GOP to counter effectively the bully pulpit of the White House.

The 104th Congress watched its public approval sink from a high of 52 percent in December 1994, shortly before its members took office, to

41 percent in June 1995 to just the high 20s in January 1996. By October 1996, moreover, Speaker Gingrich had a personal approval rating of only 27 percent and a disapproval rating of 51 percent.[43] Conservative columnist Mona Charen, however, disputed the contention that Republicans had misinterpreted the 1994 results as "weariness with liberal governance." Rather, Republicans made several major "tactical errors" that cost them dearly.[44]

To begin with, Republicans failed to use their majority status to educate the public. They assumed, erroneously, that "the case for cutting government did not need to be made—again." Congressional hearings detailing "government waste and duplication" would have helped the electorate understand what Congress was attempting to do. Second, Republicans did not concentrate on one or two key reforms that would have delineated the clear differences between the two political parties. They tried to do too much too quickly. Third, Republican leaders became "too wrapped up in their own egos." Charen referred to the famous complaint by Gingrich when he was not given an up-front seat on Air Force One to talk with the president.[45] (Far more damaging, as the two-year deliberations of the House Ethics Committee showed, was Speaker Gingrich's insistence on continuing to teach a college course on American civilization when key conservatives were urging him to get his priorities straight.)

Finally, Republicans misjudged Clinton's proclivity for twisting the truth to win the debate over budget showdowns and government closures. The president was able to convince the public that Republicans wanted to "cut" rather than reform Medicare. Still, Charen argued, Clinton was obliged to adopt GOP proposals, from a balanced budget to ending automatic benefits for welfare mothers, proving that Republican issues were "winners" rather than losers.[46]

And then there was the unhappy spectacle of the 1996 presidential nominations, with conservatives cutting each other up and characterizing venerable ideas like the flat tax as "nonsense." In his State of Conservatism essay, Feulner noted with regret that the long-held conservative belief in free trade had weakened. The solution to "lost jobs," he insisted, was expanding American exports, "not shutting U.S. borders to trade."[47]

But conservatism's "slow progress" in 1996 notwithstanding, Feulner said, its future remained far brighter than that of liberalism, which Feulner dismissed as "increasingly irrelevant." He offered examples of liberal excess such as the farcical war of the Equal Employment Opportunity Commission (EEOC) against Hooters, a restaurant chain that hires only buxom young women to wait on its customers. EEOC decided that Hooters owed at least $22 million in back pay to men denied the opportunity to work there. As one observer wrote, "Civil rights crusades have gone from allowing blacks to sit at lunch counters to allowing government employees to dictate the cup size of the person who serves lunch."[48]

Conservatism would prevail, Feulner argued, because it was grounded in "sound economic principles and a realistic understanding of human nature, not wishful thinking." He concluded by quoting Sophocles: "One must wait until the evening to see how splendid the day has been." Feulner argued that for all the mistakes and lost chances, the hour was early and the day, for conservatism, would "turn splendid."[49]

The Winner—and Still President

But first the day turned splendid for Bill Clinton, who won an easy reelection victory over Republican challenger Bob Dole in November 1996. Widely dismissed as a one-term president following the triumph of the GOP in 1994, the president engineered the most remarkable comeback of his roller-coaster career.

In the lowest turnout of eligible voters in seventy years, Clinton received 45.6 million votes to Dole's 37.9 million, a solid 49 percent to 41 percent advantage in the popular vote. But the president's electoral margin was overwhelming—379 to 159, with 270 electoral votes needed to win. Reform Party candidate Ross Perot received 7.9 million votes, less than half of his 1992 total, and no electoral votes.

The election results were filled with contradictions. Clinton was the first Democratic president since Franklin Delano Roosevelt to win reelection and the first Democrat to be elected with an opposition Congress. The president carried thirty-three states to his Republican challenger's seventeen states, but Dole won more counties than the president, 1,580 to 1,534.

Clinton's victory notwithstanding, the results of numerous state ballot initiatives confirmed that the era of big government was over. According to the *Wall Street Journal,* antitax groups achieved "a clean sweep of major initiatives" in Florida, Nevada, Oregon, South Dakota, and California. And despite a singularly vicious opposition, Californians also passed the California Civil Rights Initiative (CCRI).[50]

While campaigning as a champion of the "vital center" in 1996, the president in reality endorsed a conservative agenda that mirrored his campaign promises four years earlier: a balanced budget, a focus on family values, a get-tough attitude toward crime, an end to big government, and honest welfare reform.

For all the contradictions of the election, the nation was still locked, according to a *New York Times* headline, on a "Rightward Path, Leaving Liberals Beside [the] Road." Clinton won, political correspondent R. W. Apple concluded, by deliberately running as Ronald Reagan, "peddling the politics of good humor" and "brazenly" borrowing the 1984 Reagan slogan, "It's morning in America."[51] Clinton's mimicry acknowledged the new reality: Ronald Reagan had reshaped American politics by tapping the conservative instincts of the people. Call it the "Reagan-morphing" of Bill Clinton.

Another Chance

Despite the most virulent anti-Congress rhetoric since 1948, Republicans retained control of the House, albeit narrowly, and increased their margin in the Senate. The GOP's 1996 victory has been compared to the bloody Battle of the Bulge during World War II when the Germans counterattacked fiercely but failed to overrun the American army. When their offensive failed, the Germans knew that the war was over. Conservatives are optimistic that Republicans can make major gains in the 1998 congressional elections. In the meantime, the new lineup in the House is 227 Republicans, 207 Democrats, and one Independent who generally votes with the Democrats. The GOP had 235 seats in the old House. The breakdown in the new Senate is 55 Republicans, 45 Democrats (a pick-up of two for the GOP).

Reelected Speaker of the House (the first Republican in sixty-eight years to lead consecutive House sessions), Newt Gingrich avoided revolutionary rhetoric, talking instead of forging "a broad, center-right coalition," and pledged to find "common ground" with President Clinton. Gingrich portrayed himself as "a cross between victor and survivor," a "wiser" leader who would not repeat his mistakes. Certainly, Gingrich would no longer describe Clinton as "a counterculture McGovernik" as he had following the 1994 elections.[52]

House Majority Leader Dick Armey echoed Gingrich, expressing his hope for a more disciplined, efficient, and civil 105th Congress. "We must dare to be not sensational," he said. A former professor of economics who is comfortable with ideas, Armey offered his view of the essential difference between left and right in America. "The right," he suggested, "is teaching freedom and responsibility, and the left is teaching the politics of dependency."[53]

Gingrich was chastened by the charges of ethical violations against him. The House Ethics Committee determined that Gingrich's use of tax-deductible money for political purposes and the inaccurate information he supplied to investigators represented "intentional or . . . reckless" disregard of House rules. The Speaker admitted violating House rules and accepted the Ethics Committee's findings. The House subsequently voted to reprimand Gingrich and ordered him to pay $300,000 to defray the cost of the committee's inquiry, making him the first Speaker ever to be cited for his conduct.[54]

His ethical lapses were defended in and out of Congress. For instance, Harvard graduate Bruce Chapman, one-time liberal Republican and now head of a conservative think tank in Seattle, decided to judge for himself the Ethics Committee's finding that the Speaker had misused tax-exempt money to teach a "partisan" college course. Chapman, accordingly, seated himself before a VCR and watched all twenty hours of "Renewing American Civilization." He found the course well organized, coherent, engaging, and "less partisan" than a similar course he took at Harvard under liberal Democrat Arthur Schlesinger Jr.[55]

While conceding that Gingrich often conveyed an impression of smugness and arrogance, columnist Tony Snow argued that the House's reprimand and particularly the $300,000 payment represented "a raw deal" and an "interesting" precedent. Snow pointed out that the Progressive Policy Institute, a tax-exempt arm of the Democratic Leadership Council, had published "a political manifesto for 2000" with a foreword by Vice

President Al Gore. "If Mr. Gingrich's ambitions caused his course to breach the law," Snow asked, "why shouldn't the PPI lose its tax-exempt status and why shouldn't the vice president have to sell the family farm?"[56]

As is his wont when a conservative has been wounded, Heritage President Ed Feulner took the offensive. He argued that Gingrich was being attacked by the Washington establishment not so much because of his "ethical lapses" (which the Speaker freely admitted and apologized for) but because of his "ideas" of less government, local autonomy, lower taxes, and entitlement reform. Feulner pointed out that the conservative "revolution" had not been repudiated by the voters in 1996 "as liberals believed it would be. The 105th Congress," Feulner added, "is on the brink of truly ending the era of big government and reinstituting the era of citizen-directed self-government."[57]

One large step in that direction was the Renewal Alliance, a bicameral group of over twenty conservative Republicans dedicated to promoting nongovernmental solutions to social and economic problems. Its leaders included John R. Kasich of Ohio, James M. Talent of Missouri, and J. C. Watts of Oklahoma in the House, and John Ashcroft of Missouri, Spencer Abraham of Michigan, and Rick Santorum of Pennsylvania in the Senate. The Alliance will advance legislation in such areas as enterprise zones, deregulation, tax incentives for charitable giving, education reform, and flexible work schedules. Government will always have a role in providing "a basic social safety net to meet basic material needs," explained Senator Dan Coats of Indiana, but government doesn't usually "address the underlying needs. We think the soul and the spirit need to be addressed.... It's not enough to just feed the body and mind."[58] What alliance members and other "compassionate" conservatives were attempting to do is admittedly difficult—to find the right balance of power and responsibility between the government and private sectors in the area of poverty and welfare. But it was, as senior editor David Brooks of the conservative *Weekly Standard* put it, "a noble task."[59]

Marshall Wittmann, Heritage's director of congressional relations for the House of Representatives, said the Renewal Alliance will promote "an activist, optimistic vision which strengthens communities and families." Pollster Frank Luntz stated that the alliance "was the most important conservative development on Capitol Hill since the formation of the

Conservative Opportunity Society fifteen years ago." If that turns out to be true, the man to thank will be Wittmann, without whose efforts, says one participant, the Alliance just "wouldn't have happened."[60]

Although the House leadership sometimes seemed a little too ready to sit down and reason with President Clinton, a group of seventy House members, calling themselves the Conservative Action Team, pushed an overtly conservative agenda, including a ban on partial birth abortions, an end to federal funding for the National Endowment for the Arts (NEA) and the Legal Services Corporation, and legislation to prevent unions from using compulsory dues for political purposes. Explained Team spokesman Sam Johnson of Texas, "These common-sense items represent our view that government is too big, costs too much, and too often degrades the values of the American people.... As Ronald Reagan once said, 'If not us, who? If not now, when?'"[61]

Lott Conservatism

On the other side of the Capitol, Senate Majority Leader Trent Lott was in an aggressive mood, emboldened by the Republican gain of two seats and the knowledge that almost all nine new Senate Republicans were more conservative than the senators they were replacing. In fact, by party ratio, this new Senate was the most Republican since the one elected in 1928.

While declaring that the president was entitled to present his program first, Lott made clear that he expected Clinton to address difficult as well as easy initiatives. On Medicare, for example, the president would have to "basically admit that he demagogued" the issue, accusing Republicans of "cutting" the program to finance tax reductions for the wealthy. "Let's see how he swings at this problem," said Lott, "since he has ducked it" so far.[62]

The Senate agenda addressed the priority concerns of the American people but gave them a conservative twist, emphasizing education choice, missile defense, a tax-relief package including a $500 per child tax credit, a reduction in the capital gains tax, and reform of the unpopular estate (death) tax. Lott promised once again to offer a ban on partial birth abortion.

Both the president and Congress were aware of the November 1996 exit polls which showed that the country was still in a generally conservative mood. Asked by Voter News Service (a consortium of major print and broadcast media) which was closer to their views, that government "should do more to solve problems" or that it was "doing too many things better left to businesses and individuals," respondents chose "doing too much" by 52 percent to 41 percent. Only 18 percent of those participating in the VNS exit poll said they thought the new federal welfare law cut spending too deeply while 39 percent said it didn't cut deeply enough.[63]

In his State of the Union address, delivered in early February 1997, President Clinton seemed to cling to the center, promising, for example, a balanced budget by 2002 and urging citizen volunteerism in a wide variety of fields. He described a "new kind of government—not to solve all of our problems for us, but to give all our people the tools to make the most of their own lives."[64] One Republican aide called the president's more limited and focused approach "small packages with pretty bright ribbons."[65]

After examining the president's budget message, Heritage analysts William Beach and John Barry concluded that Clinton's "bridge to the 21st century" would cost an astounding $9 trillion (the total of the federal budgets between 1997 and 2002). They charged that the president's "blueprint" was seriously flawed and filled with highly suspect math. It used, for example, "a far rosier outlook" for budget deficits than those forecast by the non-partisan Congressional Budget Office (CBO). As a result, Clinton will have to cut $245 billion less than the CBO says he should. "As any engineer will attest," stated Beach and Barry, "if your calculations are off by even a fraction, your bridge will collapse."[66]

Republican skepticism about Clinton's supposed "centrism" was pronounced. "We'll sit down and talk," promised Congressman George P. Radanovich of California, "as long as he keeps to his pledge to end big government.... Otherwise, he's going to be in for a big budget fight."[67] Congressional leaders immediately announced plans to proceed with consideration of a balanced-budget amendment to the constitution, a proposition firmly opposed by the president. Liberal criticism of Clinton was sharp and surprising.

A *Washington Post* lead editorial faulted the president for avoiding any serious discussion of Medicare or Social Security, both of which face

financial ruin in the first part of the twenty-first century. And if simulta-
neously balancing the budget, protecting entitlements, and providing a
middle-class tax cut were as easy as Clinton suggested, said the *Post,* "you
wonder why it didn't happen long ago." Its verdict on the State of the
Union: "a disappointing speech."[68] Political reporter David Broder pointed
out that, once again, Clinton sounded like "the governor of the United
States." Every one of the major topics he discussed—crime, welfare, taxes,
health care, the environment, and especially education—are matters that
have traditionally been the province of state and local government. "But
now," wrote Broder, "they are the heart of the presidential program."[69]

Conservative columnist George F. Will was unrestrained in his scorn,
accusing Clinton of "pandering" to the people with a $51 billion education
plan. He noted that there are already more college students than high school
students, "a majority of whom will never get a degree." Clinton's plan to
increase the number of community colleges, the columnist continued ruth-
lessly, will in fact "churn out graduates unequipped to guffaw when a president utters solemnities at the expense of the education system."[70]

Liberal essayist Barbara Ehrenreich was equally sarcastic, remarking
at a Progressive Caucus seminar in Washington, "I say take a tip from Paula
Jones: Dump Bill." There were loud laughs and cheers from many in the
audience. "This is not a time for party loyalty," argued Ehrenreich. "If
anyone has been disloyal to his party and what it stands for, it is Bill
Clinton."[71]

A Different Mandate

Mandate for Leadership I helped shape the Reagan administration, which
ultimately implemented an estimated 60 percent of the study's two thousand recommendations. *Mandate for Leadership II* was called "one of the
most important books" of 1984 in detailing how the administration could
continue the conservative revolution. *Mandate for Leadership III* described
minutely (one newspaper compared it to the Yellow Pages) how to manage the federal bureaucracy in the post-Reagan era.

Mandate for Leadership IV: Turning Ideas into Action was a far different
document, reflecting the changed character of Washington politics and
of The Heritage Foundation. It was not a blueprint for a conservative

administration—the White House was held by an opportunistic Democrat who often echoed conservative themes but was in reality a "counterfeit" conservative.[72] This *Mandate* was not a long laundry list of policy recommendations; the conservative agenda had already been written in the Contract with America and publications like Heritage's *Issues '96*. *Mandate IV* was, rather, a closely reasoned political strategy by which Congress could carry out the conservative platform endorsed by the American people in the elections of 1994 and 1996, a strategy first outlined in the election of 1980.

Mandate IV assumed that the primary impetus for legislative action would come "from Capitol Hill rather than from the White House." It argued that Congress must "weigh carefully the often painful lessons of the past" in seeking conservative reform. And it stressed the importance of building "public understanding of the need for specific changes."[73]

The 51-page first chapter, "Moving Policy Through Government," written by Dave Mason, the foundation's senior fellow in congressional studies, set the realistic tone for the rest of the 760-page book. Mason pointed out that in fact the accomplishments of the 104th Congress in a number of areas, from spending restraint to welfare reform, exceeded those of the Reagan administration. Yet somehow congressional Republicans had been placed on the defensive, the Contract with America was "unmentionable," and freshman Republicans in particular were under assault. Why? Mason offered nine lessons from the past, including:[74]

Lesson #1: "A political program needs the right balance of vision and practicality." Republicans, for example, kept promising a term limits amendment, although it could not possibly pass the 104th Congress. Failure left many conservatives, in and out of Congress, disillusioned.

Lesson #2: "A successful political program must be conceptually clear and consistent." The Contract with America was relatively simple, Mason acknowledged, but it was "politically ineffective" because the concepts behind it were not clear to the public. Such blunt analysis is characteristic of Mason's chapter and most of the nineteen chapters that follow.

Lesson # 9: "Process does not sell." And since the Contract with America was essentially a process, Mason suggested, it was fated to fail. Process, he insisted, must be linked directly to "a compelling substantive goal"—for conservatives, limiting government. Mason went on to present several lessons learned from the legislative process of the preceding two years: "shutdown showdowns" almost always produce disappointing outcomes; ignoring the executive branch does not work; and successful policies have a bipartisan element.[75]

Next, drawing on one of Heritage's strengths, he offered some marketing lessons, starting with *"A vigorous and ongoing public campaign is essential to overall policy success."* Mason criticized the 104th Congress for its "inadequate marketing" and for being too "slow to respond" when President Clinton declared that he too wanted a balanced budget and then lambasted almost every significant element of the Republican plan. (Speaker Gingrich acknowledged that he and other GOP leaders had failed to allot sufficient time and energy to "selling.")[76]

"Do not treat the media as the enemy," counseled Mason, pointing out that President Reagan never publicly criticized or complained about even the most liberal reporters. When conservative politicians, from Spiro Agnew to Newt Gingrich, attacked the media, they were cheered by their "hard-core supporters" but lost public support and failed to "advance their own ideas."[77]

Party leaders, argued Mason, should concentrate on creating and managing the agenda and let others—from committee chairmen and staffers to outside agencies—handle the detailed design and marketing of legislation. They should work to build and direct public opinion through the media, interest groups, and the congressional hearing process. Conservatives had to get better, much better, at conducting "effective congressional hearings." Bipartisan commissions (like the 1982 one on Social Security) should be carefully used. They cannot serve as "fail-safe answers to every politically difficult issue."[78]

Examining the "mixed record of the 104th Congress," Mason concluded that, above all, conservatives "need to learn better how to govern." That did not mean "reflexive compromising" but "more prudence" about what was achievable in a limited amount of time and in a given set of political circumstances. At the same time, conservatives had to improve their own ideas, better manage "the governmental process," and constantly promote their proposals. He called on conservative legislative leaders to set their sights "not lower, but further out."[79]

Ensuing chapters of *Mandate IV* discussed how to close or privatize agencies and programs, devolve programs to the states, and strengthen local institutions of civil society. Three chapters suggested strategies for dealing with middle-income entitlements, including Social Security and Medicare, government regulations, and taxes.

Stuart Butler and coauthor John S. Barry argued that Congress must convince Americans, particularly the elderly, that the entitlements crisis "is real and needs decisive action and do it *before* a detailed [reform] proposal is unveiled." The American people must be informed, for example, that Social Security is not "a real account with their own money in it, like savings in a bank," but "a program in which the government spends every penny paid into the system and in which benefits have little to do with contributions made." Because public apprehension about the future of Social Security is so intense, change should not be presented as "Social Security reform," but as part of a comprehensive plan for "improving the retirement options of all Americans."[80]

In the section on foreign policy and defense, *Mandate IV* outlined America's proper objectives: to protect American national interests, promote global security and freedom, and ensure free trade and open markets. Succeeding chapters described how to maintain a strong national defense "in a budget straitjacket," plan an effective national security strategy (striking a sensible balance, as analyst John Hillen put it, between "a wasteful crusade" and "a rejectionist isolationism"), and build a consensus for a "homeland missile defense system."[81] Separate chapters were devoted to foreign aid, which has "wasted" some $2 trillion in U.S. taxpayers' money since 1945; and to the United Nations, where, in the words of analysts Brett D. Schaefer and Thomas P. Sheehy, "the United States should follow a policy of selective participation."[82]

The national security section was based in large measure on *Restoring American Leadership,* the foundation's newest foreign and defense policy "blueprint," which was edited by Kim Holmes and Thomas Moore and published in the fall of 1996. *Restoring* was described by Lawrence J. Korb of the Brookings Institution as containing "a gold mine of useful information" and by Thomas H. Henrikson of the Hoover Institution as "timely and significant to our current [foreign policy] predicament."[83]

One of the most prickly parts of that predicament is America's relations with its former archenemy, Russia. Ariel Cohen, Heritage's senior analyst in Russian and Eurasian affairs, urged a policy of realism rather than romanticism, pointing out that "Russia is reasserting itself as a great power." Already, Russia has taken the path to confrontation with the West "over Bosnia, NATO expansion, the supply of nuclear reactors to Iran, and the sale of modern weaponry to China." As Russia goes through a period of "political turbulence," said Cohen, America should support democracy, free markets, and individual rights in Russia and oppose anti-democratic solutions, "no matter who initiates them."[84]

Even before *Mandate IV* was released, congressional conservatives introduced the Defend America Act, calling for deployment of a national missile defense system as quickly as possible. The act was based in large part on the report of an eighteen-member blue-ribbon panel of military and technological experts, assembled by Heritage and led by Visiting Fellow Henry Cooper (former director of the Strategic Defense Initiative Organization) and former Senator Malcolm Wallop of Wyoming, a Heritage Distinguished Fellow. The Cooper panel, known as "Team B," recommended a two-stage plan using available technology—e.g., the Navy's Aegis system—to protect America going into the twenty-first century.[85]

Stuart Butler and Kim Holmes confidently asserted that, if congressional leaders carefully studied *Mandate IV,* they would find the ways and means to return America "to its constitutional roots" and restore its proper role of "defending freedom and democracy at home and abroad."[86]

Senate Majority Leader Trent Lott agreed. According to *Washington Times* political correspondent Donald Lambro, Lott telephoned House Speaker Newt Gingrich to ask him, "Have you read Dave Mason's chapter on moving an agenda through Congress?"[87] The Mason chapter and other parts of *Mandate IV* were also carefully studied at an orientation conference for freshman congressmen held by The Heritage Foundation and Empower America and attended by sixteen Republicans and seven Democrats. Republican senators participating in an agenda-setting strategy session at the Library of Congress were reportedly poring over the Heritage volume—further proof that *Mandate IV* had become "must reading on Capitol Hill."[88]

The State of Conservatism

Summing up the state of conservatism in his annual essay, Ed Feulner declared flatly that "a conservative attitude now pervades the American political landscape." The challenge for conservatives was to "convert" that attitude into common-sense solutions that the average American would support. That challenge could be met, at least in part, Feulner suggested, by recalling the five simple words that Ronald Reagan emphasized when he accepted the Republican Party's 1980 presidential nomination—"family, work, neighborhood, freedom, peace." Those words, signifying fundamental American values, could well form the basis for a campaign that would reassure the American people that conservatives don't just know how to balance the budget or quote from the *Federalist Papers;* they also care deeply about the future of every American.[89]

8

The Man Who
Makes It Happen

I n mid-October 1964, a twenty-three-year-old graduate student was
  seated on the stage of an auditorium at the University of Pennsylvania, listening intently as Senator Barry Goldwater called for the implementation of conservative ideas—a flat tax, an end to government
subsidies, victory over communism—to counter the prevailing liberal
ethos. Suddenly, the graduate student ducked as several tomatoes and
eggs were thrown at the Republican presidential nominee, flung by out-
raged liberals who thought that a conservative shouldn't be allowed to say
such crazy things. It was one of Ed Feulner's first public encounters with
political correctness, albeit in a most virulent form. And he never forgot
it—the assault on Goldwater was an assault on him. "He was the political
embodiment of what I believed."[1]

Cradle Conservative

If ever anyone was, Edwin J. Feulner Jr. was destined to be a conservative.
Born in Chicago on August 12, 1941, he was the oldest child of Edwin
John and Helen Joan (Franzen) Feulner. His parents, of German ances-
try, were devout Roman Catholics; all three of Helen Feulner's brothers
were parish priests. Edwin Feulner owned a successful real estate firm in
downtown Chicago and provided a good living for his wife and four

children—Ed Jr. and three sisters, Mary Ann, Joan, and Barbara. His father's deep faith and quiet charity impressed young Ed. For many years, for example, Edwin Feulner paid the rent of two elderly distant relatives who would otherwise have been homeless. No one knew he was helping them until after his death. In his son's words, "He didn't need, or expect, accolades for his good deeds."[2]

When Ed was ten, the family moved to the comfortable suburb of Elmhurst, where the young Feulner—"He was always a hard worker" and "serious."[3]—scrupulously tended a large vegetable garden next to their house and worked in a camera shop every summer. Ed attended Catholic schools from kindergarten through twelfth grade, then enrolled at Regis College, a Jesuit-run liberal arts college in Denver, Colorado, where he earned a B.A. in English with a minor in philosophy.

As an eighteen-year-old Regis freshman, Ed Feulner began delving into the conservative canon, reading *The Conservative Mind* by Russell Kirk and *Liberty or Equality* by Erik von Kuehnelt-Leddihn. These books and publications like *National Review* and *Human Events* "helped turn my conservative instincts into firm conservative convictions."[4] He became a Goldwaterite after reading the senator's bestselling 1960 manifesto, *The Conscience of a Conservative.*

Always an ardent advocate of voluntary associations, Feulner and other Regis students formed an associated club of the Intercollegiate Society of Individualists (ISI), a conservative youth group founded by libertarian writer Frank Chodorov. (Its first president was William F. Buckley Jr.) ISI, which later became the Intercollegiate Studies Institute, enabled Feulner to make many important connections and firm friendships, including his lifelong friendship with fellow midwesterner and pipe-smoker Donald Lipsett.

Starting a Society

In the fall of 1964, faced with the prospect of an overwhelming Goldwater defeat, Lipsett and Feulner conceived the idea of starting a society of conservative intellectuals. It would be an American version of the Mont Pelerin Society, begun by F. A. Hayek in Europe twenty years before. It

Trustee Thomas L. Rhodes and Vice Chairman of the Board Richard M. Scaife.

Key Heritage domestic policy staffers include, left to right, Vice President Stuart Butler, Scott Hodge, Robert Rector, and Dan Mitchell.

Developing membership strategy are, left to right, Vice President John Von Kannon; Bob Russell, counselor; Scott O'Connell; Bridgett Wagner; and Bernard Lomas, counselor.

Senate Majority Leader Trent Lott and Phil Truluck review a copy of Issues '96.

Distinguished Fellow William Bennett with Heritage members Grace and John Hoad at Heritage's Eleventh Annual Public Policy Seminar in 1996.

The Roe Institute team: Thomas A. Roe (center front), a Heritage trustee, with Roe fellows and researchers.

Heritage trustees Midget Decter, Barb Van Andel-Gaby, and J. Frederic Rench.

Ambassador William H.G. FitzGerald, right, with the William H.G. FitzGerald Fellow in Family and Cultural Issues, Patrick Fagan, and Ed Feulner.

*Discussing a draft of a foreign policy study at an early 1991
meeting, left to right, Baker Spring, Vice President Kim Holmes,
and Jay Kosminsky.*

*Distinguished Fellow Richard V. Allen with former Secretary of
Defense Caspar Weinberger.*

Ken Cribb, president of the Intercollegiate Studies Institute, left, and Bill Bennett with Heritage trustee William E. Simon.

Heritage Vice President Stuart Butler with Michael Joyce, president of the Lynde and Harry Bradley Foundation, and Robert Woodson, president of the National Center for Neighborhood Enterprise, at the 1996 congressional "advance briefing."

Heritage senior managers include Vice Presidents Mike Franc, Adam Meyerson, and Bob Blatz.

Key staffers, all with fifteen or more years with Heritage, are, left to right, Richard Odermatt, Shelia Derricott-Myles, Missy Stephens, Jim Phillips, Clair Fries, and Kathy Rowan, executive assistant to Ed Feulner.

Heritage's management team in July 1997. Seated, left to right: Adam Meyerson, Kim Holmes, Michael Franc, Lewis Gayner, Herb Berkowitz, Edwin Feulner, Phillip Truluck, John Von Kannon, Robert Blatz, Stuart Butler, Bridgett Wagner. Standing, left to right: Richard Odermatt, Ann Klucsarits, Terri Brickley, Wesley Dyck, David Mason, Matthew Spalding, Cheryl Rubin, Mark Esper, Angela Antonelli, Karen Miller, Thomas Atwood, Mary Anne Carter, Robert Moffit, Chip Griffin, Marshall Wittmann, Gretchen Kugel, Thom Golab.

would also serve as an unofficial alumni association of ISI. "We wanted to keep [ISI graduates] involved," explains Feulner, "in the battle of ideas."[5] The two young men decided that, to be successful, the group would need the participation of two key conservatives — editor-author William F. Buckley Jr., representing the traditionalist wing of the conservative movement, and economist Milton Friedman, representing the libertarian wing.

Incredibly enough, the two eminent conservatives had never met. Feulner recalls thinking, "How can we bring these people together?"[6] Fortunately, he and Lipsett had met both Buckley and Friedman through ISI, so a meeting was arranged in New York City. *National Review* 's senior editor Frank Meyer, well known for his efforts to "fuse" the different strains of conservatism, joined with them to start the Philadelphia Society.

Although only twenty-three, Ed Feulner was elected treasurer — the first but far from last time that he would take responsibility for the finances of a conservative organization. Bill Buckley put up $100 so "we could open a bank account."[7] The secretary, "Commodore" Don Lipsett, quietly and effectively ran the organization until his early death in 1995. For more than three decades, the meetings of the Philadelphia Society have provided an opportunity for conservatives of all persuasions to analyze the present and debate the future of the conservative movement.

In December 1964, after receiving his M.B.A. from the Wharton School of Commerce and Finance at the University of Pennsylvania, Feulner decided he wanted to study basic economic principles in more detail. At Regis and then at Wharton, he had studied under such conservatives as Herbert Northrup, professor of labor-management relations; Bernard Sheehan, professor of American history; and philosopher-historian Larry Stepelevitch. While at Wharton, he had also attended the lectures of Robert Strausz-Hupé, the international strategist and author of the classic work, *Protracted Conflict*. (Thirty years later Strausz-Hupé would become a Heritage Distinguished Scholar.) During this period, Feulner lunched frequently with E. Victor Milione, the strongly traditionalist president of the Intercollegiate Studies Institute who was "an intellectual mentor in a non-classroom setting."[8] These writers and thinkers enabled Feulner to leave Wharton with not only a degree in business administration but a deeper understanding of political philosophy and conservatism.

Hoping to pursue his studies at the famed London School of Economics (LSE), Feulner applied to ISI and received a Richard Weaver Fellowship, named after the author of the renowned *Ideas Have Consequences*. While at LSE during the first half of 1965, Feulner was exposed to Kenneth Minogue, former pupil of British philosopher Michael Oakeshot and author of *The Liberal Mind,* and economist Peter Bauer, later Lord Bauer of Clare Market. Bauer's seminar redefined issues like aid for developing countries, "about which I had previously gotten the conventional wisdom from 'experts' like Walt Rostow."[9] Feulner also met for the first time that giant of modern economics, Friedrich A. Hayek, who gave several lectures at LSE. Two decades later, Hayek became a Heritage Distinguished Scholar.

The young American noted that despite the school's left-wing reputation, the London School of Economics' faculty was in fact "balanced and all-encompassing" in its ideology. Not so the student body; with a few exceptions, it was "overwhelmingly left." Yet, among the students from sub-Saharan Africa, Asia, and "places that were out of the Arabian Nights," Feulner discovered some who were deeply interested in and committed to "the basic premises of a free society." Their commitment confirmed what the LSE faculty, or at least some members of it, were teaching about the universal applicability of precepts like limited government and the free market.[10] On the whole, Ed Feulner's experience at LSE reinforced his conviction that America's future depended on what happened as much outside as inside its borders.

Because he was not working toward a formal degree, Feulner found time to start an affiliated ISI club at the London School of Economics. "My fellow officers were from Portugal, India, and Scotland."[11] He also obtained a part-time job (paying five pounds a day) at the Institute of Economic Affairs (IEA), a small but influential think tank that would later provide many of the free-market ideas for Conservative Prime Minister Margaret Thatcher in the 1970s and 1980s.

Feulner learned from IEA directors Ralph Harris and Arthur Seldon that it was "absolutely essential" for a think tank to maintain the integrity of its research. Because the institute's researchers were so scrupulous, everyone from the media to the opposition took IEA's arguments seriously. If the institute issued a study that challenged the status quo, "the other side had to rebut it. Ideas were taken seriously. Ideas mattered."[12] Ed Feulner would bring to Heritage the same scrupulosity and firm belief in the ability of ideas to change minds and the direction of government.

Washington at Last

Feulner first met Richard V. Allen at a one-day ISI seminar in Indianapolis in the winter of 1963. Allen was a charismatic young academic who, the previous year, had helped start the Center for Strategic Studies at Georgetown University along with Admiral Arleigh Burke, the famed World War II naval hero, and David Abshire, a West Point graduate at ease in both the academic and political worlds of Washington. Allen was impressed with Feulner's keen mind, abundant energy, and willingness to listen; he promised to stay in touch.[13] At the London School of Economics more than a year later, Feulner received a telex from Portuguese Angola: Dick Allen wanted to have dinner with him in London. Feulner, who had not received many telexes in his life and none from the heart of Africa, was understandably intrigued.

During their dinner, Allen explained that the Noble Foundation of Ardmore, Oklahoma, had agreed to underwrite a new program at the Center for Strategic Studies (later renamed the Center for Strategic and International Studies). A graduate student would do research at the center for a year and then spend a second year as a research assistant to a senator or congressman. Ed Noble and other trustees of the Noble Foundation, "an early, major supporter of The Heritage Foundation," realized that members of Congress urgently needed more research help in the field of foreign policy and national security. Noting that the United States was engaged on an increasing number of foreign fronts—Vietnam, Cuba, China, Western Europe—the Noble Foundation offered an initial grant of $13,000. Allen asked Feulner if he would like to be CIS's "first Public Affairs Fellow."[14]

The timing was right. Now that he was finishing up as a Weaver Fellow at LSE, Ed Feulner had been reviewing his situation. He had "thought about teaching," but knew he would need a Ph.D. He could go to work for his father's real estate firm, but business per se held little appeal for him. Going to Washington and working on Capitol Hill sounded exciting to the twenty-four-year-old conservative, and he accepted Allen's offer, effective September 1965.[15]

Feulner spent a year at CIS researching and writing about American trade policy toward the Soviet Union, often in collaboration with Samuel Clabaugh, a retired colonel with a strong interest in economic strategy. They coauthored a well-received CIS monograph, *Trading with the Communists*.[16] Feulner also monitored congressional proceedings for the center's senior scholars and enrolled in Georgetown University, seeking a Ph.D. in economics. Among his favorite teachers was Professor Lev E. Dobriansky, "who had his head screwed on straight and was not all wrapped up in mathematical economics."[17] Dobriansky, a deeply informed anticommunist, was the originator of the annual Captive Nations Week, authorized by Congress and proclaimed by every president since Dwight D. Eisenhower in 1959.

In late 1966, Feulner carefully considered his congressional options: the office of Republican Senate Leader Everett M. Dirksen, where he would probably "lick postage stamps"; the office of Congressman Donald H. Rumsfeld (R-Ill.), whose primary area of international interest was Latin America, a region of marginal interest to most Americans, including Feulner; and the office of Congressman Melvin R. Laird (R-Wis.), head of the House Republican Conference. Regarded as the "idea man" of House Republicans, Laird offered the greatest opportunity.

Meanwhile, however, Dick Allen had moved from the Center for Strategic Studies to the Hoover Institution at Stanford University, and the Noble grant followed him.[18] Accordingly, Ed became Laird's Public Affairs Fellow under Hoover Institution sponsorship.

Feulner spent the next three years working for Mel Laird, first at the House Republican Conference and then as his "confidential assistant" when Nixon named Laird his Secretary of Defense in 1969. At the Pentagon, Feulner was assigned to the office of the assistant secretary responsible for political appointees. Out of three million people, civilian and military, in various Defense Department agencies, "there were about ninety-two or ninety-three [political] slots to fill." Feulner frequently found himself visiting the White House Office of Personnel to explain why his boss had appointed someone "who was right on defense" but had irritated almost "everyone else in the administration."[19]

Days at the Pentagon were exciting but frustrating. "You had to fill out a requisition form for *everything,*" Feulner recalls, "even a pad of paper." The young conservative was also frustrated by what was happening in the Nixon administration. Decisions on defining issues, like relations with China and welfare, were increasingly veering to the left of center. So, although he was learning much at the Pentagon about "the interaction of ideas and policy" in government, Feulner was receptive when, in December 1969, he received a telephone call about a possible position on Capitol Hill.[20]

Philip M. Crane, a professor of history at Bradley University, had just won a special election (defeating ten other candidates) to succeed Don Rumsfeld as the representative from the Thirteenth Congressional District of Illinois. Crane had to run again in November 1970, and needed to focus much of his attention on his reelection campaign. He wanted someone in his Washington office who knew "how Washington works" and could help him "do the conservative things he had been promising he would do." Feulner, who had already met Crane through an Intercollegiate Studies Institute summer school, interviewed with Crane.[21]

"Ed was very bright," remembers Crane, "a committed conservative, and he understood the legislative process."[22] It was an easy decision. Ed Feulner was hired as legislative assistant and then became administrative assistant after Crane was handily reelected that fall. For four years, he smoothly administered Crane's office, established close working relationships with other young congressional staffers like Paul Weyrich, and pondered how conservatives could be more effective on Capitol Hill.

Despite his deepening political involvement, Feulner regretted that he had not been able to complete his Ph.D. studies at Georgetown University. He had finished his course work, passed both his German and French exams, and begun preparing for the oral examinations which Georgetown required before a dissertation topic was assigned. While there was "no overt hostility" among the faculty, he detected subtle derogatory comments about his open conservatism and his work for Mel Laird, a well-known Republican hawk on the Vietnam War. Feulner also concedes that he became so immersed in Vietnam and other high-profile issues that it "detracted from my ability to sit down and study rigorous ideas like macroeconomic theory." For all these reasons, it soon "became very clear" that

a Georgetown doctorate "was a no-go."[23] He put aside the possibility of a
Ph.D. for the time being.

Love and Marriage

His immersion in policy and politics, however, did not leave Ed too busy
to begin dating Linda Levanthal, a slender beauty from New York City.
Linda was a graduate of Tufts University with a B.S. in occupational ther-
apy who came to Washington to intern at D.C. General Hospital. Ed and
Linda were married on March 8, 1969. In September 1971 Edwin John
III was born, and Emily Victoria arrived in April 1973. A devoted father,
Ed regularly gave the children their baths and put them to bed, and bus-
ied himself with family errands on Saturdays. "When he was here," says
Linda, "he was *here*."[24]

Ed is a "morning person," she reports, rising at 5:30 to walk the dog
and read the newspapers before going to the office. When he is not on the
road for Heritage, Ed and Linda prefer to spend their evenings at home
rather than at dinners in Georgetown or political or embassy receptions.
Sometimes, says Linda, "we go out for dinner and a movie, in our jeans."[25]

Asked why he works so hard and so long—"he brings home two or
three briefcases every night"—Linda says simply, "Because he has a great
sense of responsibility to the three things that matter most to him—his
religion, his family, and the conservative movement, with Heritage at its
center."[26]

Stalking the House

In the early 1970s, of course, there was no Heritage, and there was only
a budding conservative movement in Washington. It seemed as though
liberals had all the answers and provided all the policies, from détente to
Keynesian economics. It was incredibly frustrating for young conservatives like Ed Feulner, who knew that conservatives had better ideas, like
limited government and individual responsibility, but seemed unable to
shape them into attractive legislative alternatives.

As administrative assistant to Congressman Crane, Feulner found himself asking: Is this a good bill or a bad bill? Do we have a conservative

alternative? Do we have a strategy to pass the good legislation or stop the bad? The answer was almost always No. "What I needed, as an overworked staffer laboring away in a congressman's office, was nuts-and-bolts legislative research and off-the-shelf policy prescriptions that had a realistic chance of making their way through Congress."[27]

Two bills in particular helped convince Ed Feulner, Paul Weyrich, James Lucier, and other conservative staffers that they had to get organized—the Family Assistance Plan (FAP) and the Child Development Act (CDA). Sponsored by the Nixon administration, both proposals cut sharply against the conservative grain. FAP guaranteed an income for every citizen, seriously undermining the work ethic. CDA contained child-advocacy and child-rights programs that were incompatible with traditional American education.

FAP seemed on its way to easy House passage in March 1970 when a small group of Republican congressmen, led by Phil Crane, Ed Derwinski (R-Ill.), and John Ashbrook (R-Ohio) challenged it. On April 15, the House narrowly approved a "closed rule" (no amendments allowed) for the Family Assistance Plan by a vote of 205 to 183. More Republicans opposed the motion than supported it—a major rebuff to the Republican leadership which had lobbied hard for the closed rule. The next day, the House passed FAP, but the large number of Republican defections on the closed-rule vote demonstrated that conservatives, if organized, could make a difference in a key policy debate.

Conservatives immediately began planning a Senate strategy. Crane and Derwinski called Republican Senator Carl Curtis of Nebraska, a senior member of the Senate Finance Committee that would be considering the legislation. They suggested a meeting, which may seem a trivial and even obvious idea. But although liberals had long coordinated their House and Senate activities, conservatives had chosen to respect the independence of each House. At last, beleaguered by liberals on all sides, conservatives took Benjamin Franklin's advice and decided to start hanging together.

Jerry Preston James, legislative assistant to Congressman Floyd Spence (R-S.C.), offered an important suggestion. Why not invite Dr. Roger Freeman, a Senior Fellow at Stanford University's Hoover Institution, to testify before the Senate Finance Committee and privately brief committee members? Freeman was a nationally recognized economist and welfare expert who had served in the Nixon White House and now publicly opposed FAP. His participation in the FAP debate was crucial. As political scientist Allen Schick wrote, "Congress can more easily exploit work done by others than carry the main burden of analysis by itself."[28] That insight would be incorporated into the core mission of The Heritage Foundation.

On November 20, 1972, after months of deliberation, the Family Assistance Plan was rejected by the Democrat-controlled Senate Finance Committee by a vote of 10 to 7. With modest staff resources but a carefully conceived strategy, conservatives delayed and then buried "the keystone of the Nixon administration's legislative agenda." Seven years later, a disillusioned Senator Daniel Patrick Moynihan, who as a White House assistant to President Nixon had conceived FAP, wrote a revealing letter to his friend William F. Buckley Jr.:

> I've had a week here, reading and fussing with a great mound of research reports on the guaranteed income experiments which we started in the late 1960s. . . . Were we wrong about a guaranteed income! Seemingly it is calamitous. It increases family dissolution by some 70 percent, decreases work, etc.[29]

The coalition building, politicking, and delaying tactics all contributed to the defeat of FAP, but Feulner is convinced that the research made the difference. "We were able to change the minds of some key people."[30]

The Child Development Act (CDA) required a different strategy. The legislation had President Nixon's initial support but not the strong commitment he had given the Family Assistance Plan. So an "inside-outside" effort was mounted to secure a presidential veto. To begin with, the Emergency Committee for Children was formed to mobilize public sentiment against the bill. Crane then delegated Feulner to hire a part-time staffer who would work exclusively on the project; to enlist academic members for the committee; and to ensure that enough members of Congress would vote to sustain a presidential veto. Crane became the de facto leader of the opposition to the Child Development Act, with Feulner his chief coordinator—a crucial learning experience for the thirty-year-old aide.

The Emergency Committee for Children aggressively promoted its activities. Thomas Winter, editor of the influential conservative weekly newspaper *Human Events,* was contacted and agreed to publish an editorial urging a presidential veto of the legislation. Information packets were widely distributed, generating anti-CDA articles by conservative columnists William F. Buckley Jr., James J. Kilpatrick, and Russell Kirk. Feulner carefully noted the critical difference that effective public relations and marketing could make.

With marketing in mind, Paul Weyrich personally visited Nixon's most conservative speechwriter, Patrick J. Buchanan, and presented the case against the CDA. "We convinced Vice President Agnew's staff," remembers Feulner, "that the Child Development Act, despite its seductive name, would be a disaster for children and the traditional family."[31] Shortly thereafter, Agnew attacked the bill in a speech that had to have been cleared by the White House.

The rising chorus of demands for a veto of the bill included the clarion voice of Congressman John Ashbrook, then chairman of the American Conservative Union, an aggressive conservative lobbying group. Ashbrook was known to be considering a run against Nixon for the Republican presidential nomination in 1972, so his prominent role in the anti-CDA fight was a determining factor in the administration's decision to veto the measure.

On December 9, 1971, President Nixon sent his veto message to Congress, with special emphasis on Title V, "Child Development Programs." Using unusually strong language, Nixon stated: "The intent of Title V is overshadowed by the fiscal irresponsibility, administrative unworkability, and family-weakening implictions of the system it envisions. We owe our children something more than good intentions."[32]

The defeat of the CDA was a defining moment in the building of an effective, coordinated conservative presence in Congress. Conservatives discovered that individual members, even those without leadership or ranking committee positions, could affect the flow of legislation if they were articulate, aggressive, and well informed.

In early 1973, following two formal meetings at the Red Fox Inn in Middleburg, Virginia, and numerous discussions on and off Capitol Hill, House conservatives formed the Republican Steering Committee (renamed the Republican Study Committee after the 1974 congressional elections). "We described ourselves," Feulner says, "as a group of 'conservatives' in general agreement on policy issues, thus drawing a clear distinction between our group and other Republican Party organizations which had no clearly defined philosophical point of view."[33] Their timing was good. Forty-three new Republicans had been elected to the House in the 1972 elections, thirty of them conservative. Most of them joined the Republican Steering Committee.

Ed Derwinski, the senior congressman of the group, became chairman, although no formal election was held. As its full-time staff director, the committee appointed Dr. Albert Gilman, who had been a vice president of Western Carolina University. They then hired research and clerical staff and found an office in the House Office Building complex. But there were conflicting views about the committee's role: some congressmen expected it to provide information about bills coming to the floor; others saw it as an "in-house conservative think tank"; and still others wanted to use it as an alternative to unreliable and Democrat-dominated committee staffs. Furthermore, all committee members worried about becoming too visible and irritating the Republican House leadership. The first mailings to members were, therefore, sent in untitled orange envelopes with only the Derwinski frank on them.[34]

A New Executive Director

A major legislative agenda was drawn up, which included the elimination of the Legal Services Corporation and a conservative response to the proposed federal land-use act. But Congress's fast pace and daily demands overwhelmed the academically trained Gilman, and Ed Feulner—the man who, everyone now realized, should have been named in the first place—replaced him as executive director in February 1974. Moving quickly to get the Republican Steering Committee on track, Feulner focused on mission, staff, and finances. He made a series of courtesy calls on members to get their ideas about the direction the committee should take; insisted that every committee staffer call on the administrative assistants of RSC members at least twice a month (after all, part of the staffers' salaries came from the members); and he reassured RSC employees that they would be paid by instituting a policy of paying the executive director last. Feulner would emphasize the same three components—mission, staff, and finances—as president of The Heritage Foundation.

Over the next three years, the Republican Study Committee became a major force in the House of Representatives, the Republican Party, and the Washington political community. The committee, for example, helped House conservatives win a major victory in the 1973–1974 battle over federal land use. Research director Phil Truluck briefed members and staff, wrote speeches, arranged for a Special Order that included remarks by over twenty congressmen, and worked on language for an alternative land-use bill that was introduced by Sam Steiger (R-Ariz.). The Steiger substitute offered "incentives to the states to adopt their own [land-use] plans, thereby demoting the federal government to an advisory role."[35]

At a critical juncture, Truluck (who had been hired by Ed Feulner) briefed three White House aides about conservative objections to the Democratic bill sponsored by Morris Udall (D-Ariz.). Two weeks later, the White House sent word to House Minority Leader John Rhodes (R-Ariz.) that the administration "was withdrawing its support of the Udall bill in favor of the Steiger substitute."[36]

In June 1974, the House, despite its 243–188 Democratic majority, rejected the Udall measure by 211–204. It was clear to everyone, from Udall to the White House, that the RSC had mobilized the opposition and "was now a significant force in the House legislative process."

There was also a practical payoff for the committee. Two days after the successful floor vote, John Rhodes called RSC chairman Lamar Baker of Tennessee to advise him that the committee had been given Room 134 in the Cannon House Office Building, a space three times larger than its original quarters. Ed Feulner was delighted. His current office was a converted and not overly large kitchen, and many of the committee's files had been stacked over a bathtub in an old restroom.[37]

When Feulner left the Republican Study Committee in April 1977 to join The Heritage Foundation, the RSC had about one hundred congressional members and a staff of twelve. Its budget came from annual dues paid by members and funds raised by the chairman and the executive director. The committee had published *The Case Against the Reckless Congress,* a paperback book setting forth conservative positions on such public-policy issues as welfare and food stamp reform; *A Research Guide in Public Policy,* an annotated bibliography of scholarly articles about politics, economics, and national security; and *The Research Directory,* a listing of four hundred Washington-based policy experts, including congressional aides, lobbyists, and academics. It also established the RSC Campaign Fund, which distributed nineteen information packets to nonincumbent Republican candidates during the 1974 elections. Several new House members were introduced to the RSC through the packets and "expressed their appreciation of the Campaign Fund's efforts in their behalf." And they happily joined the committee.[38]

Ironically, when the 104th Congress undertook a number of institutional reforms in early 1995—based in large part on Heritage recommendations—it eliminated most quasi-official committees, including the Democratic Study Group and the Republican Study Committee. For most conservatives, it was a good tradeoff.

In summarizing Feulner's contributions to the Republican Study Committee, Phil Crane asserted that his entrepreneurial leadership, intimate knowledge of the House, and personal friendship with many RSC members "held the RSC together." These same qualities led the trustees of The Heritage Foundation to select Ed Feulner as their new president.

A Rare Combination

There are many different kinds of think tank presidents. Some are intellectuals. Some are political insiders. Some are public officials. Some are managers. Some are communicators. Some are fund-raisers. Some are public-policy entrepreneurs. A few, very few, are all of these things. Ed Feulner is one of those rare few, as attested by other public-policy leaders inside and outside Washington.

When Christopher DeMuth left the Kennedy School of Government at Harvard in December 1986 to become head of the then financially troubled American Enterprise Institute, the two people he "sought out" for advice were Ed Feulner and W. Glenn Campbell, the director of the Hoover Institution at Stanford University. "They were the best in the business." DeMuth notes that it is a temptation for a think tank president "to spend all your time with people who give you money, [but Feulner] spends time with pure thinkers. . . . He has never lost touch with his roots in the conservative intellectual movement."[39]

David Abshire, president of the Center for Strategic and International Studies, has known Ed Feulner since the mid-1960s when he was a Noble Foundation fellow at CIS. The two men later often worked together at the Pentagon. "He was obviously a very bright young man," Abshire recalls. By drawing on his experience with think tanks, Capitol Hill, and the Pentagon, Feulner has been able "to bridge ideas and action." He understands that "you can't ride on your oars. You must constantly seek a sense of renewal." Summing up, Abshire remarks, "Ed made Heritage."[40]

The president of the venerable Brookings Institution, Michael Armacost, seconds David Abshire's point about Feulner's ability to bridge politics and policy. "Ed has a high regard for the power of ideas," says Armacost, "but is centered in the policy environment." Such melding, he suggests, will become more prevalent in other research organizations, including the one he heads. When Brookings was founded early in the century, there were no other think tanks in Washington. "We filled a void." But Washington, Armacost admits, is now "a less reflective and more competitive place." Today, "you have to have an ear for the rhythm of the political world."[41]

Gerald Dorfman, deputy director of the Hoover Institution at Stanford University, also met Ed Feulner in the 1960s. Dorfman was then in Washington working for the State Department and the Agency for International Development (AID). Twenty years later, he had the opportunity to watch Feulner serve as chairman of the U.S. Advisory Commission on Public Diplomacy. "There is a force about him," Dorfman observes. "You pay attention to what he has to say." The Hoover official says that in life you encounter a few people like Ed Feulner, people who have a special "entrepreneurial spirit." He compares Feulner to Margaret Olivia Sage, founder of the Russell Sage Foundation, who helped shape social research and public policy during the Progressive Era. Among the multitude of think tanks in this conservative era, asserts Dorfman, "Heritage has made the most national splash."[42]

It is not only those on the right or in the center who praise Heritage. Michael Shuman, director of the determinedly liberal Institute for Policy Studies, asserts that The Heritage Foundation has had a "more profound" influence on American politics and policy "than any other conservative institution in the last generation." Noting the foundation's innovative marketing, its ability to fund-raise at all levels (not just among big donors), and its "powerful networks" at the state and local levels, Shuman says, "I have tremendous admiration for what they've done and what they are."[43]

According to Will Marshall, president of the Progressive Policy Institute (PPI), which numbers President Clinton among its founders, Heritage "pioneered a new kind of advocacy tank" that "broke the old mold" made by Brookings. Marshall freely concedes that PPI "is trying to emulate the success of Heritage" and reveals that Ed Feulner was "generous with his time" and "even encouraging" when Marshall asked for his advice. Marshall is particularly impressed with Heritage's marketing skills: It "wrote the book on how to market and popularize political ideas."[44]

At the other end of the political spectrum, Edward H. Crane, president of the libertarian Cato Institute, credits The Heritage Foundation with being the first think tank to "crack open the incestuous relationship" between research organizations like Brookings, the federal government, and academia. Ed Feulner, says Crane, "brought the public policy debate to the American people. It was no longer a closed debate." Heritage's president, he declares, "is a great entrepreneur of ideas and deserves accolades."[45]

"Heritage is *primus inter pares* of the think tanks," states Michael Joyce, president of the Lynde and Harry Bradley Foundation, a major funder of The Heritage Foundation for nearly twenty years. And it is Ed Feulner's "energy, intelligence, and will power" that are primarily responsible for Heritage's preeminence. Richard Larry, president of the Sarah Scaife Foundation, which has been supporting Heritage even longer than Bradley, agrees with Joyce's glowing assessment, remarking, "Ed has all the tickets—managerial, intellectual, and historical. He has always had a very clear idea of what Heritage should do and how to do it."[46]

The head of Newt Gingrich's favorite think tank (the Progress and Freedom Foundation) says that Ed Feulner is successful because "he believes so deeply in what he is doing.... There is that flame inside him." Jeffrey Eisenach was a visiting fellow at Heritage from 1989 to 1991 and had an opportunity to observe Feulner first hand. "[Washington] is a very sloppy city," he contends, in which "income and outgo are difficult to measure." To counteract that tendency, Eisenach says, "Ed demands excellence from his people."[47] Since 1977, when Feulner assumed the presidency,

The Heritage Foundation has been "the single most important institution in the conservative movement and has had far and away the greatest impact of any think tank on the political process." Heritage is "the standard," Eisenach states, "the *real* standard."[48]

A Formidable Challenge

But Heritage was not the standard in 1977 when Ed Feulner became its president. The foundation's mission was vague and its performance promising but uneven. It was regarded by most liberals as right-wing and irrelevant and by most conservatives as one part, and not a significant part, of the emerging conservative movement.

Faced with uncertainty, the board of trustees gave their new president "full liberty" to act. But Feulner had a daunting task. "Conservative ideas had been repudiated inside the Republican Party" in 1976, recalls Feulner, when Gerald Ford defeated Ronald Reagan for the presidential nomination. They had been repudiated again when Ford lost the presidency to moderate Democrat Jimmy Carter. Conservative candidates had lost several dozen 1974 congressional races because of Watergate. Conservatives "came back some in 1976," concedes Feulner, "but we were really a remnant."[49]

The foundation's financial base, moreover, was "very narrow," and "the niches we could fill on Capitol Hill were kind of ill-defined." Feulner had a staff of nine (twelve, if you counted the two Dobermans and the black Labrador one employee brought to work). Under the circumstances, he had "modest ambitions" and was amazed when the outgoing president, Frank Walton, told him during a transition session that he could envision The Heritage Foundation reaching out to the states and even the world, becoming "the central institution for the whole conservative movement." Don Lipsett made nearly the same point, telling Feulner that he thought Heritage could be "the anchor" for the movement.[50]

Carefully at first, and then with increasing confidence, Ed and the rest of the foundation's senior management strove to turn Frank Walton's vision into a reality. Feulner identifies several turning points in the foundation's history, starting in 1977 when he and the other "new guys" provided "a clear and coherent purpose" for the foundation, focusing on public policy in the fields of economics, foreign policy, and national security. "We made it clear that we were not going to be a Swedish smorgasbord of things that someone in the movement happened to think was good, reasonable, or worthwhile."[51]

And from the beginning, the new Heritage team promoted the foundation's studies and activities to all the news media. "As [Hugh] Newton says," remarks Feulner, "we don't keep just a list of conservative journalists. We are in touch with everybody, not only our friends at *Human Events* or the *Wall Street Journal,* but reporters at the *New York Times* and the *Washington Post.*"[52] According to think-tank historian James A. Smith, Heritage "is the salesman and promoter of ideas par excellence." Its marketing strategy down through the years has, quite simply, "reshaped the broader market in which all research organizations now compete."[53]

Another major move in Heritage's history, says Feulner, was building on an initial decision by Walton "to seek seriously a broad-based membership—through direct mail—as opposed to continuing to get a handful of major foundation or corporate supporters." The public relations impact was immediate: Heritage could no longer be dismissed as Joseph Coors' "hand-picked stooge in Washington."[54]

An outside observer might have supposed that Ed Feulner was sufficiently busy. But in 1978, John Macintosh, a professor of politics and a Labour member of Parliament from central Edinburgh, persuaded Feulner to seek a Ph.D. at his school, the University of Edinburgh. He received credit for most of his courses at Georgetown but still had to visit Edinburgh frequently to meet with Macintosh and other faculty. Three years later—after rising at 4:30 AM to work on his dissertation and squeezing in many transatlantic trips to Edinburgh—Ed Feulner received his doctorate from the University of Edinburgh's department of politics. His dissertation topic: the Republican Study Committee.

The next turning point in Heritage's evolution into a serious participant in the Washington policy process was the release of the first *Mandate for Leadership* in November 1980. Feulner credits *Mandate's* success to Chuck Heatherly, the man inside the foundation "who kept the discipline and made it happen," and to Ed Meese, the person on the outside who consistently sparked our "enthusiasm." Meese, says Feulner, was always conscious of "the seminal role that ideas play in changing public policy and making law."[55]

The 1983 decision to move the foundation to its present location at 214 Massachusetts Avenue, N.E, confirmed Heritage's eminent position. In his eighth floor office overlooking Capitol Hill, Feulner recalled, laughing, that Washington conservatives used to joke about holding meetings in a telephone booth. "Now," Feulner said, referring to the 65,000-square-foot Heritage headquarters, "look at our telephone booth."[56]

Back to Their Roots

Senator Bob Dole's pointed remark in the fall of 1987 that Ronald Reagan would not be sitting in the Oval Office after the next presidential election helped Feulner and other senior Heritage officials remember "why we were created" and sent them "back to our congressional roots." The foundation had a grand run during the Reagan years. Because it was regarded as the administration's "favorite think tank," nearly everybody in Washington listened when Heritage spoke. From 1980 to 1988, its annual budget increased nearly 300 percent, from $5.3 million to $14.6 million. Its staff nearly doubled, from 70 to 135. National leaders and eminent authorities such as Governor Dixie Lee Ray of Washington, Chairman Margaret Bush Wilson of the NAACP, Sovietologist Robert Conquest, Angolan UNITA head Jonas Savimbi, Nobel Laureate F. A. Hayek, U.N. Ambassador Jeane J. Kirkpatrick, Prime Minister Lee Kuan Yew of Singapore, Secretary of Education William J. Bennett, Congressman Jack Kemp of New York, Israeli Defense Minister Yitzhak Rabin, Senator Phil Gramm of Texas, Prime Minister Edward Seaga of Jamaica, Yugoslav dissident Milovan Djilas, and economist Walter Williams all stated their positions on leading domestic and foreign issues under Heritage auspices.[57]

But The Heritage Foundation, Feulner insists, was not "created as an adjunct to the Reagan administration" or any other administration. It was intended, rather, "to move public policy in a conservative direction, primarily by working with the Congress and its staff." As a consequence, the foundation's congressional liaison office was greatly expanded, and shrewd, fast-talking New Yorker Kate O'Beirne was placed in charge. O'Beirne had worked on Capitol Hill for Senator James Buckley of New York and had handled congressional relations for the Department of Health and Human Services before joining Heritage.

Knowing that the foundation needed senior, experienced people to represent it on the Hill, she hired senior House committee staffer Michael Franc as House liaison and Rick Dearborn, formerly with the Senate Republican Conference, as Senate liaison. "There is a serious government relations disease," O'Beirne explains, "a tendency to represent the Senate and the House at your organization. Mike and Rick operated the other way—they represented Heritage on the Hill."[58]

At about the same time in the late 1980s, Heritage made a significant adjustment in its research: while continuing to publish as many as 250 papers a year, it began singling out a handful of issues for special emphasis. Feulner did not want the foundation to be known as "a paper machine" that gives "every conservative every argument they need on every imaginable issue." He wanted it to be an institution that has a "major impact on major issues."[59]

That research shift led inevitably to the emergence of a group of senior policy analysts—Robert Rector, Dan Mitchell, and Scott Hodge in domestic studies; and James Phillips, Baker Spring, and Richard Fisher in foreign and national security affairs. Unlike Heritage's first just-out-of-grad-school analysts, these experts did not come and go. Rector and the others stayed with the foundation, accumulating experience, knowledge, and reputations that, over time, compared favorably with—and even overtook—those of senior researchers at other Washington think tanks like Brookings and AEI. This trend was reinforced in the mid-1990s when Heritage brought on board seasoned analysts William Beach and Patrick Fagan.

But the foundation is still best known for its quick response to issues before Congress. It agrees with publisher-presidential candidate Steve Forbes that "speed is of the essence in politics as in war." Forbes, who quotes frequently from Heritage materials, praises the foundation for developing an "intellectual cadre" that can engage effectively in the policy battles of the day.[60]

Congressional conservatives agree. House Majority Leader Dick Armey says that "when conservatives on Capitol Hill are looking to turn ideas into legislation, the first place they go is The Heritage Foundation." Senate Assistant Majority Leader Don Nickles asserts that the foundation's "new and innovative approaches to our country's biggest challenges ... have been the models on which many of our most effective laws have been based." Congressman Peter Hoekstra of Michigan, one of the rising conservative stars in the House, declares that "time and time again Heritage has played a key role in preventing the Clinton administration from expanding the federal bureaucracy."[61]

An Open-Door Policy

All along the way, the foundation has consciously reached out to the mainstream media. "We were not," says Feulner with emphasis, "going to be one of these conservative outfits that only sends its stuff to conservative friends." The policy of openness paid off: During one twelve-month period in the mid-1980s, Heritage had more op-ed articles in the *New York Times* than any other think tank. As a result, Heritage came into contact with important new audiences, and its success reinforced the notion among friends and allies that "our ideas are credible and influential."[62]

The foundation has come a long way, Feulner reflects, since the early days when Onalee McGraw's "little book on secular humanism" was Heritage's bestselling publication at just over seven thousand copies. FAIR, the liberal-left media watchdog organization, reported that in 1995 Heritage topped Brookings as the think tank most often cited by the news media. In a Nexis database search of major newspapers, radio shows, and TV programs, there were 2,268 references to Heritage compared with 2,192 references to Brookings. The American Enterprise Institute was a distant third, with 1,297 citations.[63]

Feulner's determination that Heritage remain at the cutting edge of mass communications led the foundation to invest nearly $2 million in Town Hall, the World Wide Web site of thirty-six conservative organizations and publications. Initially owned and operated by *National Review*, Town Hall was making minimal progress when Heritage got involved, and the World Wide Web took off. "I guess it's fair to say," Feulner concedes, "that I saw its potential." In fact, in late 1993 he predicted that "the Web is where the world is going," especially the new generation.[64] By 1997, under the sure hand of its president Charles (Chip) Griffin, Town Hall was getting over five million "hits" per month, with Heritage leading the electronic way. One Heritage trustee remarked that he didn't need to be mailed foundation materials—"I get what I want off the Heritage website."[65]

In 1996, responding to the information explosion, Feulner hired Grace-Marie Arnett, a former newspaper reporter and president of her own consulting firm, to be vice president of information marketing for the foundation. Feulner got to know Arnett when she was executive director and he was vice chairman of the National Commission on Economic Growth and Tax Reform, usually referred to as the Kemp Commission for its chairman, Jack Kemp.

Feulner's major role in the commission was predictable, given the long-standing, close friendship between the Heritage president and the former congressman and football star. Kemp met Feulner shortly after he was elected to Congress in 1970. When Kemp introduced the Jobs Creation Act in the late seventies—his first major legislative step into the supply-side world—Heritage was "the only policy organization that gave me a forum. Neither the U.S. Chamber [of Commerce] nor AEI did."[66]

Next, Kemp and Senator William Roth of Delaware introduced their three-year, 10–percent across-the-board tax cut. In response, Kemp recalls, "Ed invited me to dinner with Hayek.... Until I met Hayek, I was conservative by instinct and through my parents. Ed was responsible for much of my exposure to the Austrian School." As Kemp and others continued to develop what would be called supply-side economics, The Heritage Foundation supported them with research and analysis almost every step of the way. Says Kemp, "Heritage was at the epicenter of what turned out to be the Reagan Revolution."[67]

The one-time New York congressman is a true believer in economic freedom. Feulner remembers standing with Kemp in Moscow's Red Square in 1990. "Jack pointed out to me that the line at McDonald's was longer than the line to see Lenin's tomb."[68] It was inevitable, then, that when Bob Dole picked Jack Kemp as his running mate in 1996, the vice presidential candidate would turn to his old friend for something more concrete than advice and counsel. Ed Feulner took an unpaid leave of absence for three months to serve as "counselor" to the Kemp campaign. Even before he reported for work, Feulner stressed that he was not looking for a job in a Dole-Kemp administration. "I look forward," explained Feulner, "to this opportunity to promote conservative ideas during the campaign, and then returning to my true calling at Heritage."[69]

A typical day on the road with Kemp meant visits to three or four cities, half a dozen speeches by the candidate, meetings, heated discussions about future events, and constant communication with executive assistant Kathy Rowan and Feulner's old friend Ambassador Belden Bell back in Washington at the Dole-Kemp headquarters. Feulner wound up visiting twenty-one states and fifty-five cities, encountering supporters and users of Heritage products everywhere. Even the new Democratic senator from Louisiana, Mary Landrieu, cited Heritage research in an attack on her Republican opponent during the last days of her narrowly successful campaign. Honored to have participated in a vice presidential campaign, Feulner revealed his true feelings in a post-election report to Heritage employees: "It's really great to be back home!"[70]

Two Ears and One Mouth

Ed Feulner is a good listener who does not try to dominate every meeting or discussion. As he likes to say, "God gave us *two* ears and *one* mouth for a reason." When he has made mistakes, he says, they have usually occurred because he did not listen carefully enough to his colleagues or the foundation's trustees.

For instance, in 1989 he and Senior Vice President Burt Pines dismissed efforts by Paul Weyrich's Free Congress Foundation and other conservative groups to mobilize pro-democracy and pro-market forces inside the Soviet empire. Pines went so far as to write in *Policy Review* that "a fatigued West" was engaging in "wishful thinking" about an impending end of the Cold War. Instead of urging liberation for everyone behind the Iron Curtain, Pines endorsed Henry Kissinger's proposal to "de-Yaltafy" Europe by extending economic aid, credits, and "other appropriate help" to Moscow in exchange for its promise "to withdraw from Eastern Europe."[71] Both Pines and Kissinger seemed to accept with equanimity the ominous presence of a strengthened Soviet Union on the borders of Poland, Hungary, and all the other former members of a presumably dissolved Warsaw Pact.

Heritage trustee Robert Krieble, a financial supporter of the Free Congress Foundation's pro-democracy efforts, did not like either Kissinger's plan or Pines's *realpolitik* analysis. He saw them, said Pines, as "supporting [Mikhail] Gorbachev against the aspirations of the Baltics and the

Ukrainians and the Georgians and so forth. He brought it up before the board," Pines revealed, "and we had some very tough meetings about it. It was very heated."[72]

Krieble's low-key but determined lobbying of fellow trustees forced Feulner and Pines to reverse themselves and engage The Heritage Foundation more directly in one of the most dramatic developments of the twentieth century—the collapse of communism after a seventy-year reign of terror and intimidation. Feulner conceded that he could be faulted "for not having seen ... the desire for democracy inside the fifteen [Soviet] republics."[73] But the foundation made up for lost time by establishing a close working relationship with Boris Yeltsin and other Russian reformers and opening a Moscow office as early as November 1992.

Feulner is well paid for keeping Heritage at the top of the think tank heap. "The board sets my salary," he explains, "and they compare me not so much to the heads of other think tanks as to the head presumably of a major trade association or a major business." Surveying all that Heritage has done and its fifteenfold increase in income during Feulner's tenure as president, trustee Midge Decter says succinctly, "Ed is indefatigable and indispensable. He's worth every nickel."[74]

A Conservative Life

Ed Feulner is a big man, six feet one inch tall, and well over two hundred pounds. He wears Brooks Brothers suits and a Heritage tie every day. For many years, he wore black-rimmed eyeglasses that gave him an academic air, but has since switched to more fashionable rimless spectacles. He likes good food and choice wines and has tried more diets than Oprah Winfrey. Like Oprah, he has learned to control his weight by watching what he eats and exercising under the guidance of a personal trainer. He smokes cigars, and there are more than forty pipes of varying ages, sizes, and colors in his Williamsburg-decorated office. The office walls are crowded with photos of his public life, showing him with Ronald Reagan, George Bush, Jack Kemp, Jeane Kirkpatrick, Rush Limbaugh, Fredrich A. Hayek, Milton Friedman, and dozens of other celebrated people.

He is constantly on the go, traveling 150,000 miles a year, learning what is on the minds of conservative leaders at home and abroad, raising tens of millions of dollars for the foundation, but always finding time to buy a special gift for Linda and the children. "I've never seen," says Kenneth Sheffer, who runs Heritage's Hong Kong office, "a man with more energy and more luggage." While in Asia, Feulner will have eight to twelve meetings a day, starting with breakfast and often lasting until midnight "when he calls the Heritage office in Washington to check in."[75] He is "known and respected in capitals around the world," says Richard Allen, who asserts flatly that the Republic of China on Taiwan "owes its safe existence to a very small band of conservatives, including Ed Feulner."[76]

Feulner is renowned for his loyalty to friends. He provided a Heritage platform for Russell Kirk when that eminent conservative author was ignored by liberals and neglected by conservatives. From 1978 till his death in 1993, Kirk delivered a total of sixty lectures at Heritage. Feulner regarded him as the *"paterfamilias* of the conservative movement," says Annette Kirk.[77] And when Dick Allen was under heavy media fire as national security adviser to President Reagan in 1981, Ed Feulner filled the ballroom of the Mayflower Hotel for a "Friends of Dick Allen" luncheon.

Above all, Feulner is serious about his Catholic faith. Ken Sheffer says that in ten years and dozens of trips to Asia, Feulner has never missed Sunday Mass, "no matter how far out in the jungle we were."[78] He also remains deeply involved in the conservative movement, always checking to see that key organizations like the Philadelphia Society and the Intercollegiate Studies Institute are adequately funded and well led. While he was ISI chairman from 1989 to 1994, the organization's annual income quadrupled from $1 million to over $4 million. "ISI is the only organization," says its president, T. Kenneth Cribb Jr., "other than Heritage, for which Ed Feulner personally solicits money. We couldn't have done it without him."[79] Feulner's manifold contributions to the Mont Pelerin Society were recognized in 1996 when he was elected its president, the fifth American in fifty years to be so honored. The previous four were all Nobel Laureates in economics, and one of them, Milton Friedman, describes Feulner's contributions to the society as "an organizational miracle."[80]

In one of his last official acts, President Reagan bestowed the Presidential Citizens Medal on Ed Feulner at a simple yet solemn White House ceremony. The citation read:

As President of The Heritage Foundation, Edwin J. Feulner Jr., has been a leader of the conservative movement. By building an organization dedicated to ideas and their consequences, he has helped to shape the policy of our Government. His has been a voice of reason and values in service to his country and the cause of freedom around the world.[81]

Feulner was deeply moved because the medal honored the two most important things in his professional life—The Heritage Foundation and the conservative movement—and because it acknowledged the power of ideas to shape policy in "the cause of freedom" everywhere. The medal meant all the more because it was conferred by the president whom he admired over any other. "It was," he said, "the proudest moment of my life."[82]

9

The Next Twenty-five Years

The last twenty-five years have been full of challenge and opportunity for The Heritage Foundation. The clear and present danger of communism had to be resisted and defeated. A five-trillion-dollar welfare state had failed and was in urgent need of reform. Jimmy Carter, Walter Mondale, Michael Dukakis, and other representatives of wayward liberalism constantly had to be corrected. And for much of that time the conservative colossus of Ronald Reagan, smiling and confident, stood astride the American landscape.

But now communism has collapsed, and the "error" of big government has been acknowledged. The man who ended the Cold War without firing a shot is gone. Foolish liberals have been replaced by shrewd "centrists." It is no longer enough to cry that the emperor has no clothes. Conservatives must painstakingly construct a limited government for a penitent electorate that cries, à la St. Augustine, "Reduce my subsidies and entitlements—but not yet!"

The euphoria of the Reagan years and the jubilation of the Newt "revolution" have been replaced by the sober realization that it may take conservatives as long to reform the welfare state as it took liberals to create it.

When he was asked in 1991 where he would like The Heritage Foundation to be on its twenty-fifth anniversary, Ed Feulner replied that he hoped people would view Heritage as "a permanent institution, not unlike their college or university, and not unlike their church or synagogue, an institution that will be around for the long haul—for future generations—and that will represent their interests in Washington."[1] Today, almost no one would deny that the foundation is a permanent institution in Washington, D.C., and the nation. The young conservatives who set out to create an effective counterpart to the renowned Brookings Institution have succeeded. Indeed, Heritage has surpassed Brookings in several important aspects: It is now the most quoted think tank in the nation,[2] and Heritage's annual income is just under $30 million, one third larger than Brookings'.

In the same 1991 interview, Feulner also expressed the hope that people would regard Heritage as an institution that stood for "certain basic principles" when it was founded and "will stand for the same principles" twenty-five years from now.[3] When it was founded eighty years ago, Brookings had no fixed principles, only a fervent belief in "efficiency," so it turned liberal in the Kennedy-Johnson-Carter years and is now determinedly "centrist." But Heritage has never deviated from its conservatism. Even the foundation's severest critics will aver that Heritage stands resolutely for the free market, limited constitutional government, individual freedom and responsibility, traditional American values, and a sturdy national defense.

Moving from the general to the particular, Ed Feulner said he hoped that by 1998:

> America will have a free-trade zone from the tip of Alaska to the tip of Chile; a top marginal tax rate of 20 percent; educational choice plans in all fifty states; empowerment for the poor; a deployed SDI system; and ... fifteen independent nations where there once was a single Soviet Union.[4]

Thanks to President Bush, congressional Republicans led by Newt Gingrich and Bob Dole, and conservative institutions like The Heritage Foundation, we have a North American Free Trade Agreement (NAFTA). Ross Perot and other fervent protectionists have wound up sucking air as U.S. exports to Mexico and Canada steadily increase due to the workings of NAFTA. But significant barriers to untrammeled trade remain throughout the hemisphere, despite some progress between the United States and Chile.

And then there are taxes. Despite the Kemp Commission's call for "a flatter tax" and Bob Dole's and Steve Forbes's best efforts in behalf of a flat tax in 1996 and since, there is as yet no consensus, either in Congress or among the public, for a top marginal tax anywhere near 20 percent. Most Americans remain fixated on the annual federal deficits and the $5.4 trillion national debt, which translates into a bill of over $20,000 for every man, woman, and child in the country. The experience of the 104th and 105th Congresses showed that the conservative coalition must address the issues of taxes and spending at the same time, not separately.

As for the nation's schools, while many of them struggle to prepare their pupils for the complex informational demands of the twenty-first century, teachers unions stubbornly resist school vouchers, tuition tax credits, charter schools, and other reforms. But in spite of the unions, the determined efforts of a coalition of parents, educators, and private funders like the Bradley Foundation are bringing educational choice plans to a number of school districts. One of the most promising signs of this growing grassroots movement is the involvement of black parents, pastors, local officials, and civil rights leaders. As Nina H. Shokraii wrote in *Policy Review,* "teachers unions will find it increasingly difficult to hold back reforms that offer black children a better chance."[5]

The Welfare Scandal

As noted earlier, welfare spending in the last thirty years has cost taxpayers $5.4 trillion. This staggering sum—70 percent greater than the price tag for defeating Germany and Japan in World War II, after adjusting for inflation—has unquestionably helped America's poor in certain respects. There is, for example, little or no poverty-induced malnutrition in the United States. Poor Americans have more housing space and are less likely to be overcrowded than are average citizens in Western Europe. Analyst Robert Rector asserts that "there is little material poverty in the U.S. as the public generally understands the term."[6]

But *behavioral* poverty in America is growing at an alarming pace. The trillion-dollar welfare state has produced a breakdown in the values and conduct of the poor, leading to runaway illegitimacy, criminal activity, drug and alcohol abuse, an "eroded work ethic," and a "lack of educational aspiration."[7] To truly empower the poor, Rector, Patrick Fagan, and other Heritage analysts have proposed a wide variety of policies and programs that would, if enacted, remove the yoke of welfarism from low-income Americans and help produce a better society.

Ronald Reagan pushed hard for what became the Strategic Defense Initiative, based in large part on ideas developed by The Heritage Foundation and the late Lt. Gen. Daniel O. Graham. The need for SDI was reinforced in February 1991 when an Iraqi Scud missile killed twenty-nine American soldiers in Dharan, Saudi Arabia—the largest single loss of American life in the Persian Gulf War. Today, tragically, the nation is no better protected from missile attack than it was five or ten or twenty years ago.

In December 1995, President Clinton vetoed the fiscal year 1995 defense authorization bill because it mandated the deployment of a national missile defense system. In response, Senate Majority Leader Bob Dole and House Speaker Newt Gingrich introduced the Defend America Act of 1996—the first time ballistic missile defense ever received "the active support of the Republican leadership in both houses of Congress."[8] Dole, Gingrich, and others in Congress depended heavily on a document called *Defending America: Ending America's Vulnerability to Ballistic Missiles*, published by The Heritage Foundation. As Feulner remarked, "no think tank has done more than Heritage over the past decade to show policy-makers why missile defenses are strategically necessary and technologically feasible."[9]

Feulner's hope that fifteen independent states would replace the Soviet Union has been realized, although their "independence" admittedly varies widely, sometimes from week to week. But the Marxist-Leninist regime that launched a global revolution killing over 100 million civilian victims is no more. Heritage helped bring communism to its knees with its vigorous support of President Reagan's defense buildup and the Reagan Doctrine that put the Soviets on the defensive from Afghanistan to Nicaragua.

Words were as important as weapons in the victory over communism. "It is with words that we govern men," Disraeli once said, and Ronald Reagan, argued Feulner, governed men and nations when he had the "audacity" to call the Soviet Union the "Evil Empire." Reagan's celebration of

Captive Nations Week was another act of public diplomacy that helped give people behind the Iron Curtain "the will to continue" and ultimately prevail over tyranny.[10]

A New Conservative Establishment

It was the same will to continue in the face of adversity that sustained conservatives, particularly young conservatives like Ed Feulner and Paul Weyrich, during the 1960s and 1970s when liberalism dominated American politics and policymaking. A firm faith in the power of free individuals and free markets to make the right decisions made The Heritage Foundation a preeminent Washington institution.

Some conservatives believe that Heritage has grown too comfortable as a member of the establishment, even suggesting that it has "gone Washington." Feulner rejoins that "our goal is not to join the Washington establishment. It is to create a new conservative establishment that will supplant the old." He spells out a strategy for creating such an establishment, including forming more effective ad hoc coalitions on major political issues, improving news media coverage of conservative ideas, and building several "major academic institutions that can have a major impact on public policy." He emphasizes that in this process there are certain things that Heritage cannot and will not do. For example, "The Heritage Foundation is not a lobbying organization; we're an educational organization." Heritage's senior management seriously debated the possibility of creating a sister lobbying organization, but the idea was finally vetoed by Feulner, who decided that "lobbying would have been a great distraction from the foundation's fundamental role" of providing research for members of Congress and other policymakers.[11]

Another fundamental function of the foundation has been to encourage others—such as state-level conservative think tanks—to strengthen the conservative movement. That is why Heritage started the Resource Bank, which is now in constant touch with more than two thousand scholars and four hundred groups, large and small, worldwide. But state public-policy organizations do not require, nor do they expect, a "franchise" from Heritage. "They're independent, they're free-standing, they're self-starting," says Feulner, "and they're multiplying with extraordinary success."[12]

To further the conservative movement, Feulner promises, Heritage will continue to "hold the door open for all brands of conservatism" and make itself "a meeting place where they [can] come together." An open-door policy reflects the Heritage president's conviction that conservatism will have to become "broader-based" if it wants to be "a governing majority for the future."[13]

A governing majority. That was a bold, ambitious goal for conservatives when Ed Feulner first suggested it in 1991. Are conservatives closer to that goal as the nation approaches the year 2000? On the one hand, Clinton's easy reelection in 1996 and the Republicans' thin margin in the 105th Congress seem to suggest that a conservative majority remains elusive. Divided and *somewhat* limited government appears to be the present preference of the American people. On the other hand, President Clinton did not receive 50 percent of the popular vote, congressional Republicans did retain their majority in both Houses, and thirty-two states have Republican governors. All of which suggests that a governing conservative majority remains an achievable objective, depending upon the results of the 1998 congressional elections and the Republican presidential nominee in 2000.

But if conservatives do not attain a governing majority (that is, effective control of both the executive and the legislative branches) sometime in the early 2000s, the political viability of the conservative movement will come into serious question. Conservatism *could* be the progressivism of the early twenty-first century, a constellation of once fresh, vibrant ideas that had their day in the political sun and then slowly faded from view. The question is, If conservatism were to fade, how would Heritage fare?

The Five "M's"

In its determination to remain a permanent Washington institution, The Heritage Foundation constantly takes stock of its performance in five essential areas—Money, Management, Message, Media, and Members.

Regarding *money:* with an annual budget of about $30 million, The Heritage Foundation is a smooth-running fund-raising operation that is the envy of every other conservative organization in America. The secret, as treasurer John Von Kannon stresses, lies in the foundation's consistent conservative message, not in rhetorical tricks or technological gimmicks.

Von Kannon and his team are superb salesmen because they believe deeply in what they are selling. "Thou shalt not lie," says Von Kannon, is a good commandment for fund-raising as well as for everyday life.[14]

However, there is some concern whether a much-discussed "endowment" will affect future fund-raising, internally and externally. Will the development staff, for example, be as diligent in its efforts, or will it begin to coast, knowing it can rely on the endowment? Will donors be as generous as in the past, or will they feel that the foundation does not really need their support? As a top Heritage official put it, "How do you keep your edge?"[15]

Heritage *management*, by almost universal agreement, has been outstanding for the past twenty years, primarily because of one person— Edwin J. Feulner Jr. At fifty-six, Feulner is a seasoned, gray-at-the-temples chief executive but still enthusiastic about directing the foundation and contributing to the conservative movement. He has no thought of retiring: "Heritage is my life."[16]

But inevitably, in the next decade or so, Ed Feulner will choose to step down as president of The Heritage Foundation. What kind of person should succeed him? Feulner and other senior managers and the board of trustees have begun considering the question. Before anything else, regardless of his or her managerial or fund-raising ability, or political or communications skills, a Heritage president must be a conservative, and a more traditional than a libertarian conservative. The foundation needs a person, says Feulner, who understands and can use economics but has "a deep religious commitment to a higher order." It is "essential," remarks the head of Heritage, "to remember our place. Politics is only a part, public policy is only a part of what we are."[17]

Although it is a nonprofit research organization, Heritage functions more like a business than a university. Every year the foundation goes through a rigorous "management by objective" process that becomes its "business plan" for the next twelve months. Priority issues are agreed upon and a budget is set. At the top of the foundation's management is the chief executive officer, the CEO in corporate parlance. Ed Feulner's successor will be expected to do what Feulner has been doing: ensure the development of new ideas, uncover new talent, effectively market those ideas and talent, and raise the funds necessary to balance the budget.

And he or she must have a vision that encompasses the world. It is no accident that, at a time when some conservatives and other Americans are drifting toward neo-isolationism, The Heritage Foundation continues to analyze a broad range of foreign policy and defense issues, from the appropriate size of the U.S. military to trade with former Cold War adversaries to the uncertain future of potential flashpoints like Hong Kong and North Korea. As Feulner states in his foreword to the foundation's ambitious study, *Restoring American Leadership*, "leadership is not a luxury for America; it is a necessity."[18]

Ed Feulner is well aware of what can happen to even the best of institutions under the wrong leadership. The American Enterprise Institute nearly went under in the mid-1980s when William J. Baroody Jr., handpicked by his father to succeed him as AEI president, ran "a one-man show" and failed to "hold the confidence" of foundations and corporate sponsors.[19] In London, the retiring founders of the prestigious Institute of Economic Affairs picked "the wrong guy," a man who did not understand that the IEA was a think tank, not a trade association. He was soon replaced by John Blundell, who has done a "spectacular" job of getting the institute back on track.[20] The foundation's management and trustees are determined that Heritage will not go the way of either AEI or IEA.

The *message* of The Heritage Foundation flows from its five-fold mission: to promote conservative public policies based on the principles of free enterprise, limited government, individual freedom, traditional American values, and a strong national defense. Heritage analysts believe that:

- The private sector can be depended upon to make better economic decisions than the public sector in ninety-nine out of one hundred cases.
- Government serves the governed best when it is limited.
- Individuals need freedom to exercise responsibility.
- Good men and women produce a good society rather than the reverse.
- Peace is best protected through military strength.
- America should not hesitate to use its power and influence to shape a world friendly to American interests and values.

That is the foundation's *message*.

Too Political?

Although some conservatives have criticized Heritage positions—on health-care reform, for example—as too "governmental," the overwhelming majority of the foundation's policy proposals would significantly reduce, but *not* eliminate, the role of government in Americans' lives. Initially, Heritage opposed federal involvement in child care. But when the possibility of child-care legislation became a certainty, says Feulner, the foundation helped shape the debate so that the final bill included a voucher-type program "that could be copied in education" and even in health, welfare, and other areas. Heritage's role, says its president, is to encourage "political change at the margin," sometimes through "giant bites," often "by just nibbling away."[21]

Questions have also been raised about some of Heritage's messengers: Do they become too involved in the political process? The *Wall Street Journal* called senior policy analyst Robert Rector "one of the gurus behind the GOP's rightward swerve on welfare reform." Congressman Jim Talent (R-Mo.) sought Rector's help in writing his own welfare reform bill. Talent also consulted with the Heritage analyst when he helped draft the welfare provisions of the Contract with America. Congressional Republicans, says Talent, see Rector as "one of the foremost experts in the country."[22]

Others have charged that Heritage has functioned almost as an adjunct of the Republican Party, starting with the Reagan administration and continuing through the Gingrich revolution. Feulner explains that Heritage works more frequently with Republicans because they are more conservative than Democrats, many of whom are still enthralled with the Great Society. But the foundation has also cooperated with conservative and even occasionally with moderate or liberal Democrats who "see the light on specific issues"—Senator Daniel P. Moynihan on payroll tax cuts; Senator Lloyd Bentsen on health-care issues; Senator Bill Bradley on economic subsidies for the former Soviet Union; Senator Joseph Lieberman on defense spending; and even Senator Edward Kennedy on airline deregulation.[23]

Identifying with Republicans, in Feulner's opinion, is good for Heritage and for the conservative movement. "The future of the Republican Party, and also the future for conservatism as the driving force in the

Republican Party," he says, "is unlimited, assuming the GOP reinvigorates its grassroots operation and sticks to its articulation of conservative principles."[24]

As for lobbying, Feulner concedes that the foundation is more aggressive than other tax-exempt policy research organizations but adds, "We are free to discuss our views as outspokenly as we want, but we must discuss issues or general policy." When a study analyzes a specific bill, it outlines both the advantages and disadvantages, leaving plenty of room to maneuver. "Many other think tanks have been overly cautious in deciding just how far they can opine," Feulner told historian James A. Smith, "and the result is that their impact has not been nearly as effective as it should be. We set out to change this."[25]

Richard N. Holwill, when he was the foundation's vice president for government relations in the early 1980s, gave what is still one of the best answers to the charge that Heritage is a lobbying organization. Holwill stated that as a tax-exempt policy research organization, the foundation is not permitted to "lobby" and "in fact, we don't lobby."[26] The foundation is allowed, however, to publish studies which address policy issues facing American lawmakers. The next step in this process is crucial to an understanding of what The Heritage Foundation is and is not.

After a Heritage study is published, copies are distributed to every member of Congress, committee and congressional staff members interested in the subject, the White House, executive branch officials, and the national news media. "Though Heritage does not take a formal institutional position on any of these issues," Holwill stated, "we encourage our analysts to express their views in the clearest possible terms, and to structure their arguments in persuasive, logical ways. We don't expect everyone to agree with their findings."[27] And then Holwill added this key caveat:

> We never ask anyone to vote one way or another on a particular proposal. The line between policy analysis and lobbying is very clear. It is a line we never cross.[28]

That Heritage has never crossed the line into the mine-filled land of lobbying is attested by the fact that after twenty-five years and frequent audits, the foundation remains a tax-exempt think tank in good standing with the ever watchful Internal Revenue Service.

Keeping Up with the Media

Heritage has always been *media* savvy. As early as 1981, the foundation was marketing Heritage research to the broadcast media. Heritage analysts give hundreds of radio and television interviews each year. In 1995, a state-of-the-art radio broadcast studio was installed on the fifth floor of the Heritage building, and it is used frequently for live broadcasts by talk radio hosts from Boston to Portland. The only expense to the radio station is the cost of the long-distance telephone charges. Among the dozens of talk radio hosts who have used Heritage facilities are Blanquita Cullum, Armstrong Williams, Bob Grant, Barry Farber, Ollie North, Rabbi Daniel Lapin, Michael Medved, Ken Hamblin, and Judy Jarvis. In 1995, Heritage also began hosting an annual seminar, "Talk Radio: The Year in Review." Says Michael Harrison, editor and publisher of *Talkers* magazine, "Heritage has become the most respected, influential and user-friendly think tank in the talk radio community."[29]

Typical of Heritage's targeted approach to communications is its sponsorship of the Washington Roundtable for the Asia-Pacific Press (WRAPP), organized in 1994 by International Communications Fellow Julian Weiss and now including more than 270 members. WRAPP programs in the last two years have featured such U.S. and Asian leaders as Mitsup Sato, president of the Asian Development Bank; Congressman Doug Bereuter (R-Nebr.), chairman of the House Asia-Pacific Affairs subcommittee; Congressman Philip Crane, chairman of the House Trade subcommitte; and Martin Lee, then president of Hong Kong's Legislative Council. Mikio Haruna, Washington bureau chief for the Kyodo News Agency in Tokyo, says that WRAPP gives foreign correspondents in Washington "direct access to congressmen and other personalities—access that would otherwise be impossible."[30]

In February 1997, Heritage began a new television venture—a weekly hour-long program on NET-Political NewsTalk Network hosted by award-winning commentator-columnist Cal Thomas. Ed Feulner explained that foundation programs like its lectures and seminars in the Lehrman Auditorium and other public events would have "a second life on NET," which is available in 13.5 million households. Foundation analysts and key Washington figures are featured guests. Depending upon the demand, there could even be a "third life" for Heritage products through the sale of videotapes of the weekly programs. But, explains Feulner, the new Heritage program is not just a marketing tool. By appearing on NET, the foundation demonstrates once again that it does not insist on always being the quarterback. "When someone else has a good idea, we will happily participate in it."[31]

In all of its media undertakings, The Heritage Foundation will continue to ignore the siren song of the late Marshall McLuhan that "the medium is the message." For Heritage, the mission is the message. And the mission is to build a conservative establishment from Washington, D.C., to Washington State.

Heritage People

When Ed Feulner says that "Heritage is its people," he is referring not only to the 160 managers, analysts, and support staff who work in the building on Massachusetts Avenue, but to the more than 200,000 *members* who helped the foundation raise just under $29 million—54 percent from individual donors, 21 percent from foundations, 7 percent from corporations—in 1996. This was a slight downturn from 1995's record level. One reason for the dip was the unprecedented level of political fundraising in the Clinton-Dole race.

Heritage's contributions come from four main sources—Founders, Associates, the President's Club, and Members. Founders donate $100,000 or more per year. In 1996, twenty-six individuals, foundations, and corporations contributed at the Founder level. Associates give at least $10,000 a year, and in 1996 there were 128 Heritage Associates. The President's Club includes those who give $1,000 or more, and there were 1,186 Club members in 1996. The President's Club Executive Committee—comprising those who contribute at least $2,500—stands at 294. In 1996 $22.9 million came from some 200,000 members.

The Windsor Society is composed of individuals who provide long-range financial support for Heritage through their estates and other deferred gifts. The program is named after England's Windsor Castle, the site of its first meeting in September 1986, and is co-chaired by Heritage trustee Preston (Dick) Wells and his wife Marion. Bernard Lomas, counselor to the Heritage president, spends much of his time on the Windsor

Society. So far, some 190 gifts totaling just under $10 million have been received.

The late Donald and Helena Ibach were typical donors, neither famous nor wealthy, but the kind of people Ronald Reagan called "the countless, quiet, everyday heroes of American life." Acting on their conservative convictions, the Ibachs left the majority of their estate, almost $750,000, to The Heritage Foundation. Al and Mary Haggar, who have bequeathed 10 percent of their estate to the foundation, explain that "a bequest to Heritage can do more to protect America than anything we as individual citizens can do."[32]

But Heritage's members do far more than give money. They attend the foundation's events; read *Policy Review;* monitor Heritage activities on NET, C-SPAN, and talk radio; surf the World Wide Web (often visiting Town Hall or the Heritage website); and write letters to the editors of their local newspapers and to members of Congress. Some letters ask for information about a legislative initiative before Congress or being floated by the administration.

Many letters reveal the personal and professional importance of Heritage in their lives. Mrs. John Hoad, an Executive Committee member, says that she passes out "Heritage papers" when she invites friends over to have dinner and discuss national events. President's Club member Ardeth Blauvelt marvels at the weekly mailings of "seminal, up-to-the-minute, state-of-the-art information.... Never have I benefited more from a donation." Heritage Associate William L. Davis declares that Heritage, with its all-encompassing research, is "the 'Wal-Mart' of the think tank world."[33]

Such enthusiasm may be expected from committed conservatives, but it is unusual when the senior vice president of an airplane manufacturer is effusive in his praise, calling Heritage's work and staff "excellent," "first-rate," and "impressive." Or when the executive director of an oil company foundation pays tribute to Heritage's efforts to make "the conservative agenda ... a reality, not only in Washington but across the nation."[34]

But like the foundation's management and trustees, Heritage's members are graying: the youngest trustee, at 35, is Barb Van Andel-Gaby and the average age of a contributor is 56. The Reagan generation is passing, and the baby-boomers, comfortable with Bill Clinton, seem an unlikely source of major support for Heritage. John Von Kannon and other development officers are constantly trying to develop new audiences—through the Internet. Social conservatives and their concerns are receiving far more attention in studies by senior policy analysts like Robert Rector and Patrick Fagan and Distinguished Fellow William J. Bennett. The hiring of Lew Gayner, a former senior official of Dow Chemical, is part of the foundation's long-range plan to increase corporate support, which currently constitutes only 5 percent of annual income. (In contrast, about 40 percent of AEI's budget is derived from corporations.)

These, then, are some of the potential problems facing Heritage—complacency, the question of succession, trying to do too much, growing old. But everything in its twenty-five-year history suggests the foundation will act vigorously to solve them.

A longer-term test for Heritage, think tank historian James A. Smith suggests, will be to resist "the strongest gravitational force in Washington—the relentless pull toward the center."[35] Richard M. Weaver provided the best conservative answer for those who are attracted to the so-called "vital center." "When you drive your car," he asked, "do you drive in the middle of the road? . . . You don't, of course, if you want to stay alive and get somewhere."[36]

The Right Ideas

There are good ideas and there are bad ideas, and both have logical consequences. As Richard Weaver argued in his seminal work, *Ideas Have Consequences,* ideas like nominalism, rationalism, and materialism led inexorably to what he saw as the moral "dissolution" of the West. Man turned away from first principles and true knowledge and eagerly embraced rampant egalitarianism and the cult of the mass.[37]

But as conservative historian George Nash points out, Weaver did not write a jeremiad and leave it at that. He offered three reforms—three ideas—that would help mankind recover from modernism: the defense of private property; a purification of and respect for language; and an attitude of piety toward nature, each other, and the past. [38]

In *The Road to Serfdom,* Friedrich Hayek asserted that "planning leads to dictatorship" and the "direction of economic activity" inevitably means the "suppression of freedom." Hayek proposed a different road, the road of individualism and "classical" liberalism, which he insisted was not laissez-faire but based on a government, carefully limited by law, that encouraged competition and the functioning of a free society.[39] In their separate ways, Weaver and Hayek traced the decline of the West in the post-World War II era to "the triumph of pernicious ideas."[40]

In *The Conservative Mind*, Russell Kirk offered a passionate defense of contemporary conservatism, stating that it was "struggling for ascendancy in the United States." He declared that the essence of conservatism lay in six canons: (1) a divine intent, as well as personal conscience, rules society ("political problems, at bottom, are religious and moral problems"); (2) traditional life is filled with variety and mystery while most radical systems are characterized by a narrowing uniformity; (3) civilized society requires orders and classes ("the only true equality is moral equality"); (4) property and freedom are inseparably connected; (5) man must control his will and his appetite, knowing that he is governed more by emotion than by reason; and (6) society must alter slowly ("change and reform are not identical").[41]

In the last chapter, "The Promise of Conservatism" (its very title setting the author apart from ex-communist Whittaker Chambers, who believed that in rejecting communism he was joining the losing side), Kirk argued that the principal interests of true conservatism and old-style libertarian democracy were converging. Confronted by collectivists and the architects of the New Society, he said, conservatives must "defend constitutional democracy as a repository of tradition and order" while intelligent democrats must "espouse conservative philosophy as the only secure system of ideas with which to confront the planners of the new order."[42]

Because The Heritage Foundation rests securely on the ideas of Kirk, Hayek, Weaver, and a hundred other conservative thinkers, it has become the most influential think tank in the most important city in the most powerful nation in the world.

Appendix

Board of Trustees

1973–1997

Edwin J. Feulner Jr.	1973–
President, The Heritage Foundation, since 1977	
Marvin (Mickey) Edwards	1973–1974
Lecturer, John F. Kennedy School of Government, Harvard University	
Former Congressman from Oklahoma	
John Perrino	1973–1974
Rhode Island businessman	
J. Frederic (Fritz) Rench	1973–
President, Racine Industries, Racine, Wisconsin	
*Forrest Rettgers	1973–1974
Chairman, Heritage Board of Trustees, 1973–1974	
Executive Vice President/General Counsel, National Association of Manufacturers, Washington, D.C.	

Jack G. Wilson   1973–1980
    Former President, Television News Inc., New
        York City
    Former Assistant to the President, Adolph Coors
        Company, Golden, Colorado

Thomas C. Ellick   1974–1981
    Vice President, Corporate Relations,
        Fluor Corporation, Irvine, California

Ben B. Blackburn   1975–1984
    Chairman, Heritage Board of Trustees,
        1975–1982
    Former Congressman from Georgia
    Former President, Southeastern Legal
        Foundation, Atlanta

Walter Mote   1975–1976
    Assistant to Senator Carl T. Curtis
        of Nebraska
    Chief of Staff, Vice President Spiro Agnew

*Frank J. Walton   1975–1982
    President, The Heritage Foundation, 1975–1977
    Former Secretary of Business and
        Transportation, State of California

Joseph Coors   1977–1991
    Former President, Adolph Coors Company,
        Golden, Colorado

*J. Robert Fluor   1977–1981
    Chairman, President, CEO,
        Fluor Corporation, Irvine, California

William E. Simon   1977–
    Chairman, William Simon and Sons,
        Morristown, New Jersey
    Former Secretary of the Treasury

David R. Brown, M.D.   1978–
    Chairman, Heritage Board of Trustees, 1992 to
      present
    Chairman Emeritus, Orthopedic Associates,
      Oklahoma City, Oklahoma

*Shelby Cullom Davis   1979–1992
    Chairman, Heritage Board of Trustees,
      1985–1992
    Former U.S. Ambassador to Switzerland

Jack Eckerd   1979–1985
    Founder, Eckerd Corporation,
      Clearwater, Florida

*Joseph R. Keys   1979–1991
    President, Arch Cape Development,
      Cannon Beach, Oregon

*Robert H. Krieble, Ph.D.   1979–1996
    President, Krieble Associates,
      Washington, D.C.
    Former Chairman, Loctite Corporation,
      Newington, Connecticut

Frank Shakespeare   1979–
    Chairman, Heritage Board of Trustees,
      1982–1985
    Former Ambassador to the Vatican and to
      Portugal

Lewis E. Lehrman   1980–1994
    General Partner, Ten Squared, Greenwich,
      Connecticut

Midge Decter   1981–
    Author and lecturer, New York City
    Former Chairman, Committee for the
      Free World

Robert F. Dee   1982–1986
    Chairman, SmithKline Beckman Corporation,
        Philadelphia, Pennsylvania

*John D. (Jack) Wrather   1982–1984
    President, Chairman, Wrather Corporation,
        Los Angeles, California

*Clare Boothe Luce   1985–1987
    Author, playwright, and editor
    Former U.S. Ambassador to Italy
    Former U.S. Congresswoman from Connecticut

Thomas A. Roe   1985–
    Chairman, Roe Foundation,
        Greenville, South Carolina

Richard M. Scaife   1985–
    Publisher and Owner, Tribune-Review
        Publishing Co., Inc., Greensburg,
        Pennsylvania

Arthur Spitzer   1985–1988
    Chairman, Spitzer Investments, Los Angeles,
        California

Jay Van Andel   1985–
    Co-founder and Senior Chairman, Amway
        Corporation, Ada, Michigan

J. William Middendorf II   1988–
    Chairman, Middendorf and Company,
        Washington, D.C.
    Former Secretary of the Navy

Grover Coors   1991–
    Founder, MicroLithics, Golden, Colorado

William J. Hume   1992–
    Chairman, Basic American, Inc.,
        San Francisco, California

Thomas L. Rhodes   1993–
    President, *National Review,* New York, New York

Preston A. Wells   1993–
    President, Los Olas Development Company,
        Fort Lauderdale, Florida

Jeb Bush   1995–
    Chief Operating Officer, Codina Group,
        Miami, Florida

Barb Van Andel-Gaby   1996–
    Vice President for Corporate Affairs, Amway
        Corporation, Ada, Michigan

*Deceased

Honorary Trustees

Joseph Coors, Palm Springs, California

Kathryn Davis, Ph.D., Tarrytown, New York

Jack Eckerd, Clearwater, Florida

Henry H. Fowler, former Treasury Secretary, Alexandria, Virginia

Nancy B. Krieble, Old Lyme, Connecticut

Notes

Chapter One

1. Richard M. Nixon, television interview, January 4, 1971, in *What They Said in 1971: A Yearbook of Spoken Opinion*, Alan F. and Jason R. Pater, eds. (Beverly Hills, Calif.: Monitor Book Company, 1972), p. 191.
2. Confidential AEI memorandum, February 7, 1974, Roger Freeman Papers, Hoover Institution Archives, Stanford, Calif.
3. James Allen Smith, *Brookings at Seventy-Five* (Washington, D.C.: The Brookings Institution, 1991), p. 14.
4. James A. Smith, *The Idea Brokers: Think Tanks and the Rise of the New Policy Elite* (New York: The Free Press, 1991), pp. 130–131.
5. Timothy Adams, "Think Tank Proposals May Be Key to Reagan Policy," *Atlanta Journal-Constitution*, November 23, 1980.
6. Edwin J. Feulner Jr., *The Quiet Revolution*, unpublished 1991 manuscript.
7. *Congress and the Nation*, Vol III, *1969–1972*, Washington, D.C.: Congressional Quarterly Service, 1973, p. 168.
8. Paul Weyrich, "Laying the Right Foundations," interview by Susanna Monroney, *Rutherford* (December 1995), p. 10.
9. "Lobby Investigation," *Congressional Quarterly Almanac, 1950*, pp. 752–753.

10. Charles Lichenstein, interview with the author, March 7, 1997, Washington, D.C.

11. Feulner, *The Quiet Revolution,* p. 56.

12. Smith, *The Idea Brokers,* p. 197.

13. Ibid., pp. 197–198.

14. J. Frederic (Fritz) Rench, interview with the author, April 12, 1996, Naples, Fla.

15. Paul Weyrich, interview with the author, April 17, 1996.

16. Ibid.

17. Ibid., and Joseph Coors, interview with the author, August 18, 1996, Rancho Santa Fe, Calif.

18. Weyrich, interview, April 17, 1996.

19. Paul Weyrich, telephone interview with the author, July 18, 1996; remarks between Russell Long and Ronald Reagan, February 1, 1972, hearing of U.S. Senate Committee on Finance, Roger Freeman Papers, Hoover Institution Archives, Stanford University.

20. Lewis F. Powell, "The Powell Memorandum: Attack on American Free Enterprise System," August 23, 1971, published and distributed by the U.S. Chamber of Commerce.

21. Coors interview.

22. Stephen E. Ambrose, *Nixon: The Triumph of a Politician 1962–1972* (New York: Simon & Schuster, 1989), p. 458.

23. Coors interview; Weyrich interview.

24. Dan Joy, telephone interview with the author, May 17, 1996.

25. Weyrich interview.

26. Minutes of board of trustees meeting, March 23, 1973.

27. Weyrich interview.

28. Ibid.

29. Jeffrey B. Gayner, interview with the author, April 15, 1996, Washington, D.C.

30. Milton Friedman, notes for an afternoon panel at the National Conference on Government Responses to the Energy Crisis, January 24, 1974, Mayflower Hotel, Washington, D.C. (Provided for the author by Dr. Friedman.)

31. Smith, *The Idea Brokers,* p. 196.

32. "Prospectus for 1974," The Heritage Foundation, Inc., 415 Second Street, N.E., Washington, D.C. 20002, included in a letter from Jerry P. James to Roger A. Freeman, March 27, 1974. James was writing to Freeman to invite him to serve on Heritage's board of advisers. Roger Freeman Papers, Hoover Institution Archives, Stanford.

33. Edwin J. Feulner Jr., interview with the author, June 6, 1996, Washington, D.C.

34. Mary Elizabeth Lewis, interview with the author, July 2, 1996, Alexandria, Va.

35. Lee Edwards, *Ronald Reagan: A Political Biography* (Houston: Nordland Publishing, 1981), p. 178.

36. Ibid., pp. 182–183.

37. Milton R. Copulos, interview with the author, June 3, 1996, Washington, D.C.

38. Stuart M. Butler and Eamonn F. Butler, *The British National Health Service in Theory and Practice: A Critical Analysis of Socialized Medicine.* Public Policy Studies No. 4 (Washington, D.C.: The Heritage Foundation, June 1976), pp. 4, 37.

39. Ibid., p. 50.

40. Frank Walton, interview, *The Heritage Foundation Newsletter* I, No. 2 (November 1975), p. 2.

41. Jeffrey St. John and Jeremy Rifkin, *The Great Bicentennial Debate: History as a Political Weapon* (Washington, D.C.: The Heritage Foundation, 1976), p. 46.

42. Ibid., p. 5.

43. Lee Edwards, "The 'Real' Jimmy Carter," *Conservative Digest* (September 1976), p. 56.

44. Ibid.

45. Stephen Isaacs, "Coors' Capital Connection: Heritage Foundation Fuels His Conservative Drive," *Washington Post,* May 7, 1975.

46. Ibid.

47. *Communique II,* No. 1, published by the Heritage Foundation (January 1977), p. 3.

48. Richard Odermatt, interview with the author, March 15, 1996, Washington, D.C.

Chapter Two

1. Richard A. Viguerie, *The New Right: We're Ready to Lead* (Falls Church, Va.: Viguerie Company, 1980), pp. 76–77.
2. Ibid., p. 79.
3. J. Frederic (Fritz) Rench, interview with the author, April 12, 1996; Joseph Coors, interview with the author, August 18, 1996.
4. Lee Edwards, *Goldwater: The Man Who Made a Revolution* (Washington, D.C.: Regnery, 1995), p. 351.
5. Edwin J. Feulner Jr., *The Quiet Revolution,* unpublished 1991 manuscript, p. 60.
6. Ibid.
7. Andrew Tully, "Carter's Voting Bill Just Plain Awful," The Heritage Foundation *Communique* (June 1977), p. 6.
8. Feulner, *The Quiet Revolution,* p. 64.
9. Willa Ann Johnson, interview with the author, October 29, 1996, Washington, D.C.; Thomas C. Atwood, interview with the author, March 22, 1996, Washington, D.C.
10. Chuck Stone, "Minimum Wage Law Hurts Jobless, Economist Says," *Phildelphia Daily News,* February 2, 1978.
11. Feulner, *The Quiet Revolution,* p. 72.
12. "Freedoms Foundation Honors Heritage," The Heritage Foundation *Communique III,* No. 3 (March 1978).
13. Robert Timberg, "What the Think Tank Thought," *Baltimore Sun,* April 26, 1981.
14. In a 1986 profile of Ed Feulner, *Time* wrote that "the new 'advocacy tanks' [like Heritage] see themselves as more than merely idea incubators; they also take on the task of selling those ideas." Amy Wilentz, "On the Intellectual Ramparts," *Time* (September 1, 1986), p. 22.
15. James A. Smith, *The Idea Brokers: Think Tanks and the Rise of the New Policy Elite* (New York: The Free Press, 1991), pp. xv–xvi.
16. George H. Nash, "The Rise of Conservative Think Tanks: Some Reflections," remarks delivered at the President's Club Dinner, Indiana Policy Review Foundation, September 26, 1991, Indianapolis. Reprinted in *Indiana Policy Review* (1992), p. 3.
17. Smith, *The Idea Brokers,* p. xiv.

18. William F. Buckley Jr., ed., *Did You Ever See a Dream Walking? American Conservative Thought in the Twentieth Century* (Indianapolis: Bobbs-Merrill Company, 1970), p. xvii; George H. Nash, *The Conservative Intellectual Movement in America Since 1945* (Wilmington, Del.: Intercollegiate Studies Institute, 1996), p. xv.

19. William F. Buckley Jr. and Charles R. Kesler, eds., "Introductions" to *Keeping the Tablets: Modern American Conservative Thought* (New York: Harper & Row, 1990), pp. 6–7.

20. Ibid., p. 8.

21. Leonard W. Levy and Alfred Young, "Foreword" to *Did You Ever See a Dream Walking?* p. xi.

22. Austin Ranney, *The American Elections of 1980* (Washington D.C.: American Enterprise Institute, 1981), p. 31.

23. *Human Events*, August 25, 1979, p. 1.

24. Feulner, *The Quiet Revolution*, p. 90.

25. Ibid., pp. 92–93.

26. Robert Schuettinger and Eamonn Butler, *Forty Centuries of Wage and Price Controls: How Not to Fight Inflation* (Washington, D.C.: The Heritage Foundation, 1979).

27. Ibid., back cover.

28. *See* his "Economic Report to the U.S. Congress," delivered in January 1979, when Carter reiterated the need for "voluntary wage and price standards" to reduce inflation, *CQ Almanac* XXXV (1979), pp. 8E–9E.

29. Stuart M. Butler, "Enterprise Zones: Pioneering in the Inner City," *Critical Issues* (The Heritage Foundation, 1980), back cover.

30. Stuart Butler, "The Enterprise Zone Tax Act of 1982: The Administration Plan," Heritage Foundation *Issue Bulletin*, March 29, 1982, p. 12.

31. Phillip Truluck, interview with the author, January 30, 1997.

32. Donald J. Senese, "Indexing the Inflationary Impact of Taxes: The Necessary Economic Reform," *Critical Issues*, 1978.

33. Samuel T. Francis, "Cost Estimates of the Carter Welfare Reform Proposal," Heritage Foundation *Backgrounder*, November 11, 1977, pp. 1, 3, 5.

34. Martin Anderson, "Why Carter's Welfare Reform Plan Failed," *Policy Review* 5 (Summer 1978), pp. 37–39.

35. John Behuncik, "Heritage Study on the Backfire Bomber," April 13, 1978; "Analysis of SALT II," *National Security Bulletin,* August 1979; Jeffrey Barlow, "Study of SALT II," November 2, 1979.

36. James Phillips, "Afghanistan: The Soviet Quagmire," Heritage Foundation *Backgrounder,* October 25, 1979, pp. 1, 14, 15, 17.

37. Ibid., p. 18.

38. James Phillips, "The Soviet Invasion of Afghanistan," Heritage Foundation *Backgrounder,* January 9, 1980, p. 1.

39. *The Heritage Foundation Annual Report 1979,* inside front cover.

40. Ibid., p. 10.

41. *The Heritage Foundation Annual Report 1989,* pp. 22–26.

42. *The Heritage Foundation Annual Report 1981,* inside front cover.

Chapter Three

1. Minutes, Board of Trustees Meeting, October 9, 1979.

2. Bernard Weinraub, "Conservatives Aid Transition Plans Behind the Scenes," *New York Times,* December 15, 1980.

3. Charles Heatherly, interview with the author, August 19, 1996, Claremont, Calif.

4. Ibid.

5. Charles L. Heatherly, ed., *Mandate for Leadership: Policy Management in a Conservative Administration* (Washington, D.C.: The Heritage Foundation, 1981), p. vii.

6. Heatherly interview, August 19, 1996.

7. Ibid.

8. Ibid.

9. Robert Huberty, interview with the author, May 23, 1996, Washington, D.C.

10. Lee Edwards, *Ronald Reagan: A Political Biography* (Houston: Nordland Publishing, 1981), p. 189.

11. Heatherly interview, August 19, 1996.

12. Ibid.

13. Ibid.

14. Edwin J. Feulner Jr., statement at a news briefing about *Mandate for Leadership,* November 16, 1980.

15. Russell Kirk, "The Conservative Movement: Then and Now," The Heritage Lectures, No. 1, January 1, 1980.

16. "Executive Summary" of *Mandate,* distributed at news briefing, November 12, 1980.

17. Edwin Meese, quoted in "What the Think Tank Thought," Robert Timberg, *Baltimore Evening Sun,* April 26, 1981; E. Pendleton James and Robert Terrell, quoted in "The Heritage Report: Getting the Government Right with Reagan," Joanne Omang, *Washington Post,* November 16, 1980; David Stockman and Trent Lott, quoted in *The Heritage Foundation Annual Report 1980,* pp. 10–11.

18. Bernard Weinraub, "Conservatives Aid Transition Plans Behind the Scenes," *New York Times,* December 5, 1980; Joanne Omang, "The Heritage Report: Getting the Government Right with Reagan," *Washington Post,* November 16, 1980; Ira Allen (UPI), "Conservative Think Tank Moves into Capital Spotlight," *Los Angeles Times,* December 21, 1980.

19. Herb Berkowitz, interview with the author, July 22, 1996, Washington, D.C.

20. Omang, "The Heritage Report."

21. *Mandate,* pp. 630–631.

22. Heatherly interview.

23. Weinraub, "Conservatives Aid Transition Plans."

24. Ibid.

25. Edwards, *Ronald Reagan,* p. 254.

26. Ibid., pp. 254–255.

27. Ibid., p. 256.

28. Ibid., pp. 258–259.

29. Edwin J. Feulner, *The Quiet Revolution,* unpublished 1991 manuscript, p. 118. Feulner preached and practiced "People are policy" from his first days at Heritage. For one of many references to this maxim, see Sidney Blumenthal, *The Rise of the Counter-Establishment: From Conservative Ideology to Political Power* (New York: Times Books, 1986), p. 50.

30. Morton Kondracke, "The Heritage Model," *The New Republic* (December 20, 1980), p. 8.

31. Ibid.

32. Milton Friedman, quoted in *The Heritage Foundation Annual Report 1983*, p. 2; Edwards, *Ronald Reagan*, p. 237.

33. "Congress Enacts President Reagan's Tax Plan," *1981 Congressional Quarterly Almanac*, p. 91.

34. Thomas M. Humbert, "An Analysis of the Reagan Tax Cuts and the Democratic Alternative," Heritage Foundation *Issue Bulletin* No. 67, July 13, 1981.

35. *The Heritage Foundation Annual Report 1981*, p. 13.

36. *Congressional Quarterly Almanac* XXXVII (1981), p. 103.

37. *Annual Report 1981*, pp. 4, 8.

38. Jeffrey G. Barlow, ed., *Reforming the Military* (Washington, D.C.: The Heritage Foundation, 1981). Quotes excerpted from a summary of the monograph, May 10, 1981.

39. Burton Yale Pines, *Back to Basics: The Traditionalist Movement That Is Sweeping Grass-roots America* (New York: William Morrow and Company, 1982). For a good *Time*-like summary, see the introduction, pp. 13–27.

40. Herb Berkowitz, interview with the author, March 8, 1996, Washington, D.C.

41. Burton Yale Pines, interview with the author, May 9, 1996.

42. Ibid.

43. Ibid.

44. Burton Yale Pines, "The Case for Ignoring the World Court," Heritage Foundation *Executive Memorandum*, April 12, 1984.

45. Pines interview.

46. Milton R. Copulos, "Finally We Come Together," Heritage Foundation essay, March 19, 1982.

47. Charles A. Murray, interview with the author, June 27, 1996, Washington, D.C.

48. Charles A. Murray, *Safety Nets and the Truly Needy: Rethinking the Social Welfare System* (Washington, D.C.: The Heritage Foundation, 1982), p. 25.

49. Ibid., pp. 30, 34–35.

50. *The Heritage Foundation Annual Report 1981*, p. 10; Phillip Truluck, interview with the author, March 6, 1996, Washington, D.C.

51. Richard Larry, interview with the author, August 1, 1996, Pittsburgh, Pa.
52. John Von Kannon, interview with the author, March 8, 1996, Washington, D.C.
53. Phillip Truluck, interview with the author, January 30, 1997.
54. Richard V. Allen, interview with the author, June 7, 1996, Washington, D.C.
55. Michael Johns, telephone interview with the author, May 14, 1996.
56. Allen interview.
57. "New National Strategy Based on U.S. Lead in Space Recommended to Reagan Administration and Congress," Heritage news release based on summary of *High Frontier,* March 3, 1982.
58. Ibid.
59. Lou Cannon, *President Reagan: The Role of a Lifetime* (New York: Simon & Schuster, 1991), p. 319.
60. Ibid, p. 320.
61. Martin Anderson, *Revolution* (New York: Harcourt Brace Jovanovich, 1988), p. 96.
62. Ibid., p. 96; Feulner, *The Quiet Revolution,* p. 186.
63. Feulner, *The Quiet Revolution,* p. 186; George A. Keyworth, interview, September 28, 1987, Oral History Project, Ronald Reagan Presidential Library, Simi Valley, California.
64. Keyworth interview.
65. Cannon, *President Reagan,* p. 332.
66. Richard Gid Powers, *Not Without Honor: The History of American Anticommunism* (New York: The Free Press, 1995), p. 429.
67. Kathy Rowan, interview with the author, July 18, 1996, Washington, D.C.
68. Midge Decter, interview with the author, April 13, 1996, Naples, Fla.
69. "A Nobel Winner Assesses Reagan," *New York Times,* December 1, 1982.
70. Ibid.
71. Richard N. Holwill, ed., *The First Year* (Washington, D.C.: The Heritage Foundation, November 1981), p. 1.

72. Letter from Ronald Reagan to Edwin J. Feulner Jr., February 8, 1982, Ronald Reagan Presidential Library.

73. Dom Bonafede, *National Journal*, March 20, 1982, "Issue-oriented Foundation Hitches Its Wagon to Reagan's Star"; Kondracke, "The Heritage Model," p. 8.

Chapter Four

1. *The Heritage Foundation Annual Report 1983*, p. 20.

2. Phil McCombs, "Building a Heritage in the War of Ideas: The Tigers in the Think Tank Celebrate 10 Years," *Washington Post*, October 3, 1983.

3. Edwin J. Feulner Jr., interview with the author, June 26, 1996, Washington, D.C.

4. *The Heritage Foundation Annual Report 1985: Where the New Ideas Are Coming From*, p. 29; *The Heritage Foundation Annual Report 1986*, p. 29; *The Heritage Foundation Annual Report 1987*, p. 31.

5. *The Heritage Foundation Annual Report 1983*, p. 20.

6. *Annual Report 1986*, p. 2.

7. *The Heritage Foundation Annual Report 1984*, p. 5.

8. Peter J. Ferrara, "The Social Security System," *Mandate for Leadership III: Policy Strategies for the 1990s* (Washington, D.C.: The Heritage Foundation, 1989), p. 274.

9. Ibid., p. 275.

10. Ibid., p. 276.

11. For a discussion of the widespread attack on Goldwater, see the author's *Goldwater: The Man Who Made a Revolution* (Washington, D.C.: Regnery, 1995), ch. 10, "A Choice, Not an Echo"; ch. 14, "Anything Goes."

12. Stephen Moore, "Managing the Federal Budget," *Mandate for Leadership III*, p. 63.

13. John M. Palffy, "How to Slash $119 Billion from the Deficit," Heritage Foundation *Backgrounder*, January 1, 1984.

14. *Annual Report 1984*, p. 4.

15. Gregg Easterbrook, "Ideas Move Nations; How Conservative Think Tanks Have Helped to Transform the Terms of Political Debate," *Atlantic Monthly* (January 1986), p. 66.

16. *Annual Report 1984,* p. 9.

17. "Summit Excitement," *New York Times,* November 27, 1985; *Annual Report 1985,* p. 14. Also see Lou Cannon, *President Reagan: The Role of a Lifetime* (New York: Simon & Schuster, 1991), p. 751.

18. *Annual Report 1985,* p. 14.

19. Ibid., p. 19.

20. Lee Edwards, "The US and UNESCO: Is It Time to Rejoin?" *International Library Review* 22 (1990), pp. 109, 111.

21. Richard Bernstein, "U.S. Aide Suggests Members Take the U.N. Elsewhere If Dissatisfied," *New York Times,* September 20, 1983.

22. Stanley J. Michalak Jr., *UNCTAD: An Organization Betraying Its Mission* (Washington, D.C.: The Heritage Foundation, 1983), p. 2.

23. *Annual Report 1985,* p. 19.

24. "Washington Talk: Mandate and the Sequel," *New York Times,* December 5, 1984; "Mandate for Leadership II," book review, *Saturday Review* (February 1985); *Heritage Today* (November/December 1984), p. 9.

25. From the introduction of "Mandate for Leadership II: From Public Relations to Policy," a presentation of the Heritage Foundation to the Public Relations Society of America, March 1, 1985.

26. "Washington Talk: Scores on State of Union," *New York Times,* February 22, 1985.

27. *Annual Report 1984,* p. 3.

28. Richard Corrigan, "A National Agenda," *The National Journal* (January 12, 1985), p. 108.

29. Stuart M. Butler, Michael Sanera, and W. Bruce Weinrod, eds., *Mandate for Leadership II: Continuing the Conservative Revolution* (Washington, D.C.: The Heritage Foundation, 1984), p. 3.

30. Ibid., pp. 4, 8.

31. Ibid., pp. 223–224, 228.

32. Joanne Omang, "Reagan Urged to Oust Shultz," *Washington Post,* July 3, 1985.

33. Don Oberdorfer, "Foggy Bottom Woos Its Critics," *Washington Post,* December 29, 1985.

34. Jim Anderson, "Heritage Foundation: State Department Undermining Reagan," UPI, February 11, 1986; Bryan Brumley, "State

Department Official Criticizes Conservative Think Tank," AP, 10 March 1986.

35. Ibid.

36. Cannon, *President Reagan,* pp. 656, 661.

37. Ibid., p. 653.

38. Burton Yale Pines, "Policy on Iran: Right and Wrong," *New York Times,* December 5, 1986.

39. James A. Phillips, "The Continuing Need for a U.S. Opening to Iran," Heritage Foundation *Backgrounder,* March 5, 1987, p. 1.

40. Edwin Meese III, *With Reagan: The Inside Story* (Washington, D.C.: Regnery Gateway, 1992), p. 271.

41. Cannon, *President Reagan,* p. 704.

42. Richard Gid Powers, *Not Without Honor: The History of American Anti-communism* (New York: The Free Press, 1995), p. 411.

43. Ibid.

44. Meese, *With Reagan,* p. 286.

45. Ibid., pp. 302–303.

46. Powers, *Not Without Honor,* p. 415.

47. Feulner, *The Quiet Revolution,* unpublished 1991 manuscript, p. 202.

48. Ibid., p. 205.

49. *Washington Post,* January 25, 1985; *Annual Report 1987,* p. 27.

50. "Washington Update: Policy and Politics in Brief," *National Journal* 24, No. 51–52, December 19, 1992, p. 2899; Karl Vick, "Two Sides to Congress' Orientation," *St. Petersburg Times,* November 16, 1992; John McCaslin, "Inside the Beltway," *Washington Times,* November 9, 1992.

51. Paul Starobin, "In Town to Further Conservative Ideals," *National Journal* (December 7, 1996), p. 2649.

52. Ibid.

53. Russell Kirk, "May the Rising Generation Redeem the Time?" The Heritage Lectures, No. 371, December 11, 1991.

54. Ronald Reagan testimonial for *The Third Generation: Young Conservative Leaders Look to the Future,* ed. Benjamin Hart (Washington, D.C.: Regnery Gateway, 1987), back cover.

55. Thomas Atwood, interview with the author, March 22, 1996, Washington, D.C.

56. John Andrews, interview with the author, April 25, 1996, Chicago, Ill.

57. James Peyser, interview with the author, April 26, 1996; Andrews interview; Byron Lamm, interview with the author, April 26, 1996, Chicago, Ill.

58. Thomas A. Roe, interview with the author, April 13, 1996, Naples, Fla.

59. Joe Bast, interview with the author, April 25, 1996, Chicago, Ill.

60. Terrence M. Scanlon, interview with the author, August 5, 1996, Washington, D.C.

61. Michael S. Joyce, interview with the author, April 13, 1996, Naples, Fla.

62. Marvin Olasky, telephone interview with the author, July 25, 1996.

63. Ibid.

64. Ernest van den Haag, *Smashing Liberal Icons: A Collection of Debates* (Washington, D.C.: The Heritage Foundation, 1984), pp. 48, 51.

65. George Nash, *The Conservative Intellectual Movement in America Since 1945* (Wilmington, Del.: Intercollegiate Studies Institute, 1996), pp. 57–58.

66. Remarks by Edwin J. Feulner Jr., at luncheon meeting of Conservative Women's Network, June 21, 1996, The Heritage Foundation.

67. Remarks by Frank Shakespeare, Clare Boothe Luce Award Dinner, September 23, 1991, Washington, D.C.

68. Ibid.

69. Stuart Butler and Anna Kondratas, *Out of the Poverty Trap: A Conservative Strategy for Welfare Reform* (New York: The Free Press, 1987), p. 150.

70. Ibid., pp. 151–159.

71. Ibid., p. 243.

72. Robert Rector and Michael Sanera, eds., *Steering the Elephant: How Washington Works* (New York: Universe Books, 1987), back cover.

73. Ibid., pp. 143–144.

74. Ibid., p. 338.

75. Ibid., p. 344.

76. Ibid., pp. 346–347.

77. Edwin J. Feulner Jr., interviews with the author, June 12, 26, 1996, Washington, D.C.

78. *The Heritage Foundation Annual Report 1988: Architects of Public Policy,* p. 31.
79. Charles L. Heatherly and Burton Yale Pines, eds., *Mandate for Leadership III: Policy Strategies for the 1990s* (Washington, D.C.: The Heritage Foundation, 1989), p. xi; Peter Osterlund, "Homework for Mr. Bush," *Christian Science Monitor,* December 8, 1988; Tom DeLay, Memorandum to the Heritage Foundation, January 10, 1989.
80. Ibid., p. 14.
81. Ibid., pp. 15–16. For an extended analysis of the historical and political basis of this problem, see *The Imperial Congress: Crisis in the Separation of Powers* (New York: Pharos Books, 1989), eds. Gordon S. Jones and John Marini.
82. *Mandate for Leadership III,* p. xii.

Chapter Five

1. Edwin J. Feulner Jr., "Conservatism in a New Age," distributed by The Heritage Foundation, January 1991.
2. Ibid.
3. Ibid.
4. Ibid.
5. Remarks by Vice President George Bush, October 3, 1983, Office of the Press Secretary to the Vice President.
6. *The Heritage Foundation Annual Report 1989,* p. 6.
7. Edwin J. Feulner Jr., interview with the author, June 13, 1996, Washington, D.C.
8. Stuart M. Butler and Edmund F. Haislmaier, eds., *A National Health System for America* (Washington, D.C.: The Heritage Foundation, 1989), p. 57.
9. "Conservatives Unveil Plan for National Health-Care System," Heritage Foundation news release, June 1, 1989.
10. Ibid; see also *A National Health System for Americans,* p. 47.
11. Edmund F. Haislmaier to Stuart Butler, memorandum, June 26, 1989.
12. Stuart M. Butler, "From Welfare Recipients to Owners of Homes," *Washington Post,* October 26, 1988.

13. *The Heritage Foundation Annual Report 1988,* p. 15.
14. Robert Rector to Stuart Butler, impact statement, May 18, 1989.
15. Robert Rector, interview with the author, May 23, 1996, Washington, D.C.
16. *Annual Report 1989,* p. 17.
17. "Quayle Urges More Aid to Cambodian Rebels," *New York Times,* June 23, 1989; "Quayle Urges Peking to End Executions Now," Central News Agency, June 23, 1989.
18. "Heritage Foundation to Undertake U.S. Congress Assessment Project," Heritage Foundation news release, March 13, 1989.
19. Phillip N. Truluck, Heritage Foundation news release, March 13, 1989.
20. Dick Armey to Adam Meyerson, correspondence, April 10, 1989.
21. Meg Hunt to Kim Holmes, memorandum, September 19, 1989.
22. Senator Joseph I. Lieberman to James Phillips, November 7, 1989; James Phillips to Kim Holmes and Burt Pines, memorandum, November 30, 1989.
23. Adam Meyerson to Burt Pines, memorandum, November 22, 1989. *See also* Dan Quayle, "SDI and Its Enemies," *Policy Review* 50 (Fall 1989), pp. 2–5.
24. Adam Meyerson, interview with the author, March 6, 1996; *see* Charles R. Kesler, "The Case Against Congressional Term Limitations," *Policy Review* 53 (Summer 1990), p. 20–25.
25. Dan Balz and Ronald Brownstein, *Storming the Gates: Protest Politics and the Republican Revival* (Boston: Little, Brown and Company, 1996), p. 320.
26. "Adam Meyerson's Intellectual Journey," *Heritage Today* (September/October 1989), p. 5.
27. *Annual Report 1989,* p. 10.
28. Ronald Reagan, keynote address at The Heritage Foundation Annual Board Meeting and Public Policy Seminar, June 1990, Carmel, Calif.
29. Ibid.
30. Edwin Meese III, "The Reagan Legacy," The Heritage Foundation Annual Board Meeting and Public Policy Seminar, June 1990, Carmel, Calif.

31. Ibid.

32. Ronald W. Reagan, "The March of Freedom: The Westminster Speech," June 8, 1982, reprinted in "The President's Essay," The Heritage Foundation (December 1996), p. 30.

33. Ibid.

34. Edwin J. Feulner Jr., "The State of Conservatism 1992: Bush Recession Needs Conservative Cure," January 23, 1992. See "George Bush: Do We Need Another Establishment Candidate?" *Conservative Digest*, January 1984.

35. Edwin J. Feulner Jr., "A Conservative Manifesto: Bush Can Do for the Right What Reagan Couldn't," *Washington Post*, December 4, 1988.

36. "New Taxes Threaten Recesssion, Could Lead to Higher Spending, Study Says," Heritage Foundation news release, May 17, 1990; "Economics Panel Labels Tax Hike 'Unnecessary,'" Heritage Foundation news release, May 30, 1990.

37. Daniel F. Mitchell, "Bush's Deplorable Flip-Flop on Taxes," Heritage Foundation *Executive Memorandum*, June 28, 1990.

38. Edwin J. Feulner Jr., "The State of Conservatism 1991: Fashionably Out of Fashion Again," January 7, 1991; E. J. Dionne Jr., "Conservatives Denounce President; Heritage Foundation Cites 'Political Void,'" *Washington Post*, January 8, 1991; Phillip Truluck, interview with the author, March 13, 1996; Edwin J. Feulner Jr., "The State of Conservatism 1992: Bush Recession Needs Conservative Cure," January 23, 1992.

39. Burton Yale Pines, interview with the author, May 9, 1996.

40. Feulner, "The State of Conservatism 1992."

41. *See* Russell Kirk, "Prospects for Conservatives Part III: The Behemoth State: Centralization," The Heritage Lectures, No. 293, September 19, 1990.

42. Ibid.

43. Ibid.

44. Ibid.

45. Scott Hodge, interview with the author, April 5, 1996, Washington, D.C.

46. *The Heritage Foundation Annual Report 1990,* p. 3.

47. Frank Staar, "What Will the U.S. Fight For?" *Baltimore Sun,* January 20, 1991.

48. *The Heritage Foundation Annual Report 1991,* p. 17.

49. Michael Kinsley, "The Right Cure," TRB from Washington, *The New Republic* (July 29, 1991), p. 4; "Editorial," *National Review* (August 12, 1991), p. 10.

50. David Lauter and Edwin Chen, "Health Care for All—Three Plans Compete," *Los Angeles Times,* November 11, 1991.

51. George Archibald, "Mellowing in the Warmth of Establishment Respect," *Washington Times,* December 2, 1991.

52. William J. Bennett, "The War Over Culture in Education," The Heritage Lectures, No. 341, October 19, 1991.

53. *The Heritage Foundation Annual Report 1992,* p. 9.

54. Russell Kirk, "Renewing a Shaken Culture," The Heritage Lectures, No. 434, December 11, 1992.

55. William J. Bennett, *The Index of Leading Cultural Indicators* (Washington, D.C.: Empower America, The Heritage Foundation, and the Free Congress Foundation, March 1993), pp. i–iii.

56. Kim R. Holmes and Thomas G. Moore, "America's Proper Role in the World," *Issues '96: The Candidate's Briefing Book* (Washington, D.C.: The Heritage Foundation, 1996), p. 461.

57. Kim R. Holmes, interview with the author, March 8, 1996.

58. Kim R. Holmes, ed., *A Safe and Prosperous America: A Foreign and Defense Policy Blueprint* (Washington, D.C.: The Heritage Foundation, 1993), pp. 9–12.

59. *See* Joshua Muravchik, *Exporting Democracy: Fulfilling America's Destiny* (Washington, D.C.: AEI Press, 1991); *see also* Ben J. Wattenberg, *The First Universal Nation: Leading Indicators and Ideas about the Surge of America in the 1990s* (New York: The Free Press, 1991).

60. Russell Kirk, "Prospects for Conservatives Part I: Prospects Abroad," The Heritage Lectures, No. 274, June 14, 1990.

61. Malcolm Wallop, quoted in memorandum, Foreign Policy and Defense Studies Department, The Heritage Foundation, second quarter, 1993, p. 1.

62. *The Heritage Foundation Annual Report 1993,* p. 14.

63. Holmes, *A Safe and Prosperous America,* p. 2.

64. *The Heritage Foundation Annual Report 1994,* p. 19.

65. *Annual Report 1993,* p. 18.

66. Baker Spring, "Clinton's Defense Budget Falls Far Short," Heritage Foundation *Backgrounder Update,* March 15, 1994; Baker Spring, "The Army's Budget Choice: A Force Too Small or Hollow," Heritage Foundation *Backgrounder Update,* March 28, 1994.

67. Ibid.

68. *See* John Luddy, "This Is Defense? Non-Defense Spending in the Defense Budget," Heritage Foundation *F.Y.I.,* March 30, 1994; "More Non-Defense Spending in the Defense Budget," Heritage Foundation *F.Y.I.,* December 30, 1994.

69. Luddy, "More Non-Defense Spending," p. 3.

70. *CQ Almanac, 103rd Congress, 1st Session—1993* (Washington, D.C.: CQ Press, 1993), pp. 171–179.

71. Holmes interview.

72. *Kommunist,* 1986, *Mezhdunarodnaya Zhizn,* 1986, *Heritage Foundation Annual Report 1986,* p. 10; Kim Holmes, interview with the author, August 19, 1997. Based on Holmes' 1996 conversation with Alexander Yakovlev, Gorbachev's top aide, in Moscow.

73. *Annual Report 1991,* p. 5.

74. *Annual Report 1992,* p. 11.

75. *Annual Report 1993,* p. 17.

76. Ibid., p. 18.

77. Margaret Thatcher, remarks at The Clare Boothe Luce Award Dinner sponsored by the Heritage Foundation, September 23, 1991. The Clare Boothe Luce Award, the foundation's highest honor, was presented to Ambassador Shelby Cullom Davis and Dr. Kathryn Davis.

78. Ibid.

79. Ibid.

80. Ibid.

81. Ibid.

82. Ibid.

83. Ibid.

Chapter Six

1. Lee Edwards, "Why Bush Lost—and What It Means," *The World & I* (February 1993), 28–29.
2. Edwin J. Feulner Jr., "A New 'Mandate' for Limited Government" (January 4, 1993) in "The State of Conservatism 1993," distributed by the Heritage Foundation.
3. Ibid.
4. Ibid.
5. Ibid.
6. Ibid.
7. Ibid.
8. Ibid.
9. Ibid.
10. David S. Broder, "Urban Recipe: From Back Burner to Hot Spot," *Washington Post,* May 24, 1992.
11. Ibid.
12. Ibid.
13. Stuart Butler, interview with the author, February 26, 1997.
14. Ibid.
15. Theda Skocpol, *Boomerang: Clinton's Health Security Effort and the Turn Against Government in U.S. Politics* (New York: W. W. Norton & Company, 1996), p. 1.
16. *CQ Almanac 1993, 103rd Congress, 1st Session* (Washington, D.C.: Congressional Quarterly, 1994), p. 335.
17. Skocpol, *Boomerang,* p. 2.
18. *CQ Almanac 1994, 103rd Congress, 2nd Session* (Washington, D.C.: Congressional Quarterly, 1995), p. 355.
19. Ibid., p. 319.
20. Burdett Loomis, University of Kansas political scientist, quoted in *CQ Almanac 1994,* p. 320.
21. Skocpol, *Boomerang,* p. ix.
22. Butler interview.
23. Edwin J. Feulner Jr., "Good for What Ails You?" *Chief Executive,* May 1991.

24. "Tax Credits for Health: Wrong Rx," *New York Times* editorial, December 16, 1991.

25. John Hood, "Healthy Disagreement: The Struggle to Offer a Politically Palatable Alternative to Hillarycare," *Reason* (October 1993), 30.

26. Stuart M. Butler, "Have It Your Way: What the Heritage Foundation Health Plan Means for You," *Policy Review* 66 (Fall 1993), p. 54.

27. Ibid.

28. Ibid.

29. The following description of the Federal Employees Health Benefits Program (FEHBP) is taken from "Health Care," John C. Liu and Robert E. Moffit, ch. 10 of *Issues '96: The Candidates Briefing Book* (Washington, D.C.: The Heritage Foundation, 1996), pp. 314–315.

30. Ibid.

31. Hood, "Healthy Disagreement," p. 31.

32. James J. Kilpatrick, "A Good Idea—for Health Care," *San Diego Union-Tribune*, June 15, 1989; Michael Kinsley, "The Right Cure," *The New Republic* (July 29, 1991), 4.

33. Kinsley, "The Right Cure."

34. Hood, "Healthy Disagreement," p. 32.

35. Ibid., p. 33.

36. Michael S. Joyce, interview with the author, April 13, 1996, Naples, Fla.; John Fund, interview with the author, April 30, 1996, New York City.

37. Edwin J. Feulner Jr., "Sweet Smell of Success," *Heritage Today* (September 1996), p. 3.

38. Stuart Butler, interview with the author, February 26, 1997.

39. Butler interview, March 21, 1997.

40. "The Clinton Health Plan: A Prescription for Big Government," *A Special Report of the Heritage Foundation*, November 1993, p. 1.

41. Robert Moffit, interview with the author, March 22, 1996, Washington, D.C.

42. Skocpol, *Boomerang*, p. 148.

43. Robert E. Moffit, "A Guide to the Clinton Health Plan," Heritage Foundation *Talking Points* (November 19, 1993), pp. 1–5; "Clinton Health Plan Amounts to 'Canadian-Style, Nationalized System in

Disguise,'" Heritage Foundation news release, November 22, 1993.

44. "The Clinton Health Plan: A Prescription for Big Government," *Heritage Foundation Special Report*, November 1993.

45. *The Heritage Foundation Annual Report 1994*, p. 11.

46. Moffit, "A Guide to the Clinton Health Plan," pp. 29–30.

47. Grace-Marie Arnett, "What's in Store for Health Care," a report of The Heritage Foundation Physicians Council, September 30, 1996.

48. *The Heritage Foundation Annual Report 1993*, p. 3.

49. Ibid.

50. James Fallows, "Farewell to Laissez-Faire! Clinton Pulls a Reagan on Free-Market Republicans," *Washington Post Outlook*, February 28, 1993.

51. Impact Statement, Domestic and Economic Policy Studies, The Heritage Foundation, First Quarter—1993, p. 2.

52. Ibid.

53. Ibid., p. 3.

54. "Contract with America" (Washington, D.C.: House Republican Conference), p. 3.

55. *See*, for example, *America's Failed $5.4 Trillion War on Poverty* (Washington, D.C.: The Heritage Foundation, 1995).

56. Robert Rector, "Combatting Family Disintegration, Crime and Dependence: Welfare Reform and Beyond," Heritage Foundation *Backgrounder*, April 8, 1994, p. 3.

57. Ibid.

58. Robert Rector, "Understanding the Welfare Reform Bill," Heritage Foundation *F.Y.I.*, August 7, 1996.

59. Rick Dearborn, interview with the author, April 1, 1996, Washington, D.C.

60. Edwin J. Feulner Jr., interview with the author, September 27, 1996, Washington, D.C.

61. Kim R. Holmes, "Preface" to *The Index of Economic Freedom*, Bryan T. Johnson and Thomas P. Sheehy (Washington, D.C., The Heritage Foundation, 1995), p. vi.

62. Bryan T. Johnson and Thomas P. Sheehy, *The Index of Economic Freedom* (Washington, D.C.: The Heritage Foundation, 1995), p. v.

63. Kim R. Holmes, "In Search of Free Markets," *Wall Street Journal*, December 12, 1994.

254 The Power of Ideas

64. James K. Glassman, "Making 'Economic Freedom' an Investing Benchmark," *Washington Post,* December 11, 1994.
65. Bryan T. Johnson and Thomas P. Sheehy, *1996 Index of Economic Freedom* (Washington, D.C.: The Heritage Foundation, 1996), p. ix.
66. Bryan Johnson, interview with the author, September 5, 1996, Washington, D.C.
67. Kim R. Holmes, Bryan T. Johnson, and Melanie Kirkpatrick, eds., *1997 Index of Economic Freedom* (Washington, D.C., and New York City: The Heritage Foundation and Dow Jones & Company, Inc. 1997), p. xiv.
68. "The Wealth of Nations," *Detroit News* editorial, December 30, 1996.
69. Fred Armentrout to Julian Weiss, comment, Washington, D.C., December 15, 1996.
70. *1997 Index of Economic Freedom,* p. xii.

Chapter Seven

1. David Mason, "A Real Revolution," *The World & I* (April 1995), pp. 26–27.
2. Ibid.
3. Edwin J. Feulner Jr., interview with the author, June 11, 1996.
4. Representative Newt Gingrich, "Foreword" to *The Imperial Congress: Crisis in the Separation of Powers,* Gordon S. Jones and John A. Marini, eds. (New York: Pharos Books, 1988), p. x.
5. Representative Newt Gingrich, "What the Elections Mean to Conservatives," *Heritage Lecture,* November, 15, 1994, Washington, D.C., p. 2.
6. Rick Dearborn, interview with the author, April 1, 1996; David Mason, interview with the author, March 7, 1996; *The Heritage Foundation Annual Report 1994,* p. 25.
7. Anthony Flint, "New Republican Order Dims Harvard's Star," *Boston Globe,* November 18, 1994.
8. Walter Mears, "New Trainers for the New Herd," *Washington Times,* November 26, 1994.
9. John Von Kannon, interview with the author, January 23, 1997.
10. Edwin J. Feulner Jr., interview with the author, June 12, 1996, Washington, D.C.

11. Kevin Merida and Kenneth J. Cooper, "New Heritage Emerges in Orientation: Hill Newcomers Hear Conservative Gospel," *Washington Post,* December 10, 1994.

12. Kevin Merida, "Rush Limbaugh Saluted as a 'Majority Maker,'" *Washington Post,* December 11, 1994.

13. Katharine Q. Seelye, "Republicans Get a Pep Talk from Rush Limbaugh," *New York Times,* December 12, 1994.

14. Ibid.

15. Mears, "New Trainers for the New Herd."

16. Stuart M. Butler and Kim R. Holmes, eds., *The New Member's Guide to the Issues* (Washington, D.C.: The Heritage Foundation, 1994), p. vii.

17. Ibid., pp. 10, 15.

18. Mason, "A Real Revolution," p. 31.

19. Tamar Lewin, "Liberal Urging Has Given Way to Eerie Hush," *New York Times,* November 24, 1995.

20. Guy Gugliotta, "A Bold 'Budget Plan to Rebuild America': Heritage Foundation Wants to Set GOP's Course," *Washington Post,* April 17, 1995.

21. Peter F. Drucker, *Managing in a Time of Great Change* (New York: Truman Talley Books/Dutton, 1995), p. 306.

22. "Farm Policy Changes Praised," Heritage Foundation news release, March 29, 1996.

23. Adam D. Thierer, "Telecommunications Unbound," *The World & I* (November 1995), pp. 68–69.

24. Ibid., p. 71.

25. William Beach, interview with the author, May 14, 1996.

26. Grace-Marie Arnett, interview with the author, September 12, 1996.

27. Ibid.

28. Edwin J. Feulner Jr., interview with the author, September 27, 1996.

29. Hilary Stout, "GOP's Welfare Stance Owes a Lot to Prodding from Robert Rector," *Wall Street Journal,* January 23 1995.

30. Robert Rector and William F. Lauber, *America's Failed $5.4 Trillion War on Poverty* (Washington, D.C.: The Heritage Foundation, 1995), p. 2.

31. *See* Bill Broadway, "The Social Blessings of Believing," *Washington Post,* February 10 1996.

32. Patrick F. Fagan, "Why Religion Matters: The Impact of Religious Practice on Social Stability," Heritage Foundation *Backgrounder,* January 1996, pp. 1, 28.

33. Midge Decter, quoted in an interview with Adam Meyerson, December 30, 1996, Washington, D.C.; "Welcome to Policy Review: The Journal of American Citizenship," *Policy Review* (January/February 1996), p. 5.

34. Ibid.

35. Ibid., p. 6.

36. William A. Schambra, "By the People: The Old Values of the New Citizenship," *Policy Review* (Summer 1994), p. 32.

37. Adam Meyerson, interview with the author, March 15, 1996, Washington, D.C.

38. Dan Coats, "Can Congress Revive Civil Society?" *Policy Review* (January/February 1996), p. 25–27.

39. Edwin J. Feulner Jr., "Did We Win or Lose?" *1996 State of Conservatism,* April 11, 1966.

40. Ibid.

41. Ibid.

42. Ibid.

43. Kevin Phillips, "The Rise and Folly of the GOP: As Voter Disgust Rises, So Do Clinton's Chances," *Washington Post,* August 6, 1995, p. C1; Morton Kondracke, "Debate That Tilted to Gingrich," *Washington Times,* October 7, 1996.

44. Mona Charen, "Can the Revolution Recover?" *Washington Times,* May 17, 1996.

45. Ibid.

46. Ibid.

47. Ibid.

48. Ibid.

49. Ibid.

50. "Clear Signals," *Wall Street Journal* editorial, November 7, 1996.

51. R.W. Apple Jr., "Nation Is Still Locked onto Rightward Path, Leaving Liberals Beside Road," *New York Times,* November 5, 1996.

52. Kevin Merida, "Gingrich Pledges to Find 'Common Ground' with Clinton," *Washington Post,* November 7, 1996.

53. Stephen Goode, "Majority Leader Dick Armey Dares To Be Not Sensational," *Insight* (March 10, 1997), pp. 19–20.

54. John E. Yang and Helen Dewar, "Ethics Panel Supports Reprimand of Gingrich, $300,000 Sanction for House Rules Violations," *Washington Post*, January 18, 1997.

55. Bruce Chapman, "The Gingrich Case: At Most a Minor Failing," *Washington Post*, January 2, 1997.

56. Tony Snow, "Punishment with Side-effects and Cures," *Washington Times*, January 24, 1997.

57. Edwin J. Feulner Jr., "Defending Gingrich," Heritage News Forum, No. 2, January 23, 1997, distributed by The Heritage Foundation.

58. Cheryl Wetzstein, "GOP's Renewal Alliance Has a Vision," *Washington Times*, February 9, 1997.

59. David Brooks, "The New Bleeding Hearts," *Washington Post*, February 16, 1997.

60. Marshall Wittmann, Frank Luntz, and David Mason, remarks to The Heritage Foundation Management Meeting, January 20, 1997.

61. Laurie Kellman, "House Conservatives Adopt Agenda," *Washington Times*, February 14, 1997; "A New Conservative Agenda," Manifesto of the Conservative Action Team, *Washington Times*, February 14, 1997.

62. Helen Dewar, "Senate Takes More Conservative Bent," *Washington Post*, November 7, 1996.

63. Everett C. Ladd, "The 1996 Elections," *The World & I* (January 1997).

64. James Bennett, "President, Citing Education as Top Priority of 2nd Term, Asks for a 'Call to Action,'" *New York Times*, February 5, 1997.

65. Helen Dewar, "Republicans Take on New Challenge," *Washington Post*, February 9, 1997.

66. William Beach and John Barry, "This Bridge Needs Work," *Washington Times*, February 19, 1997.

67. Donald Lambro, "House GOP Leaders Push Positive Message on Budget," *Washington Times*, February 12, 1997.

68. "The State of the Union," *Washington Post*, February 6, 1997.

69. David S. Broder, "Bill Clinton: Community Cheerleader," *Washington Post*, February 5, 1997.

70. George F. Will, "Infantile Spectacle," *Washington Post,* February 6, 1997.
71. Ralph Brownstein, "Outpouring of Ideas from Left, Right Reflects Parties' Unsettled Agendas," *Los Angeles Times,* January 13, 1997.
72. Stuart M. Butler and Kim R. Holmes, eds., *Mandate for Leadership IV: Turning Ideas into Action* (Washington, D.C., Heritage Foundation, 1996), p. xvi.
73. Ibid., pp. xvii–xviii.
74. Ibid., p. 4.
75. Ibid., pp. 13, 18–19.
76. Ibid., pp. 26–27.
77. Ibid., p. 28.
78. Ibid., pp. 40–46.
79. Ibid., pp. 53–54.
80. Stuart M. Butler and John S. Barry, "Solving the Problem of Middle-Class Entitlements," *Mandate IV,* pp. 279, 282, 295.
81. John Hillen, "Planning a Coherent Military Strategy," *Mandate IV,* p. 543.
82. Brett D. Schaefer and Thomas P. Sheehy, "Reforming and Working with the United Nations," *Mandate IV,* p. 722.
83. Lawrence J. Korb to Kim Holmes, October 7 1996; Thomas H. Henrikson to Kim Holmes, October 8, 1996.
84. Kim R. Holmes and Thomas G. Moore, eds., *Restoring American Leadership: A U.S. Foreign and Defense Policy Blueprint* (Washington, D.C.: The Heritage Foundation, 1996), p. 67.
85. *The Heritage Foundation Annual Report 1996,* p. 21.
86. Ibid., p. xxi.
87. Donald Lambro, "Learning from Last Year's Errors," *Washington Times,* January 16, 1997.
88. Ibid.
89. Edwin J. Feulner Jr., "The Conservative March: A Long View," March 3, 1997.

Chapter Eight

1. Lee Edwards, *Goldwater: The Man Who Made a Revolution* (Washington, D.C.: Regnery, 1995), p. 351.

2. Linda Feulner, interview with the author, June 6, 1996, Belle Haven, Va.

3. Ibid.; Rex Nelson, "Building a Conservative Juggernaut," *Arkansas Democrat Gazette*, November 5, 1995.

4. Edwin J. Feulner Jr., *The Quiet Revolution*, unpublished 1991 manuscript, p. 43.

5. Edwin J. Feulner Jr., interview with the author, June 6, 1996, Washington, D.C.

6. Ibid.

7. Ibid.

8. Ibid.

9. Edwin J. Feulner Jr., interview with the author, June 11, 1996, Washington, D.C.

10. Feulner interview, June 6, 1996.

11. Feulner, *The Quiet Revolution*, p. 43.

12. Feulner interview, June 6, 1996.

13. Richard V. Allen, interview with the author, June 7, 1996, Washington, D.C.

14. Ibid.

15. Edwin J. Feulner Jr., interview with the author, June 5, 1996, Washington, D.C.

16. *See* Samuel F. Clabaugh and Edwin J. Feulner Jr., *Trading with the Communists: A Research Manual* (Washington, D.C.: Center for Strategic Studies, January 1968).

17. Feulner interview, June 11, 1996.

18. Feulner, *The Quiet Revolution*, p. 44.

19. Feulner interview, June 6, 1996.

20. Ibid.

21. Ibid.

22. Philip M. Crane, interview with the author, July 25, 1996, Washington, D.C.

23. Feulner interview, June 6, 1996.

24. Linda Feulner interview.

25. Ibid.

26. Ibid.

27. Feulner, *The Quiet Revolution*, p. 49.

28. Allen Schick, "The Supply and Demand for Analysis on Capitol Hill," *Policy Analysis* 2 (Spring 1976), p. 228.

29. Edwin J. Feulner Jr., *Conservatives Stalk the House: The Story of the Republican Study Committee 1970–1982* (Ottawa, Ill.: Green Hill Publishers, 1983), p. 4; Daniel P. Moynihan to William F. Buckley Jr., September 4, 1978, quoted in *National Review* (September 29, 1978), p. 1196.

30. Feulner, *The Quiet Revolution*, p. 51.

31. Ibid., p. 53.

32. Richard M. Nixon, "Veto of Economic Opportunity Amendments of 1971," Message to Senate, December 9, 1971, *Weekly Compilation of Presidential Documents* (Washington, D.C.: General Services Administration, December 13, 1971), p. 1615.

33. Feulner, *The Quiet Revolution*, p. 53.

34. Feulner, *Conservatives Stalk the House*, pp. 64–65.

35. Ibid., p. 91.

36. Ibid., p. 93.

37. Ibid., p. 95; Phillip Truluck, interview with the author, March 6, 1996, Washington, D.C.

38. Feulner, *Conservatives Stalk the House*, p. 150.

39. Christopher DeMuth, interview with the author, July 9, 1996, Washington, D.C.

40. David Abshire, interview with the author, July 15, 1996, Washington, D.C.,

41. Michael Armacost, interview with the author, June 21, 1996, Washington, D.C.

42. Gerald Dorfman, interview with the author, August 23, 1996, Stanford, Calif.

43. Michael Shuman, interview with the author, April 29, 1996, Washington, D.C.

44. Will Marshall, interview with the author, May 10, 1996, Washington, D.C.

45. Edward Crane, interview with the author, April 24, 1996, Washington, D.C.

46. Michael S. Joyce, interview with the author, April 13, 1996, Naples,

Fl.; Richard Larry, interview with the author, August 1, 1996, Pittsburgh.

47. James Rosenthal, "Heritage Hype: The Second-Generation Think Tank," *The New Republic,* September 2, 1985, p. 14.

48. Jeffrey Eisenach, interview with the author, June 3, 1996, Washington, D.C.

49. Feulner interview, June 11, 1996.

50. Feulner interviews, June 10, 1996 and September 27, 1996.

51. Ibid.

52. Feulner interview, June 26, 1996.

53. James A. Smith, *The Idea Brokers* (New York: The Free Press, 1991), p. 200.

54. Ibid.

55. Ibid.

56. Bernard Weintraub, "Heritage Foundation 10 Years Later," *New York Times,* September 30, 1983.

57. Feulner interview, June 26, 1996.

58. Kate O'Beirne, interview with the author, April 3, 1996, Washington, D.C.

59. Ibid.

60. Steve Forbes, interview with the author, February 3, 1997, New York City.

61. Dick Armey, quoted to the author in e-mail correspondence, March 11, 1997; Don Nickles, statement to the author, March 9, 1997; Pete Hoekstra, quoted to the author in e-mail correspondence, March 7, 1997.

62. Feulner interview, June 26, 1996.

63. Michael Dolny, "The Think Tank Spectrum," *Extra!* (May/June 1996), p. 21.

64. Feulner interview, June 26, 1996; Cloyd Laporte, interview with the author, September 19, 1996.

65. Laporte interview, September 19, 1996.

66. Jack Kemp, interview with the author, August 6, 1996, Washington, D.C.

67. Ibid.

68. Robert Dodge, "Kemp Preaches Free-Market Ideal Like a Religion," *Dallas Morning News,* August 12, 1996.

69. "Feulner Joins Kemp Campaign," *Heritage Member News* (Summer 1996), p. 1.

70. Edwin J. Feulner Jr., "It's Great to Be Back Home," *Heritage Employee News* (November/December 1996), 2.

71. Burton Yale Pines, "Waiting for Mr. X," *Policy Review* 49 (Summer 1989), pp. 2, 4.

72. George Archibald, "Mellowing in the Warmth of Establishment Respect," *Washington Times,* December 2, 1991.

73. Ibid.

74. Christopher George, "Conservative Heritage Foundation Finds Recipe for Influence: Ideas + Marketing = Clout," *Wall Street Journal,* August 10, 1995; Midge Decter, interview with the author, April 13, 1996, Naples, Fla.

75. Kenneth E. Sheffer Jr., interview with the author, September 23, 1996, Washington, D.C.

76. Ibid.

77. Annette Kirk, November 23, 1996, Williamsburg, Va.

78. Sheffer interview.

79. T. Kenneth Cribb Jr., interview with the author, November 23, 1996, Williamsburg, Va.

80. Milton Friedman, interview with the author, August 23, 1996, San Francisco, Calif.

81. Presidential Citizens Medal, awarded to Edwin J. Feulner Jr. at the White House, January 18, 1989.

82. Linda Feulner, telephone interview with the author, October 18, 1996.

Chapter Nine

1. Adam Meyerson, "Building the New Establishment: Edwin J. Feulner Jr. on Heritage and the Conservative Movement," *Policy Review* 58 (Fall 1991), p. 16.

2. Michael Dolny, "The Think Tank Spectrum: For the Media, Some

Thinkers Are More Equal Than Others," *Extra!* (May/June 1996), p. 21.

3. Ibid.

4. "Building the New Establishment," *Policy Review* (Fall 1991), p. 16.

5. Nina Shokraii, "Free at Last: Black America Signs Up for School Choice," *Policy Review* (November/December 1996), p. 20.

6. Robert Rector, "Welfare Reform," *Issues '96: The Candidate's Briefing Book* (Washington, D.C.: The Heritage Foundation, 1996), p. 207.

7. Ibid.

8. *Defending America: Ending America's Vulnerability to Ballistic Missiles,* Update of the report of the Missile Defense Study Team ("Team B") (Washington, D.C.: The Heritage Foundation, 1996), p. 1.

9. "Building the New Establishment," p. 6.

10. Ibid.

11. Ibid., pp. 10, 8.

12. Ibid., p. 9.

13. Ibid., pp. 10, 13.

14. John Von Kannon, interview with the author, March 8, 1996.

15. Edwin J. Feulner Jr., interview with the author, September 27, 1996.

16. Ibid.

17. Ibid.

18. Edwin J. Feulner Jr., "Foreword" to *Restoring American Leadership: A U.S. Foreign and Defense Policy Blueprint,* Kim R. Holmes and Thomas G. Moore, eds. (Washington, D.C.: The Heritage Foundation, 1996), p. ix.

19. James A. Smith, *The Idea Brokers* (New York: The Free Press, 1991), p. 204.

20. Feulner interview, September 27, 1996.

21. "Building the New Establishment," p. 11.

22. Hilary Stout, "GOP's Welfare Stance Owes a Lot to Prodding from Robert Rector," *Wall Street Journal,* January 23, 1995.

23. "Building the New Establishment," p. 15.

24. Ibid.

25. Smith, *The Idea Brokers,* p. 201.

26. *The Heritage Foundation Annual Report 1992,* p. 12.
27. Ibid.
28. Ibid.
29. *The Heritage Foundation Annual Report 1995,* p. 26.
30. Julian Weiss to the author, memorandum, November 25, 1996.
31. Edwin J. Feulner Jr., interview with the author, January 23, 1997, Washington, D. C.
32. *Windsor* newsletter (Summer 1992), p. 3; *Heritage Foundation Annual Report 1996,* p. 43.
33. From the files of the Development Office of the Heritage Foundation.
34. Ibid.
35. Smith, *The Idea Brokers,* p. 207.
36. Richard A. Weaver, "The Middle of the Road—Where It Leads," *The Best of Human Events: Fifty Years of Conservative Thought and Action,* James C. Roberts, ed. (Lafayette, La.: Huntington House Publishers, 1995), p. 23.
37. George H. Nash, *The Conservative Intellectual Movement in America Since 1945* (Wilmington, Del.: Intercollegiate Studies Institute, 1996), pp. 34–35.
38. Ibid.
39. Friedrich A. Hayek, *The Road to Serfdom* (Chicago: University of Chicago Press, 1944), pp. xx, 70.
40. Nash, *The Conservative Intellectual Movement in America,* p. 35.
41. Russell Kirk, *The Conservative Mind from Burke to Santayana,* rev. ed. (Chicago: Henry Regnery Company, 1953), pp. 7–8.
42. Ibid., pp. 413, 424.

Selected Subject Bibliography

Key

(AS) Asian Studies, (ASB) Asian Studies Backgrounder, (B) Backgrounder, (BEI) Business/Education Insider, (BU) Backgrounder Update, (CB) Committee Briefing, (CI) Critical Issues, (EM) Executive Memorandum, (EU) Education Update, (FBR) Federal Budget Reporter, (FI) Fiscal Issues, (HL) Heritage Lecture, (IB) Issue Bulletin, (Intl. Br.) International Briefing, (M) General Monograph, (NSR) National Security Record, (PR) Policy Review, (SDI) The SDI Report, (TP) Talking Points, (UN) United Nations Studies, (USSR) U.S.S.R. Monitor.

Domestic Issues

General

Butler, Stuart M., Michael Sanera, and W. Bruce Weinrod, eds. *Mandate for Leadership II: Continuing the Conservative Revolution.* 1984.

Heatherly, Charles L., ed. *Mandate for Leadership: Policy Management in a Conservative Administration.* 1981.

Heatherly, Charles L., and Burton Yale Pines, eds. *Mandate for Leadership III: Policy Strategies for the 1990s.* 1989.

Hodge, Scott A. "Putting Families First: An Alternative to Higher Taxes and More Spending." (TP) 1993.

Holwill, Richard N., ed. *Agenda '83: A Mandate for Leadership Report.* 1983.

———. *The First Year: A Mandate for Leadership Report.* 1982.

Agriculture

Armey, Dick. "Moscow on the Mississippi: America's Soviet-Style Farm Policy." (PR) Winter 1990.

Frydenlund, John. *Freeing America's Farmers: The Heritage Plan for Rural Prosperity.* 1995.

Economics

General

Feulner, Edwin J., Jr. *Congress and the New International Economic Order.* (M). 1976.

Hudgins, Edward L. "Private Property: The Basis of Economic Reform in Less Developed Countries." (B 770) 1990.

Johnson, Bryan T., and Thomas P. Sheehy. *The Index of Economic Freedom.* 1995.

————. *1996 Index of Economic Freedom.* 1996.

Kemp, Jack. "Shaping America's Economic Course." (HL 451) 1993.

McKenzie, Richard B. *Constitutional Economics.* Lexington, Mass.: Lexington Books, 1984.

Mitchell, Daniel J. "Tax Rates, Fairness, and Economic Growth." (B 860) 1991.

Rumsfeld, Donald. "Thoughts from Business on Downsizing." (CB 15) 1995.

Sheldon, Arthur. *Corrigible Capitalism, Incorrigible Socialism.* (CI) 1981.

Singer, S. Fred. *Free Market Energy: The Way to Benefit Consumers.* New York: Universe Books, 1984.

Van den Haag, Ernest, ed. *Capitalism: Sources of Hostility.* New Rochelle, N.Y.: Epoch, 1979.

Banking & Monetary Issues

Bartlett, Bruce R. *Reaganomics—Supply-Side Economics in Action.* New York: Quill, 1982.

Colberg, Marshall R. *The Consumer Impact of Repeal of 14b.* (M) 1978.

Ely, Bert. "Confronting the Saving and Loan Industry Crisis." (IB 126) 1986.

England, Catherine. *Banking and Monetary Reform.* (CI) 1985.

Fossedal, Gregory. "The Lehrman-Mueller Hypothesis: A Theory of Deficits, Stagflation and Monetary Disorders." (PR) Winter 1992.

Germanis, Peter, Thomas Humbert, and David Raboy. *Understanding Reaganomics.* (M) 1982.

Martino, Antonio. *Constraining Inflationary Government.* (M) 1982.

Meltzer, Allan, and Alan Reynolds. *Towards a Stable Monetary Policy: Monetarism vs. the Gold Standard.* (FI) 1982.

Raboy, David G., ed. *Essays in Supply Side Economics.* (M) 1982.

Schuettinger, Robert L. *A Brief History of Price and Wage Controls from 2800 BC to AD 1952.* (M) 1974.

Schuettinger, Robert L., and Eamonn Butler. *Forty Centuries of Wage and Price Controls: How Not to Fight Inflation.* Ottawa, Ill.: Caroline House, 1979.

Budget & Deficit

Ascik, Thomas R. "The Balanced Budget Amendment." (IB 59) 1980.

Butler, Stuart M. *Privatizing Federal Spending: A Strategy to Eliminate the Deficit.* New York: Universe Books, 1985.

Butler, Stuart M., and Scott A. Hodge. "The Politics of Cutting Spending." (FYI 41) 1994.

Butler, Stuart M., and Stephen Moore, eds. *Privatization: A Strategy for Taming the Federal Budget: Fiscal Year 1988.* (M) 1987.

———. *Taming the Federal Budget: Fiscal Year 1985.* (M)

Buttarazzi, John E. "A Spending Freeze, Not New Taxes, Will Solve the Budget Crisis." (EM 181) 1987.

"Facts About the Deficit." (FRB 6) 1990.

Hale, David. "World's Largest Debtor." (PR) Fall 1986.

Hodge, Scott A. "A Lawmaker's Guide to Balancing the Federal Budget." (B 901) 1992.

————. *A Prosperity Plan for America: Fiscal 1993.* (M) 1992.

Humbert, Thomas M. "The Reagan Budget: Still Too Timid." (B 166) 1982.

Kemp, Jack. "My Plan to Balance the Budget." (PR) Spring 1986.

McAllister, Eugene J., ed. *Agenda for Progress: Examing Federal Spending.* 1980.

McAllister, Eugene J. "Balanced Budgets, Spending Limitations, and the Economy. " (B 80) 1979.

————. *Congress and the Budget: Evaluating the Progress.* (CI) 1979.

Moore, Stephen, ed. *Slashing the Deficit: Fiscal 1987.* (M) 1986.

————. *Slashing the Deficit: Fiscal 1990.* (M) 1989.

Moser, Charles A. *An Other Budget: Toward a Reordering of National Priorities.* (M) 1974.

"New Deficit Estimates to Show More Red Ink than Expected." (FBR 7) 1990.

Palffy, John M. *Slashing the Deficit.* (M) 1984.

Truluck, Phillip N., ed. *Balancing the Budget: Should the Constitution Be Amended?* (CI) 1979.

Industrial Policy

McKenzie, Richard B., ed. *The Blueprint for Jobs and Industrial Growth.* (M) 1984.

Pejovich, Svetozar. "Industrial Democracy: Conflict or Cooperation?" (B 342) 1984.

Zinsmeister, Karl. "MITI Mouse: Japan's Industrial Policy Doesn't Work." (PR) Spring 1993

Taxation

Armey, Dick. "A Republican Agenda to Reverse the Clinton Crunch." (HL 556). February 27, 1996.

Beach, William W. "Balanced Budget Talking Points #2: Who Will Benefit from Cuts in Capital Gains Taxes?" (FYI 76) 1995.

Butler, Stuart M., and Robert Rector. "Reducing the Tax Burden on the Embattled American Family." (B 845) 1991.

Christ, Carl, and Alan Walters. "The Mythology of Tax Cuts." (PR) Spring 1981.

Friedman, Milton. "The Limitations of Tax Limitations." (PR) Summer 1978.

Germanis, Peter G. "New IRA Proposal Means Bigger Savings." (EM 6) 1983.

Hodge, Scott A. "Conferees' $500 Per-Child Tax Credit Frees 3.5 Million Families from Income Tax Rolls." (FYI 71)

Humbert, Thomas M. "An Analysis of the Reagan Tax Cuts & the Democratic Alternative." (IB 67) 1981.

Liedl, Mark B., ed. *Taxation of Capital Gains: Hearing before Members of the Committee on Ways and Means, House of Representatives.* (M) 1988.

McAllister, Eugene J. "The Value Added Tax." (IB 56) 1979.

Mitchell, Daniel J. "A Brief Guide to the Flat-Tax." (TP) 1995.

———. "The State and District Impact of the Clinton Tax Increase." (BU 221) 1994.

Norquist, Grover. "Tax-Slashing 1981." (PR) Fall 1984.

Payne, James L. "The $600 Billion Tax Rip-Off." (PR) Winter 1992.

Roe Institute for Economic Policy Studies. "A Guide to Crafting a Tax Package for the Budget Resolution." (B 1043) 1995.

Senese, Donald J. *Indexing the Inflationary Impact of Taxes: The Necessary Economic Reform.* (CI) 1978.

Sennholz, Hans F. *Death and Taxes.* (M) 1976.

Ture, Norman B. *The Value Added Tax: Facts and Fancies.* (FI) 1979.

Trade & Development

Cobb, Joe. "A Guide to the New GATT Agreement." (B 985) 1994.

———. "The Real Threat to U.S. Sovereignty." (HL 497) 1994.

Hudgins, Edward L., ed. *Making America More Competitive: A Platform for Global Economic Success.* (M) 1986.

Martin, Thomas L. "The Eight Myths of Protectionism." (B 297) 1983.

Saxonhouse, Gary. "Sony Side Up: Japan's Contribution to the U.S. Economy." (PR) Spring 1991.

Smith, Wesley R., and Michael G. Wilson. "The North American Free Trade Agreement: Spurring Prosperity and Stability in the Americas." (HL 400) November 13–14, 1991.

Energy & Natural Resources

Bennett, James T., and Walter E. Williams. *Strategic Minerals.* (CI) 1981.

Copulos, Milton R. *Closing the Nuclear Option: Scenarios For Social Change.* (CI) 1978.

————. *Confrontation at Seabrook.* (CI) 1978.

————. *Domestic Oil: The Hidden Solution.* (CI) 1980.

————. *Energy Perspectives.* (M) 1978.

————. "Energy Security: The Free Market Solution." (EM 42) 1984.

————. "A Review of the Carter Energy Program." (IB 27) 1978.

————. *Securing America's Energy and Mineral Needs.* (CI) 1989.

Kahn, Herman, and Julian L. Simon. *The Resourceful Earth.* 1984.

Enterprise Zones

Beirne, Kenneth J. "The Rebirth of Urban America." (B 613) 1987.

Butler, Stuart. *Enterprise Zones: Greenlining the Inner Cities.* New York: Universe Books, 1981.

————. "How to Design Effective Enterprise Zone Legislation." (HL 215) September 21, 1989.

————. *Enterprise Zones: Pioneering in the Inner City.* (CI) 1980.

————. "Time to Enact Real Enterprise Zones." (EM 438) 1995.

————. "Urban Renewal: A Modest Proposal." (PR) Summer 1980.

Horowitz, Carl F. "How the Senate Should Strengthen the Enterprise Zone Bill." (EM 337) 1992.

————. "New Life for Federal Enterprise Zone Legislation." (B 833) 1991.

Environment

Baden, John, ed. *Earth Day Reconsidered.* (M) 1980.

Bandow, Doug, ed. *Protecting the Environment: A Free Market Appoach.* (CI) 1986.

Kahn, Herman, and Ernest Scheider. "Globaloney 2000." (PR) Spring 1981.

Krug, Edward C. "Fish Story: The Great Acid Rain Flimflam." (PR) Spring 1990.

Laffer, William G., III. "Protecting Valuable Wetlands Without Destroying Property Rights." (B 840) 1991.

Langerman, Paul. "The Clean Air Act." (B 200) 1982.

Ray, Dixie Lee. "The Greenhouse Blues." (PR) Summer 1989.

Shanahan, John. "The Conservative as Environmentalist." (HL 358) November 19, 1991.

————. "A Guide to Wetlands Policy and Reauthorization of the Clean Water Act." (IB) 1994.

Simmons, Randy T., and Urs P. Kreuter. "Herd Mentality: Banning Ivory Sales Is No Way to Save the Elephants." (PR) Fall 1989.

Simon, Julian L., and Herman Kahn, eds. *Introduction to Global 2000 Revised.* (M) 1980.

Smith, Robert J. "Privatizing the Environment." (PR) Spring 1982.

Stavins, Robert. "Clean Profits." (PR) Spring 1989.

Trevino, Victor. "Zebra Territory." (PR) Spring 1994.

Wittwer, Sylvan. "Flower Power." (PR) Fall 1992

Judicial Issues

Carrington, Frank. *Crime and Justice: A Conservative Strategy.* (CI) 1983.

Minogue, Kenneth. "Madness and Guilt: The John Hinckley Story." (PR) Summer 1983.

Labor

Galenson, Walter. *The International Labor Organization: Mirroring the U.N.'s Problems*. (CI) 1982.

Germanis, Peter G. "Creating Real Jobs: A Ten Point Strategy." (B 252) 1983.

Norquist, Grover. "Four Million New Jobs." (PR) Spring 1984.

Peterson, Wiliam H. "Six Bills Penalizing Working Americans." (IB 133) 1987.

Thierer, Adam. "Preparing for the 'Jobs Summit': The Five Principles of Job Creation." (B 982) 1994.

Tucker, Allyson M. "Six Reasons Why Bill Clinton's National Service Program Is a Bad Idea." (IB 178) 1993.

Wildavsky, Ben. "McJobs." (PR) Summer 1989.

Williford, Frederick L. *The OSHA Dilemma: An Analysis of the Citation and Penalty System as an Incentive to Comply with the Occupational Safety and Health Act*. (M) 1974.

Wilson, Mark. "Why Raising the Minimum Wage Is a Bad Idea." (B 1033) 1995.

Political Science

General

Atwood, Thomas C., ed. *Guide to Public Policy Experts: 1993–1994* and *1995–1996*. 1993, 1995.

Bennett, William J. *The Index of Leading Cultural Indicators*. (M) 1993.

Butler, Stuart M. *Agenda for Empowerment: Readings in American Government and the Policy Process*. 1990.

Butler, Stuart M., and Kim R. Holmes. *The New Member's Guide to the Issues*. (M) 1994.

D'Souza, Dinesh. "The New Liberal Censorship." (PR) Fall 1986.

Feulner, Edwin J., Jr. *Looking Back*. Edited by Herb B. Berkowitz. 1981.

Hohbach, Barbara D., and Robert Huberty, eds. *Annual Guide to Public Policy Experts*. 1989 through 1992.

Huberty, Robert, and Catherine Ludwig, eds. *The Annual Guide to Public Policy Experts.* 1982 through 1988.

———. *The Annual Insider 1981: An Index to Public Policy.* 1982.

Kirk, Russell, Paul Weyrich, George Gilder, Paul Johnson, and Ben Wattenberg. "Objections to Conservatism." (HL 3) 1981.

Limbaugh, Rush. "Why Liberals Fear Me." (PR) Fall 1994.

Meyerson, Adam. "Conservatives and Black Americans." (PR) Fall 1984.

Munn, Lynn E., ed. *The Annual Insider 1980: An Index to Public Policy.* 1981.

Parker, Fred E., Jr., ed. *The Annual Insider Index to Public Policy Studies: 1983.* 1984.

Perkins, Joseph. "Boom Time for Black America." (PR) Summer 1988.

———. *A Conservative Agenda for Black Americans.* (CI) 1986.

Perkins, Joseph, ed. *A Conservative Agenda for Black Americans.* 2nd ed. (CI) 1990.

Rifkin, Jeremy, and Jeffrey St. John. *The Great Bi-Centennial Debate.* (M) 1976.

Sutphin, Mary, ed. *The Annual Insider Index to Public Policy Studies: 1982.* 1983.

Symposium. "The Vision Thing: Conservatives Take Aim at the Nineties." (PR) Spring 1990.

Thomas, Clarence. "Why Black Americans Should Look to Conservative Policies." (HL 119) June 18, 1987.

"Two Hundred and Fifty Quotes Censored from Bartlett's." (PR) Fall 1993.

Election & Political

Ascik, Thomas R. "Restricting Political Action Committees." (IB 50) 1979.

Blackman, Paul H. *Third Party President: An Analysis of State Election Laws.* (M) 1976.

D'Souza, Dinesh. "How Conservatives Win in Liberal Districts." (PR) Summer 1984.

Ferrara, Peter J. *Issues '94: The Candidate's Briefing Book.* 1994.

———. *Issues '94: A Pocket Guide to Election Issues.* (M) 1994.

Gingrich, Newt. "Building the Conservative Movement After Reagan." (HL 167).

———. "The Life of the Party." (PR) Winter 1990.

———. "What the Elections Mean to Conservatives." (HL 510) November 15, 1994.

Kesler, Charles. "Bad Housekeeping: A Case Against Congressional Term Limits." (PR) Summer 1990.

Left and Right: Emergence of a New Politics in the 1990's? A conference by The Heritage Foundation and the Progressive Foundation. (M) 1992.

Liedl, Mark, ed. *Issues '88: Platform for America.* 3 vols. 1988.

Mason, David M. "House Term Limit Options: Good, Better, Best." (EM 406) 1995.

Mason, David M., ed. "Term Limits: Sweeping the States?" (HL 397) November 18, 1991.

Moritz, Amy. "Family Feud: Is the Conservative Movement Falling Apart?" (PR) Summer 1991.

Nash, George H. "Pilgrims Progress: America's Tradition of Conservative Reform." (PR) Fall 1991.

"The National Endowment for the Arts: Congress Avoids Responsibility." (EM 291) 1990.

Nisbet, Robert. "The Dilemma of Conservatives in a Populist Society." (PR) Spring 1978.

Schwalm, Steven A. "Back to Congress: Campaign Finance Reform." (B 885) 1992.

"Ten Years That Shook the World : A Decade of Conservative Victories, 10th Anniversary Edition." (PR) Spring 1987.

Weber, Vin. "The GOP's Idea Vacuum." (PR) Summer 1992.

Wittman, Marshall N., and Charles P. Griffin. "Restoring Integrity to Government: Ending Taxpayer-Subsidized Lobbying Activities." (B 1040) 1995.

Government & Federalism

Bradford, M. E. "Collaborators with the Left: The Monstrosity of Big-Government Conservatism" (PR) Summer 1991.

Coats, Sen. Dan, Gertrude Himmelfarb, Don Eberly and David Boaz. "Can Congress Revive Civil Society?" (PR) January–February 1996.

Felten, Eric. *The Ruling Class: Inside the Imperial Congress.* Special Abridged Edition. (M) 1993.

———. *The Ruling Class: Inside the Imperial Congress.* Washington, D.C.: Regnery Gateway. 1993.

Feulner, Edwin J., Jr. *Conservatives Stalk the House.* Ottawa, Ill.: Green Hill Publishers, Inc., 1983.

Jones, Gordon S., and John A. Marini, eds. "Foreword" by Newt Gingrich. *The Imperial Congress: Crisis in the Separation of Powers.* 1988.

Martin, David. *Screening Federal Employees: A Neglected Security Priority.* (CI) 1983.

Moynihan, Sen. Daniel Patrick. "The Most Important Decision-Making Process." (PR) Summer 1977.

Nash, George. "Completing the Reagan Revolution." (PR) Spring 1986.

Symposium. "Black America Under the Reagan Administration." (PR) Fall 1985.

Symposium. "'I Have a Dream': Ideas for Rebuilding American Society." (PR) March–April 1996.

Symposium. "Where We Succeeded, Where We Failed." (PR) Winter 1988.

Truluck, Phillip N., ed. *Private Rights and Public Lands.* (M) 1983.

Privatization

Frazier, Mark. "Privatizing the City." (PR) Spring 1980.

Glass, Stephen. "Happy Meals: School Lunch Subsidies." (PR) Summer 1995.

Hodge, Scott A. *Rolling Back Government: A Budget Plan to Rebuild America.* Washington, D.C.: Heritage Foundation, 1995.

Horowitz, Carl F. "Jack Kemp's Perestroika: A Choice Plan for Public Housing Tenants." (B 888) 1992.

Hudgins, Edward L., and Ronald D. Utt, eds. *How Privatization Can Solve America's Infrastructure Crisis.* (CI) 1992.

Shenfield, Arthur. *The Failure of Socialism: Learning from the Swedes and English.* (CI) 1980.

Regulation

Block, Frederick, and David Rivkin. "You Ain't the Right Color, Pal: The Affirmative Action Policy." (PR) Winter 1990.

Eckerly, Susan M. *A Citizen's Guide to Regulation.* (M) 1994.

England, Catherine. "Don't Cry for the Pilots—Deregulation Works." (EM 35) 1983.

Richardson, Craig E., and Geoff C. Ziebart. *Red Tape in America: Stories from the Front Lines.* (M) 1995.

———. *Strangled by Red Tape.* Special Abridged Edition. Washington, D.C.: Heritage Foundation, 1995.

Shanahan, John, and Adam Thierer. "Can We Save Even More Lives? Understanding the Opportunity Costs of Regulation." (FYI 11) 1994.

Thierer, Adam D. "A Policy Maker's Guide to Deregulating Telecommunications Part 1: The Open Access Solution." (TP) 1994.

Williams, Walter E. "Government Sanctioned Restraints That Reduce Economic Opportunities for Minorities." (PR) Fall 1977.

Ronald Reagan

Ambrose, Stephen E. et al. "How Great Was Reagan?" (PR) Fall 1988.

Bennett, William, Edwin J. Feulner Jr., Adam Meyerson et al. *Reagan Commemorative Issue.* (PR) Spring 1989.

Hackett, James T. "The State Department vs. Ronald Reagan: Four Ambassadors Speak Out." (HL 44) July 2, 1985.

Hale, David. "Reagan Versus Thatcher." (PR) Winter 1982.

Kirkpatrick, Jeane J. *The Reagan Doctrine and U.S. Foreign Policy.* (M) 1985.

Meese, Edwin, III. *With Reagan: The Inside Story.* Washington, D.C.: Regnery, 1990.

Pines, Burton Yale. "How Conservative Is Reagan's Foreign Policy?" (HL 22) September 1, 1983.

Reagan, Ronald. "Keynoting the Conservative Decade: 10th Anniversary Banquet." (HL 23) October 3, 1983.

———. "On the Eve of My Meeting with Gorbachev." (HL 141) November 20, 1987.

Symposium. "What Conservatives Think of Reagan." (PR) Winter 1984.

Symposium. "Who Should Succeed Reagan?" (PR) Summer 1986.

Weyrich, Paul. "The Reagan Revolution That Wasn't." (PR) Spring 1987.

Social Issues

General

Bennett, William. "Lost Generation." (PR) Summer 1985.

Campbell, Thomas, Michael Carvin, and Charles Grassle. "Civil Rights: Gauging Congressional Reaction." (HL 243) October 2, 1989.

Canon, David. "Abortion and Infanticide: Is There a Difference?" (PR) Spring 1985.

Carlson, Tucker. "That Old-Time Religion: Why Black Men Are Returning to Church." (PR) Summer 1992.

Decter, Midge. "The State of Our Culture." (HL 488) 1994.

———. "Why American Families Are So Unhinged." (HL 455) 1994.

Fagan, Patrick F. "Why Religion Matters: The Impact of Religious Practice on Social Stability." (B 1064) 1996.

Gramm, Phil. "Freedom and Virtue." (HL 523).

Hart, Benjamin, ed. *The Third Generation: Young Conservative Leaders Look to the Future.* Washington, D.C.: Regnery Books, 1986.

Hayek, F. A. "Our Moral Heritage." (HL 24) 1983.

Kemp, Jack. "An Inquiry into the Nature and Causes of Poverty in America and How to Combat It." (HL 263) 1990.

Kersten, Katherine. "What Do Women Want?" (PR) Spring 1991.

Kirk, Russell. *The Politics of Prudence.* The Heritage Lectures. Bryn Mawr, Pa.: Intercollegiate Studies Institute. 1993.

―――. *The Wise Men Know What Wicked Things Are Written on the Sky.* The Heritage Lectures. Washington, D.C.: Regnery-Gateway, 1986.

McGraw, Onalee. *The Family, Feminism and the Therapeutic State.* (CI) 1980.

Richardson, Heather. "The Politics of Virtue: A Strategy for Transforming the Culture." (PR) Fall 1991.

Symposium. "Sex and God in American Politics." (PR) Summer 1984.

Uzzell, Lawrence. "Abortion: Narrowing the Court's Jurisdiction." (IB 15) 1977.

Van den Haag, Ernest. "Against Natural Rights." (PR) Winter 1983.

Crime

Carlson, Tucker. "Thy Neighbor's Rap Sheet." (PR) Spring 1995.

Fagan, Patrick F. "The Real Root Causes of Violent Crime: The Breakdown of Marriage, Family, and Community." (B 1026) 1995.

Greenberg, Reuben. "Less Bang-Bang for the Buck: The Market Approach to Crime Control." (PR) Winter 1992.

Hodge, Scott. "The Crime Bill: Few Cops, Many Social Workers." (IB) 1994.

Joel, Dana C. "Time to Deal with America's Prison Crisis." (B 738) 1989.

McGuigan, Patrick. "Loose Cannons: The Self-Inflicted Wounds of the NRA." (PR) Summer 1989.

Schlesinger, Steven R. *Federalism and Criminal Justice.* (M) 1975.

Drugs

Eisenach, Jeffrey A., and Andrew Cowin. *How to Ensure a Drug-Free Congressional Office.* (M) 1991.

Eisenach, Jeffrey, ed. "Winning the Drug War: New Challenges for the 1990's." (M) (HL 297) March 20–21, 1990.

Murphy, Cait. "High Times in America: Why Our Drug Policy Can't Work." (PR) Winter 1987.

Olson, William J. "Why Americans Should Resist the Legalization of Drugs." (B 993) 1994.

Education

Allen, Jeane, ed. "Can Business Save Education? Strategies for the 1990's." (HL193) February 23, 1989.

Ascik, Thomas R. "The Equity and Choice Act: Vouchers to Give the Poor an Education Option." (IB 122) 1985.

Brock, David. "The Big Chill: P. C. on Campus." (PR) Spring 1985.

Carlson, Allan. "Sex According to Social Science." (PR) Spring 1982.

"Do Schools Contribute to Declining Moral Standards." (EU) Vol. 5, No. 5. 1984.

D'Souza, Dinesh. "National Endowment for Pornography." (PR) Spring 1982.

———. "National Endowment for Pornography Part II." (PR) Summer 1982.

"Excellence in the Schools: What Works?" (EU) Vol. 7, No. 4, 1984.

Gardner, Eileen M. *A New Agenda for Education.* (CI) 1985.

Hulsey, Angela. *School Choice Programs: What's Happening in the States, 1993 Edition.* (M) 1993.

———. *School Choice Programs 1995: What's Happening in the States.* (M) 1995.

Marshner, Susan M. *Man: A Course of Study—Prototype for Federalized Textbooks?* (M) 1975.

McGraw, Onalee. *Family Choice in Education: The New Imperative.* (CI) 1978.

———. *Secular Humanism and the Schools: The Issue Whose Time Has Come.* (CI) 1976.

Rector, Robert. "The American Family and Daycare." (IB 138) 1988.

"School Choice Initiative Expands in 1992." (BEI 28)

Tucker, Allyson M. and William F. Lauber, eds. *School Choice Programs: What's Happening in the States.* (M) 1994.

Wallis, Stephen. "How State and Local Officials Can Restore Discipline and Civility to America's Public Schools." (B 1018) 1995.

West, E. G. *The Economics of Education Tax Credits.* (CI) 1981.

Health Care Reform

Beach, William W. "The Costs to the States of Not Fundamentally Reforming Medicaid." (CB 22) 1996.

Butler, Stuart M. *The British National Health Service in Theory and Practice: A Critical Analysis of Socialized Medicine.* (M) 1974.

———. "Have It Your Way." (PR) Fall 1993.

Butler, Stuart M., ed. "Is Tax Reform the Key to Health Care Reform?" (HL 298) October 23, 1990.

Butler, Stuart M., and Edmund Haislmaier. "The Consumer Choice Health Security Act (S. 1743, H.R. 3698)." (IB 186) 1993.

Butler, Stuart M., and Edmund F. Haislmaier, eds. *A National Health Care System for America.* Revised edition. (CI) 1989.

Copeland, Lois. "Please Do No Harm." (PR) Summer 1993

Docksai, Ronald. "Putting the Patient First." (PR) Winter 1989.

Gingrich, Newt. "The Best Health Care for Everyone." (PR) Summer 1984.

Goodman, John. "More Than the Doctor Ordered." (PR) Fall 1989.

Moffit, Robert E. "Clinton's Frankenstein." (PR) Winter 1994.

———. "A Guide to the Clinton Health Plan." (TP) 1993.

———. "Overdosing on Management: Reforming the Health Care System Through Managed Competition." (HL 441) 1993.

———. "Why the Maryland Consumer Choice Health Plan Could Be a Model for Health Care Reform." (B 902) 1992.

Wolfson, Adam. "Profits with Honor." (PR) Spring 1985.

Religious Right

Atwood, Thomas. "Through a Glass Darkly." (PR) Fall 1990.

Bauer, Gary. "The Moral of the Story." (PR) Fall 1986.

D'Souza, Dinesh. "Jerry Falwell's Renaissance." (PR) Winter 1984.

———. "Out of the Wilderness." (PR) Spring 1987.

Haberman, Rabbi Joshua O. "The Bible Belt Is America's Safety Belt." (PR) Fall 1987.

Hart, Benjamin. "The Wall That Protestantism Built." (PR) Fall 1988.

Laconte, Joe. "Lead Us Not into Temptation." (PR) Winter 1995.

Reed, Ralph. "Casting a Wider Net." (PR) Summer 1993.

Social Security

Carlson, Allan. "Is Social Security Pro-Family?" (PR) Fall 1987.

Ferrara, Peter J. *Social Security Reform: The Family Plan.* (CI) 1982.

Mitchell, Daniel J. "The Facts about Cutting Social Security Taxes." (B 817) 1991.

Moser, Charles A. *The Maturity of Social Security.* (M) 1975.

Schobel, Bruce. "Sooner Than You Think: The Coming Bankruptcy of Social Security." (PR) Fall 1992.

Symposium. "Rebuilding Social Security." (HL 18) 1982.

Welfare

Butler, Stuart M. *Philanthropy in America: The Need for Action.* (FI) 1980.

Gilder, George. "The Coming Welfare Crisis." (PR) Winter 1979.

Hobbs, Charles D. *The Welfare Industry.* (M) 1978.

Kirkpatrick, Jeane. "Welfare State Conservatism." Interview by Adam Meyerson. (PR) Spring 1988.

Meyerson, Adam. "Adam Smith's Welfare State." (PR) Fall 1989.

Murray, Charles A. *Safety Nets and the Truly Needy.* (CI) 1982.

Olasky, Marvin. "Beyond the Stingy Welfare State." (PR) Fall 1990.

———. "The Right Way to Replace the Welfare State." (PR) Spring 1996.

Rector, Robert. "Combatting Family Disintegration, Crime, and Depedence: Welfare Reform and Beyond." (B 983) 1994.

———. "Why Expanding Welfare Will Not Help the Poor." (HL 450) April 28, 1993.

Rector, Robert, and William F. Lauber. *America's Failed $5.4 Trillion War on Poverty.* (M) 1995.

Symposium. "Rethinking Policy on Homelessness." (HL 194) December 14, 1988.

Unz, Ron. "Immigration or the Welfare State." (PR) Fall 1994.

Wilson, James Q., and Kathleen Sylvester. "No More Home Alone: End Money for Teen Moms Who Evade Adult Supervision." (PR) Spring 1996.

Transportation
Semmens, John. "End of the Line for Amtrack." (B 226) 1982.

Foreign Policy

General
Bandow, Doug, ed. *U.S. Aid to the Developing World: A Free Market Approach.* (CI) 1985.

Bauer, Peter, and John O'Sullivan. "Ordering the World About: The New International Economic Order." (PR) Summer 1977.

Butler, Stuart M., Michael Sanera, and W. Bruce Weinrod. *Mandate for Leadership II: Continuing the Conservative Revolution.* 1984.

"Creating a Reaganite State Department." (NSR 48) 1982.

Goldman, Morris B. *Debt/Equity Conversion: A Strategy for Easing Third World Debt.* (M) 1986.

Heatherly, Charles L. *Mandate for Leadership: Policy Management in a Conservative Adminstration.* 1981.

Heatherly, Charles L., and Burton Yale Pines, eds. *Mandate for Leadership III: Policy Strategies for the 1990's.* 1989.

The Heritage Staff. *Making the World Safe for America: A U.S. Foreign Policy Blueprint.* (M) 1992.

Holmes, Kim R., ed. *A Safe and Properous America.* 2nd ed. (M) 1994.

Kirkpatrick, Jeane. "Defining Conservative Foreign Policy." (HL 458) 1993.

Kissinger, Henry. "Observations on U.S.-Soviet Relations." (HL 174).

Menges, Constantine. "The Diplomacy of Defeat." (PR) Fall 1988.

Moore, Stephen, and Julian Simon. "Communism, Capitalism, and Economic Development: Implications for U.S. Economic Assistance." (B 741) 1989.

Pines, Burton Yale. "Ten Principles of Conservative Foreign Policy." (TP) 1991.

Pipes, Daniel. "Fundamentalists Muslims and U.S. Policy." (Intl. Br. 13) 1985.

Thatcher, Margaret, The Right Honorable. "Freedom and the Future." (HL 304) March 8, 1991.

———. "Unfinished Business, New Challenges." (HL 340) September 23, 1991.

Former Soviet Union

Bessmertnykh, Aleksandr, His Excellency. "Toward Global Cooperation Between the Soviet Union and the United States." (HL 300) November 21, 1990.

Cohen, Ariel. "Russia's Draft Constitutions: How Democratic Are They?" (B 949) 1993.

Costick, Miles M. *The Economics of Detente and U.S.-Soviet Grain Trade.*

Francis, Samuel T. *The Soviet Strategy of Terror.* (CI) 1981.

Kemp, Jack. "An Open Letter to Yeltsin." (PR) Winter 1992.

Pilon, Juliana Geran. "Closing the U.S.-Soviet Diplomatic Gap." (IB 99) 1983.

Pines, Burton Yale. "An American Conservative Views U.S.-Soviet Relations." (HL 283) September 1, 1990.

Pines, Burton Yale, and W. Bruce Weinrod. eds. *President Reagan's Summit Meeting in Geneva: Briefing Book.* 1985.

Starrels, John. *The U.S.-Third World Conflict: A Glossary.* (UN) 1983.

Symposium. "Beyond Containment? The Future of U.S.-Soviet Relations." (PR) Winter 1985.

Weinrod, W. Bruce. *Confronting Moscow: An Agenda for the Post-Detente Era.* (CI) 1985.

Weinrod, W. Bruce, ed. *Arms Control Handbook: A Guide to the History, Arsenals and Issues of U.S.-Soviet Negotiations.* (M) 1986.

"Will the Commonwealth Survive?" (USSR 28) 1992.

Latin America & The Caribbean

Ashby, Timothy. "A Nine-Point Strategy for Dealing with Castro." (B 472) 1985.

Castellanos, Sylvia. "The Cuban Refugee Problem in Perspective 1959–1980." (B 124) 1980.

DiGiovanni, Cleto, Jr. *The Inter-American Foundation: A Mandate for Leadership Report.* (M) 1981.

Gayner, Jeffrey B. "Panama: Terms of the Treaty." (B 40) 1977.

Gayner, Jeffrey B., and Lawrence D. Pratt. *Allende and the Failure of Chilean Marxism.* (M) 1974.

Inter-American Conference on Freedom and Security. Compiled by L. Francis Bouchey. (M) 1976.

Lynch, Edward A. "Bold Action in Grenada: Countering a Soviet Threat." (B 303) 1983.

Rosett, Claudia. "Economic Paralysis in El Salvador." (PR) 1984.

St. John, Jeffrey. *The Panama Canal and Soviet Imperialism: War for the World Waterways.* (CI) 1978.

Sweeney, John P. "Why the Cuban Trade Embargo Should Be Maintained." (B 1010) 1994.

"The U.S. and Mexico: Setting a New Agenda." A Heritage Foundation Conference. (HL 210) 1989.

Europe

Aron, Leon. "Gorbachev's Brest-Litovsk: The Kremlin's Grand Compromise in Eastern Europe." (B 724) 1989.

Burton, John. "Britain's Industrial Policy: Valuable Lessons for the U.S." (Intl. Br. 11) 1994.

Holmes, Kim R., and Jay Kosminsky, eds. *Reshaping Europe: Strategies for a Post-Cold War Europe.* (CI) 1990.

Hudgins, Edward L. "For Eastern Europe—An Agenda for Economic Growth." (EM 290) 1990.

Martino, Antonio. "The Future of Europe." (HL 521).

Phillips, James A. "Lift the Arms Embargo on Bosnia." (EM 421) 1995.

Pines, Burton Yale. "Waiting for Mr. X." (PR) Summer 1989.

Spring, Baker. "Assessing Clinton's Military Options in Bosnia." (B 939) 1993.

Sub-Saharan Africa

Ayittey, George B. "The End of African Socialism." (HL 250) January 24, 1990.

Buthelezi, Mangosuthu G., Chief of the Zulu Nation. "The Future of South Africa: Violent Radicalism or Negotiated Settlement." (HL 81) November 24, 1986.

———. "My Vision for South Africa." (HL 326) June 19, 1991.

Savimbi, Jonas. "The Coming Winds of Democracy in Angola." (HL 217) October 5, 1989.

———. "The War Against Soviet Colonialism." (PR) Winter 1985.

———. "Why Freedom Must Prevail in Angola." (HL 289) November 4, 1990.

Starrels, John. *East Germany: Marxist Mission in Africa.* (CI) 1981.

U.S. and Africa Statistical Handbook: 1991 Edition. Revised. Compiled and edited by Michael Johns. (M) 1991.

The Middle East & North Africa

Butterfield, Ian. "Neutralizing Qaddafi: Containing Libyan Aggression." (B 157) 1981.

Cohen, Samuel T. "Should America Defend the Persian Gulf?" (PR) Fall 1983.

Harris, George S., ed. *The Middle East in Turkish-American Relations.* (M) 1985.

Holmes, Kim R. "Fighting to Win in the Persian Gulf." (BU 153) 1991.

Holmes, Kim R., and Jay Kosminsky. "How to Defeat Iraq." (EM 279) 1990.

Muravchik, Joshua. "Misreporting Lebanon." (PR) Winter 1983.

Phillips, James A. "As Israel & the Arabs Battle, Moscow Collects the Dividends." (B 291).

———. "The Iranian Revolution: Long Term Implications." (B 89) 1979.

———. "Maintaining a Balanced U.S. Policy on Middle East Peace." (EM 318) 1992.

Rabin, Yitzhak, Defense Minister of Israel. "Middle East Update: Peace Prospects and the Danger of War." (HL 69) September 11, 1986.

Asia and the Pacific

Alves, Dora. "The South Pacific Islands: New Focus Needed for U.S. Policy." (ASB 34) 1985.

Brick, Andrew B., ed. "The Washington-Taipei Relationship: New Opportunities to Reaffirm Traditional Ties." (HL 269) October 25, 1989.

Brooks, Roger A., ed. "U.S. Policy in Asia: The Challenges for 1990." (HL 233) 1990.

Feulner, Edwin J., Jr., and Hideaki Kase, eds. *U.S.-Japan Mutual Security: The Next Twenty Years.* (M) 1981.

Fisher, Richard, Jr. "A Job Strategy for America: Expanding Free Trade with Asia." (ASB 126) 1993.

Goldwater, Senator Barry M. *China and the Abrogation of Treaties.* (CI) 1978.

Gregor, A. James, ed. *The U.S. and the Philippines: A Challenge to a Special Relationship.* (M) 1983.

Lasater, Martin L., ed. "Beijing's Blockade Threat to Taiwan." (HL 80) July 30, 1985.

———. *Taiwan: Facing Mounting Threats.* Revised 1987. (AS) 1986.

————, ed. "The Two Chinas: A Contemporary View." (M) (HL 55) January 28, 1986.

————. *U.S. Policy Toward China's Reunification.* (AS) 1988.

Lho, Shin-yong. "Prime Minister of Korea. The U.S.-Korea Success Story." (HL 52) October 25, 1985.

President Reagan's Trip to Asia: Briefing Book. Compiled by Asian Studies Center Working Group. (AS) 1983.

Scully, William L. "The Korean Peninsula Military Balance." (ASB 2) 1983.

————. "Why Japan Needs More Defense Muscle." (ASB 5) 1983.

U.S. and Asia Statistical Handbook: 1989 Edition and *1990 Edition.* Compiled and edited by Thomas Timmons. (M).

U.S. and Asia Statistical Handbook: 1991 Edition through *1995 Edition.* Compiled and edited by Kenneth J. Conboy et al. (M).

Defense

General

Armey, Dick. "Base Maneuvers." (PR) Winter 1988.

"Arms Control Violations—The 1985 Report." (NSR) 1985.

Barlow, Jeffrey G. *Reforming the Military.* (CI) 1981.

"Build More B-1s." (NSR 84) 1985.

Codevilla, Angelo et al. "A Symposium on Defense." (PR) Summer 1983.

Di Rita, Lawrence T. "Thumbs Down to the Bottom-Up Review." (B 957) 1992.

Donley, Michael B., ed. *The SALT Handbook.* (M) 1979.

Graham, Daniel O. *A New Strategy for the West.* (M) 1977.

Gray, Colin S. "The End of SALT? U.S.-U.S.S.R. Negotiations." (PR) Fall 1977.

————. "SALT II: The Real Debate." (PR) Fall 1979.

————. *Strategy and the MX.* (CI) 1980.

Kagan, Robert W. "Why Arms Control Failed." (PR) Winter 1984.

Katz, Amrom. *Verification and SALT: The State of the Art and The Art of the State.* (CI) 1979.

Kosminsky, Jay P. "Arms Control: The End of an Era." (HL 366) 1992.

Luddy, John. "Charting a Course for the Navy in the 21st Century." (B 979) 1994.

"Public Opinion & the Defense Debate." (NSR 54) 1983.

"Soviet Treaty Violations & U.S. Compliance Policy." (NSR 63) 1983.

Spring, Baker. "Clinton's Defense Budget Falls Far Short." (BU 217) 1994.

———. "A Game Plan for Restoring America's Defenses." (B 1019) 1995.

Stanmeyer, William. "Toward a Moral Nuclear Strategy." (PR) Summer 1982.

Symposium. "The Defense Budget: A Conservative Debate." (PR) Summer 1985.

Zakheim, Dov. "Yesterday's War." (PR) Summer 1989.

Strategic Defense

"Administration Victories on SDI." (SDI 3) 1988.

Defending America: A Near- and Long-Term Plan to Deploy Missile Defenses. Report by the Missile Defense Study Team. (M) 1995.

Foelber, Robert, and Brian Green. "Space Weapons, the Key to Assured Survival." (B 327) 1984.

Holmes, Kim R., and Baker Spring, eds. *SDI at the Turning Point: Readying Strategic Defenses for the 1990s and Beyond.* (CI) 1990.

Lehrman, Lewis E. "The Case for Strategic Defense." (PR) Winter 1985.

Robinson, Clarence, Jr. "Is Strategic Defense Obsolete?" (PR) Summer 1986.

Savelyev, Alexander. "Toward U.S.-Russian Strategic Defense: Ban the ABM Treaty Now." (B 921) 1992.

The Strategic Defense Initiative: A Sourcebook of Heritage Foundation Studies. (M) 1987.

Terrorism & Espionage

Pines, Burton Yale. *Report on the U.S. and U.N.: A Balance Sheet.* (UN) 1984.

———. *A World Without a U.N.* (M) 1984.

Starrels, John. *The U.S.-Third World Conflict: A Glossary.* (UN) 1983.

———. *The World Health Organization: Resisting Third World Ideological Pressures.* (UN) 1985.

U.N. Assessment Project. *The United Nations: Its Problems and What to Do About Them.* (M) 1985.

Index